WINNING THE
BOARD
GAME

WINNING THE BOARD GAME

HOW WOMEN CORPORATE DIRECTORS MAKE *THE* DIFFERENCE

BETSY BERKHEMER-CREDAIRE

ANGEL CITY PRESS

Winning the Board Game: How Women Corporate Directors Make THE Difference

By Betsy Berkhemer-Credaire

Copyright © 2019 Betsy Berkhemer-Credaire

Design by Lentini Design & Marketing, Inc.

10 9 8 7 6 5 4 3 2 1

ISBN 978-1-62640-057-3 (print edition)
ISBN 978-1-62640-058-0 (e-pub edition)

Library of Congress Cataloging-in-Publication Data is available.

ANGEL CITY PRESS

Published by Angel City Press
www.angelcitypress.com

Printed in USA

For our thirty-five-year romance, I dedicate this book to my husband Cris Credaire who died suddenly of a heart attack on Labor Day 2018. He was my voyage mate, my champion, my love. We shared a remarkable life together as private pilots, tennis players, and supporting each other's careers and goals. We thought we had many years yet to come, but it was not to be. I miss him every minute, every day.

CONTENTS

MEET THE WOMEN DIRECTORS

INTRODUCTION
Winning

The Board Game

I FELT LIKE I WAS CHANNELING SUSAN B. ANTHONY.
The day was May 31, 2018. The historic vote on SB 826 was about to take place in the California Senate Chamber in the State Capitol building in Sacramento. State senators were going to decide whether or not every publicly held corporation in California would be required to have a minimum of one woman on its board of directors by the end of 2019. And whether, by July 2021, at least two independent women directors would be required on boards with five directors and at least three women on boards with six or more directors. This day was the culmination of seven years of volunteer work, frustration, and fears mixed with confidence because we knew we were fighting for a very serious business issue.

Based in Los Angeles, I was unable to be in Sacramento that day due to my work schedule. I had previously testified at three senate committee hearings in the state capitol building, sharing with legislators how board searches work from an executive search perspective. Many women CEOs from the National Association of Women Business Owners of California (NAWBO-CA) had also testified, along with women corporate directors and business leaders. So I was disappointed not to be in Sacramento for this critical moment.

Ironically, I was attending a luncheon at the California Club in Los Angeles, the venerable bastion of male dominance of the city's business elite, where I was listening to a presentation about board governance. My smartphone was in my hand under the table and I was watching the vote on C-SPAN. I heard our champion Senator Hannah-Beth Jackson present an impassioned speech on the senate floor just before the vote was taken. Friends of mine at the luncheon table knew what was happening and watched me as I gasped and held my breath. The suspense was killing all of us. To pass, the bill had to have a simple majority of the forty state senators. Courting and cajoling senators over the previous months had not secured all the votes needed, so we were on pins and needles.

SB 826
was named for **August 26,** when women won the right to vote **in 1920**

I could not clearly hear the actual votes as they were spoken and recorded on the electronic vote board above the podium of the Senate President Pro Tem, Toni Atkins. I was hearing a lot of "No" votes, so I was scared, nervous that we were losing. I excused myself to go into the hallway so I could hear the votes being cast. There I was sitting under the vaulted ceilings, with my heart pounding, as I strained to listen. At last the gavel was brought down by Toni Atkins, fittingly the first woman to ever lead the senate. I couldn't believe my ears—she said SB 826 had passed by a majority plus two votes!

Suddenly, I was overwhelmed by tears of joy and shock. My heart was racing. SB 826 had passed the Senate! Then came a text from a jubilant Senator Jackson who said just three words: "We did it!" I knew the ghost of Susan B. Anthony was there next to me, smiling.

I had to pull myself together, dry my eyes, try to breathe normally, and return to the presentation. My friends in the presentation audience were ecstatic as I silently nodded to let them know that SB 826 passed. I was still shaking with emotion.

Wait a minute, though—the battle was far from over. The following week, SB 826 was submitted to the California State Assembly—which has eighty members, twice as many as the Senate! This was going to be even harder. Our legion of California women business owners, members of the National Association of Women's Business Owners-California (NAWBO-CA), then had to start again to visit district offices of Assembly members and book meetings in Sacramento to convince them that SB 826 would be extremely important to business and to the state's economy. Over the summer of 2018, we had to testify again—to three more Assembly committee hearings. The sessions were brutal, but we survived—and SB 826 passed all three committees. The Assembly floor vote came on August 30. Once again, we were glued to C-SPAN on our computers and our smartphones back in our offices throughout the state, all watching the vote countdown.

This time, Senator Jackson was not confident we had the votes. Our statewide board members from NAWBO-CA, which sponsored the bill, had canvassed district offices of Assembly members over the summer to gain their support; and countless friends and business leaders sent letters of support to the committees that had to pass our bill before it went to the floor. The committees in the Assembly had the same titles as those that passed our bill before the Senate vote: Banking, Judiciary, and Appropriations. Each committee required a separate campaign of support letters and phone calls. Our lobbyist Lori Kammerer was running from office to office in the capitol to tally votes in advance. Again, pins and needles.

Surprisingly, the Assembly voting process was stopped about halfway through. All of us watching on TV thought *Oh no, it's not going to pass.* Apparently, the senator and her staff determined that we were not getting "Aye" votes from some of the key Assembly members who had assured us of their approval. So a recess suspended the vote temporarily to allow supporters to run back to those members and once again urge their yes votes, citing the research and all the business reasons why the state's economy would benefit from this historic law.

About twenty minutes later, the recess ended and the vote was continued. We won! Once again, the tally was only two votes over majority—but that's all it took to win. Another round of tears and jubilation burst forth in the offices of women business owners and supporters around the state. The emotion was high—I've never in my life felt the sheer exultation I felt at that moment. That was August 30, 2018, a date I will always cherish. It was a moment we thought would never come—and yet it did!

Next, after these huge hurdles, we had to secure one final approval—Governor Jerry Brown's signature. He could veto SB 826, sign it into law, or just ignore it, which would have been almost as fatal as a veto. He had the whole month of September to sign or veto all of the bills that had been passed during the year.

These were his last signatures as governor—he would be termed out of office on December 31, 2018. So the final legacy of the only California governor to have served four terms, whose storied father Pat Brown had been governor decades earlier, would be his signature on the last few bills for the year. And SB 826 was one of them.

We hoped he would sign SB 826 because we wanted him to make history as the first governor in the nation to sign a law ensuring that at least one woman director would be on the board of every public company headquartered in the state. The new law would mean about 180 board seats added for women by year-end 2019, and approximately 1,060 seats by year-end 2021. To ensure compliance, the bill included fines of $100,000 for the first year and up to $300,000 by year-end 2021.

The month of September was almost over, yet Governor Brown had not yet signed. We kept waiting—and writing letters—and waiting. To show the governor we had widespread support, we enlisted many more companies and individuals to write letters to him urging his signature on the bill. Meanwhile, the opposition, the California Chamber of Commerce and the California Manufacturers and Technology Association (CMTA), were lobbying him to veto it. We were scared— afraid that we had come this far over seven years, worked so hard, and then might lose if the governor didn't sign.

What a tragedy that would have been! We all committed to each other that we would introduce the bill again and again until some future administration would sign it into law. But we were all fairly exhausted from our intense efforts throughout 2018. I don't know if we could have gathered the energy and stamina to do it all over again. (Yes, of course we would have, if we had to! After all, Susan B. Anthony died before women got the right to vote with the Nineteenth Amendment on August 26, 1920, almost one hundred years ago. Then other women took up the torch and kept going for another half-century to finish what Susan B. had started.)

We waited and waited. No word. We will never know why Governor Brown delayed signing the bill until the very last moment. Sunday, September 30 was the legal deadline when all bills had to be signed, vetoed, or pocketed. Finally, to our great joy and relief, we learned that he had signed SB 826 into law—the night before the deadline.

News of our complete victory spread fast through texts, emails, social media, and the NAWBO-CA grapevine. We were beyond ecstatic, emotional, excited, and grateful to Jerry Brown forever.

The national news media started to call. I was already scheduled for a CNBC interview Monday, October 1, whatever the governor's decision. That was my first interview after he signed the bill. Other newspaper, radio, and TV followed. *Bloomberg, Wall Street Journal, Los Angeles Times,* and more. Suddenly our California law was like rocket fuel across the country; the business community woke up to the fact that investors will no longer settle for all-male boards of directors. Investors know that with women on boards, there's an increased chance of a good return on their investments.

Many media outlets published opinion pieces railing against SB 826. All of them echoed the same old complaint: they didn't want companies to be told what to do by the government. I responded that we women would prefer not to have to have such laws either. But research shows that if proactive efforts are not taken, it will take decades for companies to put women directors on their boards, if ever.

Fortunately, passing the new law in California meant we had already won a victory in the war of public opinion. The ominous warnings by the opposition of taking SB 826 to the Supreme Court proved to be empty threats. This sea change in history was no longer a pipe dream. It was real. Shareholders, women in the workforce, and retirees who invest in companies were responding with loud cheers from the sidelines.

No all-male corporate board would ever again be acceptable to shareholders, investors, and the public. The business perspectives of experienced women directors on boards will help companies perform better and have a more engaged workforce and thus benefit the state's economy.

The business world is forever changed, and women in the workplace will have more opportunities for generations to come. Suffragists Susan B. Anthony, Elizabeth Cady Stanton, and Carrie Chapman Catt are all smiling down from the cosmos. And the women who currently serve on boards are delighted that there will be more women joining them. Their talents and experience will add value and innovation to boards.

Oh, glorious victory! We are full of gratitude and admiration for Senator Jackson, Senate President Pro Tem Toni Atkins, Assembly Speaker Anthony Rendon, the California State Senators and Assembly Members who voted for SB 826, and the statewide board of NAWBO-CA. And our deep thanks go to all of the people and corporate leaders who wrote letters of support to their legislators.

Coincidentally, 2018 was my first year as CEO of 2020 Women on Boards, the national education and advocacy campaign that tracks the number of women directors in Russell 3000 companies—the largest 3000 public companies in the U.S.—and ranks the companies from "Winning" to "Zero," depending upon the percentage of women on their boards. And my retained executive search firm Berkhemer Clayton was celebrating twenty-five years in business and still going strong. I am very fortunate to have been on the scene at the right time with this important business mission so I could help make a difference.

Just a coincidence, during this process of getting the law passed, I discovered that I was born the same year that women's suffrage leader Carrie Chapman Catt died. She led the final phase of the movement, fighting against opposition from President Woodrow Wilson, to get the Nineteenth Amendment ratified on August 26, 1920. It's for August 26 that we named SB 826—to honor the women who fought for the vote in the U.S. just one hundred years ago.

My goal for this book, *Winning the Board Game—How Women Corporate Directors Make the Difference,* is to recognize and applaud outstanding women corporate directors who have made the difference on their boards. Many are well known directors of large corporations; others are directors of smaller corporations that are not household names. Their stories will inspire and encourage working women to simply expect—and plan their careers toward—corporate board service as the ultimate phase of their careers, just as men do.

One of the most ludicrous objections to SB 826 from both legislators and news media alike was, "But there are not enough qualified women to serve on all these corporate boards." Another was, "Adding women to boards will reduce the caliber and quality of corporate boards." A third was, "This will cause more California companies to move out of the state to avoid having to put women on their boards."

Now that three generations of women have been in management and executive ranks over the last forty years and have climbed the ladder to achieve success in business, there are literally thousands of capable and experienced women candidates for boards. The pipeline is overflowing with board-qualified women candidates. But open board seats do not occur often, and when they do, men turn to their personal networks of trusted colleagues that often do not include women. That's why half of all public companies in the country still have only one—or no—women on their boards.

Research by Credit Suisse, McKinsey, and other independent sources has proved that corporations with women directors on their boards are more profitable, more productive, and their workforce is better engaged. That's why shareholders are now clamoring for companies they invest in to bring women on board. It's logical; shareholders want and deserve the best chance for a positive return on investment. Women corporate directors do make the difference.

As the owner of a retained executive-search firm, I know firsthand how board searches are done and how board candidates are selected—through trusted networks of board members. Most often, only candidates (women or men) who are already known to the current board members are selected.

With that knowledge, we at 2020WOB educate women about this inside secret: relying upon and expanding your own networks of contacts is the best way to be remembered for board nominations. Just as men do, women must build long-term and trusted relationships with people who have seen them in action—either on advisory boards, nonprofit boards, private company boards, government commissions, or industry trade associations. And women must intentionally let their contacts know the specific value-added experience they will bring to a corporate board. Even though board openings are rare, when board members see people who bring experience that they are missing on the board, the members have the option to add a new seat any time.

Women held 17.7% of board seats in the Russell 3000 in 2018

Yes, women make the difference on boards. Ironically, when I interviewed the women directors featured in this book, I came to realize that women directors do not want to claim victory for the impact they have had, because they don't want to boast or offend other board members. Corporate board actions are based on consensus and teamwork, not individual performance. Women are especially good at anticipating unintended consequences. I asked many questions about what specific differences women directors have made, hoping for examples such as not closing a factory when it might put people out of work or advising a CEO about how to better manage the global supply chain. These women preferred to discuss the teamwork that resulted in such victories, rather than claim that their individual leadership made something happen. They based their success on reaching consensus—not like the jury

1/1/2019

date that California became the **first state** to implement law mandating women on corporate boards

in the movie *12 Angry Men,* but rather through effective communications to encourage buy-in toward action.

We highlight several examples where a CEO has asked a woman director for counsel on certain issues where he might have felt less comfortable or less appropriate asking for help from male directors. Some of those questions relate to diversity in the workplace or other people issues such as how to engage employees, especially those with diverse backgrounds.

Our California law SB 826, effective as of January 1, 2019, has caused a ripple effect across the country, with CEOs, board members, and shareholders realizing that change is coming.

As of June 2019, New Jersey, Michigan, and Massachusetts have similar bills going through their state legislatures. The Illinois House of Representatives considered a bill requiring at least one woman, one African American, and one Latino on every public company board in Illinois. But it was amended to require simply that companies report their diversity numbers.

Someday, sometime in the near future, it will be inconceivable for a public corporation to have an all-male board, especially an all-Anglo male board. It's just not good for business governance or reputation. Women bring innovation, communication, and valuable perspectives to boards. After all, research says our gender helps companies perform better. Women are also more than half the population and make the majority of financial and purchasing decisions.

Finally, women are shareholders in companies. We invest our hard-earned money and 401 K retirement savings in corporations. As more men from the Baby Boomer generation die over the next few years, there will be greater and greater wealth in the hands of women. Women investors deserve to have the best return on investment.

Here's where you start *Winning the Board Game.* You may have read my first book, *The Board Game—How Smart Women Become Corporate Directors,* to learn how to get a seat on a board. Now you will see the big difference women make on boards they serve. Start your own journey and make the difference, too!

START HERE...

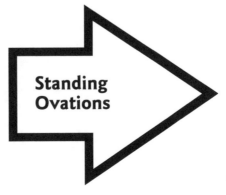

Standing Ovations

STANDING OVATIONS
Three Remarkable

BONNIE HILL

She is one of the most iconic corporate directors in the business world today, a woman who has served on more boards over the last twenty-five years than most men or women have. To those who know her, Bonnie G. Hill is the epitome of what a great corporate director should be. I admire Bonnie for her leadership, her steady integrity, and her generous spirit as a mentor and friend. Whether you aspire to be on boards, want to be a better board member, or simply want to be a classy executive woman, you want to be like Bonnie.

Somehow, despite her hectic board schedule, Bonnie finds time to be a mentor and coach to women, simply as a favor. She has spoken at countless conferences including 2020 Women on Boards. And she has made certain to bring new women board members onto the boards where she serves and when she steps down. She gives her time and deep knowledge unselfishly to help other women advance. She only asks for a rain check whenever a member of her large family that's sprawled across the U.S. needs her. With her schedule, I always marvel at how she balances work, family, and educating others. Yet somehow, she does.

Bonnie chose to retire from her last four public boards when she reached the retirement age, even when there was an opportunity to continue serving. Her public boards have included Home Depot, Yum! Brands, California Water Service Group, Hershey Foods, Albertsons, and AK Steel Holding Corporation. Although Bonnie had an opportunity to continue serving beyond retirement age, she says she believes it is good governance to make room for the next generation of directors.

These days, Bonnie serves on the board of Banc of California, which is a public company. Her nonprofit boards include the RAND Corporation, the advisory

Trailblazers

board of Millstein Center at Columbia Law School, and Boards That Lead advisory board at the Wharton School. Her "unplanned" but successful career has covered business, government, academia, and philanthropy.

President Ronald Reagan appointed Bonnie as commissioner of the Postal Rate Commission and assistant secretary of the Department of Education. President George H.W. Bush appointed her as special advisor for consumer affairs. She has also served as chair of the Consumer Affairs Advisory Committee of the Securities and Exchange Commission (SEC). Prior to her government work, Bonnie served as a vice president at Kaiser Aluminum and Chemical Corporation. After six years in Washington, she returned to California to serve in Governor Pete Wilson's cabinet as secretary of the California State and Consumer Services Agency. Her career took an unexpected turn when she was named dean of the McIntire School of Commerce at the University of Virginia. We in Los Angeles got to know Bonnie when she was named CEO of the Los Angeles Times Foundation.

Her ultimate recognition as a board director came when the National Association of Corporate Directors (NACD) honored her with its 2015 B. Kenneth West Lifetime Achievement Award and named her one of America's most influential directors in corporate governance. She was also named Outstanding Director by the *Financial Times,* and in 2019 was named Director of the Year by Directors Forum.

Bonnie deserves our applause and gratitude for being a remarkable role model for all women who aspire to make their mark in the business world. Bonnie succeeded as a professional and a corporate board member when she herself had no role models to follow. That in itself is an achievement worth applauding. Cheers to you, Bonnie Hill!

SUSAN STAUTBERG

Susan Stautberg is an innovator, multidimensional leader and bridge builder on a global scale. She created the first and most powerful global network of women who serve on corporate boards, called WomenCorporateDirectors (WCD). To those who have worked with her, it's no surprise that one of her favorite quotes is an old proverb: "They tried to bury us, but they didn't know we were seeds."

Seeds, indeed! Because of Susan's determination, in just fifteen years WomenCorporateDirectors took root from a small group of women directors gathered around her dining room table and flourished to more than 2,500 members in eighty chapters around the world. The combined market capitalization of public companies with WCD members on their boards totals almost $8 trillion. Local, regional, national, and international WCD forums generate dialogue on issues facing women directors and their companies. Members share best practices and personal stories to help each other navigate the challenges of governance in today's competitive and volatile global economy.

Susan retired from WCD in 2018 and was named governance advisor to the private equity firm Atlantic Street Capital, where she recruits women to be CEOs, COOs, CFOs, board members, and advisory counselors for its portfolio of companies.

Where did her drive and focus first appear? Susan learned to raise her voice and speak her mind while attending an all-girls high school and eventually, an all-girls college. That early training paid off throughout her career, especially when communicating with men.

She broke her first glass ceiling early—as a journalist. A Westinghouse Group-W television correspondent covering the White House and Capitol Hill, Susan was the first woman—and one of the youngest—to head a Washington TV bureau. She ventured beyond journalism, as she puts it, "trying to make changes in government and create organizations to help women succeed and make a difference in business."

In 1995, Susan started PartnerCom to assemble and manage global advisory boards for businesses, governments, and nonprofits. She then established a preëminent retreat for women leaders from around the world called the Belizean Grove. Every other year, she invites a cross section of influential women to discuss global issues, explore solutions, and learn from each other. After launching WCD, she created OnBoard Bootcamps to educate women about how to be selected by corporate boards.

She has served on various presidential commissions, boards, and foundations including the Commission on Presidential Scholars, US/Japan Fellowship, the Institute for Educational Affairs, the Defense Advisory Council on Women in the Armed Services, and the White House Fellows Association.

Susan is also a member of the Committee of 200 and the International Women's Forum. She has received countless awards, including an honorary doctorate of law from Wheaton College, the Director's Choice Award, and WCD's Visionary Award for Strategic Leadership. She has also written eight books, including *Selected Quotations that Inspire Us to Think Bigger, Live Better and Laugh Harder,* as well as *Women on Board: Insider Secrets to Getting on a Board and Succeeding as a Director.* With her wry sense of humor, she has even tackled what can go wrong in political and personal lives by co-authoring the book *Betrayed: A Survivor's Guide to Lying, Cheating & Double Dealing (2019).*

One of her fondest moments, she says, was when she launched the first WCD chapter in Chile. The head of the Chilean Stock Exchange called her to invite members of the chapter to ring the opening bell, an honor with great visibility. She said "No thanks" because there were no women on the stock exchange board of eleven white men. Taken aback, the surprised exchange president called back a few days later and promised to put a woman on the board within a month, which happened (installing a WCD member). So Susan trusted the board and together with WCD members in Chile, showed up and rang that bell!

Susan has been ringing bells on behalf of women throughout her career. We applaud you, Susan Stautberg, for being a true pioneer—and a treasure for all women who are currently serving or aspiring to serve on boards.

STATE SENATOR HANNAH-BETH JACKSON

When Governor Jerry Brown signed historic Senate Bill SB 826 into law on September 30, 2018, California became the first state in the country to require publicly traded companies headquartered within its borders to include women on their boards of directors. And at that moment, California State Senator Hannah-Beth Jackson heard her phone ringing in celebration. She had just shattered another glass ceiling. Without HBJ, as we refer to her in shorthand, this unprecedented state law would never have become reality. She championed SB 826 from pipe dream to passage, carefully orchestrating delicate steps along the seven-year timeline it took to get it done.

Senator Jackson saw the research confirming that public companies with women on their boards are more profitable and productive than those with all-male boards, and she immediately knew something had to be done to turn a business and economic problem into a success story. So she took on this long-shot concept, first with the joint Senate Concurrent Resolution (SCR) 62 in 2013, urging all public corporations to have at least one woman on every board of directors. But unfortunately, the resolution had no penalties for non-compliance. Five years later, after the needle didn't move, Senator Jackson championed SB 826, which made adding women to public boards the law. The bill was sponsored by the National Association of Women Business Owners, California (NAWBO-CA) where I am proud to have served on the statewide board for many years.

Even while she was mapping the way to get more women on corporate boards, Senator Jackson had already taken more steps to even the playing field for women. She authored SB 358, the California Fair Pay Act, one of the nation's most successful gender-pay-equity bills, which then-Governor Jerry Brown signed into law in 2015 and we all watched it take effect in 2016.

Hannah-Beth learned long ago that the playing field wasn't even—the literal field, that is. Growing up in a small town in Massachusetts, she was just seven years old when she signed up to try out for the local Little League baseball team. Officials told her she couldn't join the team because she was a girl. But she knew she was an excellent baseball player, better than most of the boys. So with the advice of her parents and grandfather—an immigrant from Russia who taught her that in America, if you work hard, you can succeed—she channeled her disappointment into her first steps as an activist. The seven-year-old carried a petition door-to-door in her neighborhood for signatures, then mailed a strongly worded letter to the Little League Association of America, suggesting that qualified girls should be allowed on Little League teams. With great anticipation, she waited for the mailman every day, but never received a reply. That very lack of response ignited her lifelong passion for seeking justice and gender equality.

HBJ graduated from all-women Scripps College in Claremont, California, and Boston University School of Law. She started her legal career in Santa Barbara County as a deputy district attorney. Even as a full-fledged lawyer, she was labeled one of the "girls," among the twenty attorneys in the office. She quickly gained everyone's respect when she prosecuted difficult domestic violence cases, fighting against the painful indignities faced by women victims in courtrooms dominated by men.

She wanted to do more for public service, so she switched to politics. Over the decades, she won five terms in California state government, three in the Assembly, then two in the Senate. She has protected privacy rights and the environment, managed through the devastating fires and floods of Santa Barbara County in 2017 and 2018, advanced legislation to reduce gun violence, and improved access to early childhood education. And throughout her career, she has steadfastly championed equality for women, passing laws to require affirmative consent, the "Yes Means Yes" law, as well as Title IX legislation to ensure that equity in education and athletic opportunity are realities for California's women and girls.

Senator Jackson does not ask for permission. She learned from Little League—and years of experience—that if you want something done, you take strong and decisive action. She forges ahead with her passion, commitment, and expertise to make the changes needed for women in many aspects of society, and the results of her actions reach far beyond the borders of California.

This political trailblazer deserves our applause! Thank you, Senator Hannah-Beth Jackson!

GO IMMEDIATELY TO

Chapter I

1

NOW

Is Your Time

FOR THE FIRST TIME IN U.S. HISTORY, IT HAS BECOME A BUSINESS IMPERATIVE THAT WOMEN SERVE ON BOARDS OF DIRECTORS OF PUBLIC COMPANIES. If you are a professional woman who has the right career experience and aspire to make a difference in business, your time is *now*. You are already board-ready.

Yet, even with state governments and shareholders pressuring boards for more gender diversity, it remains an uphill battle for women to win seats on public company boards. Highly qualified women with the critical knowledge and abilities to bring value have not been "in the board game" and thus have been overlooked. The traditional hand-off from male board members to their trusted male friends who are waiting in the wings has been a very confidential and accepted practice.

Today, however, the business case has been proven, the pipeline of qualified women is overflowing, and a board of directors that ignores the facts does so at its own peril. Research shows that companies with women on their boards perform better, are more productive, more profitable, and their workforce is better engaged. Pressure from investors and shareholders, the primary motivator for any change, is beginning to make a difference. And if various states pass laws following California's Senate Bill 826 enacted January 1, 2019 it could soon become *mandatory* in many states to add women directors to boards.

National statistics in 2018 showed that women held 4,477 (just 17.7%) of the 25,250 board seats in the Russell 3000 companies (Equilar research analyzed by 2020 Women on Boards), which includes the largest public companies in the United States. Granted, this is an increase from 16% in 2017, when 4,082

50% of the largest 3000 companies have **only one or NO women directors**

of 25,510 Russell 3000 board seats were held by women. But half of those 3000 companies had only one or no women directors. One-fourth had no women on the boards.

The time is *now*. You can be one of the women who will make the critical difference on a corporate board. The journey to pursue corporate boards is a self-directed path. Your journey begins with a single step—and you took it when you picked up this book. Now dive in!

How YOU Can Make *the* Difference on a Corporate Board of Directors

Corporate boards have the power to change the companies they govern. Actions of boards can benefit institutional investors as well as individual shareholders, the economy, the company's employees, and the business environment that affects all of us.

The fifty-four women interviewed in these pages have had significant impact on each of their boards. Their stories show consistent themes about how their corporations benefit from having women directors on the board:

- Women bring customer dimension and depth into the boardroom. In addition to making up more than half of the population, women are the primary purchasers of healthcare services, insurance, consumer products, automobiles, and technology devices. Women are always conscious of their family's budget. As a result, costs for groceries, medicines and utilities are followed more closely by women than men. And because women live longer than men, they are more inclined to plan for the long term.
- Women bring varied perspectives to the board and thus, more robust debate and better solutions. Women look at problems from different angles and bring an undeniable diversity of viewpoints. They are raised to multi-task, so their brains are wired differently. They call upon intuition, collaboration, and insight to interpret the facts and figures they receive in the boardroom. Rather than being disruptive (as some all-male boards have feared), senior-level professional women know how to pose questions and find solutions.

They've had to be cognizant of timing throughout their careers, and they know how to communicate with both genders in order to advance to senior levels.

- Women have empathy for the workforce of all ages and levels. Typically, they have worked their way up the ladder by mastering a variety of jobs along the way. From early in their careers, they have remained closely in tune with the realities of the workforce environment regarding pay, benefits, and culture. Their own diverse experiences add to consensus building on the board. Women have had to *do* the work along the way, and not simply *direct* the work. They've had to outperform their male peers in order to move up. The person who knows *how* as well as *why* makes a good leader and a darn good board member.

- Women demonstrate Environment, Social, and Governance (ESG) sensibilities. Corporations are increasingly judged on the bigger impact their companies are having on the world around them. Beyond their own internal profit-making purpose, boards must be vigilant about the universe of ESG responsibilities. Not all corporations are involved with solving global problems for humankind, like making healthcare and electric cars affordable. But even small companies play a part in achieving the greater good. Women are naturally focused on the greater good and are not concerned solely with the bottom line. This talent is increasingly valuable as corporations focus on social responsibility and solving broad, external, global issues as well as becoming more profitable by being part of the solution, not part of the problem.

- Women use their communications and team-building skills to collaborate and achieve shared goals. This is critically important today as corporate organizations evolve from traditional hierarchical to more flattened, matrixed, and cross-silo structures. The board determines the compensation of senior management executives based on whether or not they have achieved shared goals across multiple disciplines. In all corporate functions—quality control, legal, operations, global supply chain, technology, and finance—shared goals drive compensation. Whether they have worked in human resources or other career pathways, women have advanced by meeting goals. So they are well-versed in assessing how achieving specified goals should impact the compensation of executive officers.

- Women anticipate unintended consequences. Credit Suisse research indicates that companies with women on their boards are more productive and profitable not because women are risk averse, but because women tend to take risks after calculating the many ramifications that might occur—including human and workforce costs.

- Women's intuition makes a difference in the boardroom. Women's "Emotional Quotient" (EQ) goes a long way toward problem-solving, especially in a consensus-driven environment like a board of directors.

- Women directors also monitor and advocate for progress of women employees and managers in the company where they serve. They identify women leaders, encourage them to participate in speaking engagements at the company, and mentor younger women so they may advance in their careers and maybe even someday serve on boards of directors.

You will make the difference on corporate boards by bringing your perspective as a woman, your industry expertise, and your communications ability to get things done. You will bring a new tone to the boardroom as a woman and that alone will change the conversation.

How YOU Will Benefit Professionally from Being in The Board Game:

Why should women invest time and training to become corporate board members? While the compensation and prestige of serving on corporate boards can be significant, women are also motivated by the desire to make a difference and bring their unique value-added experience to bear where it will have the greatest impact. In pursuing a board seat, women should ask themselves "Where will I do the greatest good?" The answer to that question will determine which contacts and which boards to pursue. This question should be the North Star guiding your steps to attaining a board seat. When you serve on a corporate board:

- Your circles of business contacts expand exponentially. You gain respect from business leaders and co-workers because you have reached the pinnacle of business success at the board level.

- You make a positive difference in the corporation's culture, growth, and Return on Investment (ROI).

- You become a well-rounded executive and bring back best practices to the company where you work.

- You have the satisfaction of augmenting and complementing your own productive work experience with a late-stage career during your fifties, sixties, and potentially beyond retirement, into your seventies.

- You earn the lucrative board compensation that men have earned for decades, including cash compensation, stock, and trips to appealing destinations for board meetings.
- You have the prestige of being a corporate director as well as carrying the fiduciary responsibility for shareholders and the enjoyment of governing a business from the highest level.
- You are a role model, encouraging other women in the workforce and demonstrating that they, too, can rise to the top of the corporation.
- You accept the responsibility of helping companies perform better, be more profitable, and be more vigilant about workplace culture and how all employees are treated.

The Time is *NOW.*

This is certainly the most exciting time in U.S. history for professional women to rise to the highest level of business success: corporate directorship. Finally, *your* time has come. There have never been more opportunities or more access for seasoned professional women to make the move onto corporate boards.

The enactment of California Law SB 826 paved the way for at least one woman director to be added to all public company boards headquartered in California by year-end 2019. Then, by year-end 2021, public companies are required to have three seats for women (for boards with six or more members).

More than one thousand board seats in California were required to be added for women directors in the 632 publicly held companies in the state. Those companies include 438 Russell 3000 corporations plus 194 micro-cap public companies that are smaller than Russell 3000 companies. The law states that unless there is a natural opening caused by a director's retirement or decision to step down, a director position must be added to the board and filled by a woman. The fine for non-compliance is $100,000 by year-end 2019, and up to $300,000 by year-end 2021. Fines will be administered by the California Secretary of State's Office.

There is no question that California—the fifth largest economy in the world and home to more public company headquarters than New York, Connecticut, and New Jersey combined—sets the bar for the rest of the country. Similar laws in other states will follow, so that more mandatory board seats for women will be opening up in other states as well. For example, in early 2019, New Jersey initiated its own women director legislation using the California template.

In 2015, long before California's law passed, the U.S. Government Accountability Office estimated that it could take more than forty years for the number of women on corporate boards to be equal to that of men. That would mean 2055! A 2017 study by research firm Equilar suggested that it could take until the year 2055 (almost four decades) for the boards of Russell 3000 companies nationwide to reach gender parity. That's just too long. Why should businesses lose out on all those years when women directors could have brought great value to boards? The time is *now*.

There are more board retirements happening in the next few years than ever before, primarily due to the aging of the enormous Baby Boomer population. This unusual wave of retirements, the new laws, and the pressure from investors add up to many more opportunities for women who are prepared to join corporate boards.

Although opportunities for women directors may not be opening up fast enough, there has been significant recent research to bolster arguments in favor of having more women hold corporate board seats, including:

- A 2017 study by MSCI found that U.S. companies that began the five-year period from 2011 to 2016 with three or more women directors reported earnings per share that were 45% higher than those companies with no women directors at the beginning of the same period.

- Credit Suisse conducted a six-year global research study from 2006 to 2012 with more than two thousand companies worldwide that showed that women directors improve business performance by a number of key metrics including stock performance. For companies with a market capitalization of more than $10 billion, those with women directors outperformed the share price of comparable businesses with all-male boards by 26%.

- Additionally, the Credit Suisse report concluded: 1) there has been a greater correlation between stock performance and the presence of women on boards since the financial crisis in 2008; 2) companies with women on their boards of directors significantly outperformed others when the recession occurred; 3) companies with women on their boards tend to be somewhat risk averse and carry less debt, on average; and 4) net income growth for companies with women on their boards averaged 14% over a six-year period, compared with 10% for companies with no women directors.

- In 2014, Credit Suisse found that companies with at least one woman on the board had an average Return on Equity (ROE) of 12.2%, compared to 10.1% for companies with no women directors. Additionally, the price-to-book value of these firms was greater for those with women on their boards: 2.4 times the value in comparison to 1.8 times the value for all-male boards.
- A 2012 University of California Berkeley study called "Women Create a Sustainable Future" found that companies with more women on their boards are more likely to "create a sustainable future" by, among other things, instituting strong governance structures with a high level of transparency.
- A 2016 McKinsey and Company study entitled "Women Matter" showed that nationwide, the companies where women are most strongly represented at board or top-management levels are also the companies that perform the best in terms of profitability, productivity, and workforce engagement.
- According to another study entitled "Women Directors on Corporate Boards: From Tokenism to Critical Mass" (by M. Torchia, A. Calabrò, M. Huse, *Journal of Business Ethics,* 2011) and a report entitled "Critical Mass on Corporate Boards: Why Three or More Women Enhance Governance":

  Attaining critical mass—going from one or two women directors to at least three women directors—"creates an environment where women are no longer seen as outsiders and are able to influence the content and process of board discussions more substantially. When there are at least three women on corporate boards with an average membership of ten directors, performance increases significantly."
- More male CEO champions are seeing and believing the research and are standing up for women directors. Warren Buffett said in the May 20, 2013 issue of *Fortune:*

  When America comes to fully employing the talents of *all* its citizens, the greater its output of goods and services will be. We've seen what can be accomplished when we use 50% of our human capacity. If you visualize what 100% can do, you'll join me as an unbridled optimist about America's future.

There are many more reasons to feel a sense of urgency. If you want to join the women who are making the difference on corporate boards, the time is now. Tectonic changes in our society and the political world have made gender diversity headline news. A record-breaking one hundred congresswomen were sworn in on January 2019—nearly a fourth of the House of Representatives and women leaders of countries around the world have grown in numbers and influence. In 2016, one of the two major political parties in the United States elected a woman to head the presidential ticket. All of these shifts in our public consciousness bolster the call for legions of qualified women to assume power in the boardroom, just as they have in other capacities.

- Sexual harassment and work environment issues are now front and center since the "#MeToo" and "Time's Up" movements have made it clear that women's voices must be heard. Women board members will be more vigilant about fair treatment for women employees. And it will be encouraging when women look up and see women directors on their company's board. (It is worth noting that in the sexual harassment cases brought against Harvey Weinstein and Steve Wynn, there were no women on the boards of directors of their respective companies at the time.)

- Global disruption of traditional industries has resulted from the digital revolution generated by advancing technology. Board members must stay current to help companies adapt, survive, and thrive. Directors who have served on boards for twenty or thirty years may not be able to keep up with how technology affects all aspects of doing business today. Many of the women profiled in these pages have brought critical skills in cybersecurity and digital marketing to their boards. This type of current experience is mandatory in today's competitive corporate world. Few longtime board members are prepared to deal with the workforce upheaval brought on by robotics and artificial intelligence (AI).

- In today's saturated news media environment, more coverage is calling attention to the oversight of corporate boards, and not all of that coverage has been positive. We have all read news stories, investigative reports, and commentaries calling for the ouster of particular boards as companies have floundered or have been hit with devastating lawsuits. "Where was the board while all this was going on?" "Why wasn't the board keeping management in check?" "Didn't the board know about these problems?" These are all relevant and legitimate questions. Boards of directors are more aware that they must be alert to the red flags of enterprise risk, preferably long before the CEO and management have to face the resulting crises.

- As corporate boards endure more consistent public scrutiny, investors and shareholders are definitely paying closer attention. They rely upon the "independent" directors to do one primary job—to represent and protect shareholders' interests. Institutional investors and shareholders have threatened to vote their proxies against boards with fewer than two women directors. Some of the country's largest institutional investors, including CalPERS (California Public Employees Retirement System) and CalSTRS (California State Teachers Retirement System) have written urgent letters to CEOs insisting, but not requiring, that they add women to their boards.

- In the past, men often served on multiple boards—sometimes six or eight. Vanguard, the world's second largest asset manager, announced in 2019 that because so much more time and expertise is required of all corporate directors these days, *it will not support corporate executives seeking to serve on more than two boards in addition to their full-time executive job.* Vanguard also said it will vote against former executives seeking to serve simultaneously on more than four boards. This should translate to more opportunities for women to move into board seats formerly occupied by men.

California law SB 826 was named to honor August 26, the anniversary of the day when women won full voting rights in U.S. elections. The Nineteenth Amendment was passed by Congress in 1919 and ratified by the states in 1920, finally granting women the right to vote on August 26. Still, today—*a century* after women won the right to vote—a pervasive gender gap exists on boards, as well as gaps in equal pay and advancement opportunities in corporations for working women of all ethnic backgrounds.

You will be among the women who will change this picture. *Winning the Board Game* will help you make sure that it does not take another hundred years before women have equal representation on corporate boards.

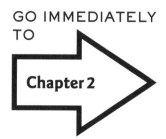

GO IMMEDIATELY TO

Chapter 2

2 A NATIONAL

A Global

CHALLENGE
Imperative

At THE TURN OF THE MILLENNIUM, SERVING ON PUBLIC COMPANY BOARDS OF DIRECTORS WAS NOT THE ULTIMATE CAREER GOAL OF MOST WOMEN EXECUTIVES, women business owners, or senior women working in government. For most, serving on corporate boards wasn't even on the radar. That was then.

Awareness was heightened in 2001 when the Enron debacle occurred, the largest corporate bankruptcy in U.S. history. Then after additional accounting scandals devastated WorldCom, Global Crossing, Tyco, and Arthur Andersen, Congress passed the Sarbanes-Oxley Act in 2002, designed to protect investors from the possibility of fraudulent accounting activities by corporations. Also known as the Corporate Responsibility Act of 2002, Sarbanes-Oxley mandated strict reforms to improve financial disclosures from corporations and increase the number of directors on boards who understood corporate finances.

Sarbanes-Oxley requires at least one "financial expert" on the audit committee of every public board. The Securities and Exchange Commission (SEC) defines "financial expert" as an independent director with experience in analyzing and evaluating financial statements that are comparable in complexity to the financial statements of the company governed by the board. Sarbanes-Oxley opened the door for a wave of women considered "financial experts" who were current or previous chief financial officers (CFOs). Practically for the first time, board nominating committees began looking beyond the preferred CEO title to find new board prospects with the requisite financial credentials.

About the same time, a new organization emerged, founded by Susan Stautberg: WomenCorporateDirectors (WCD). Today, WCD is a global community of women board members of public and large private companies who network with one another, coach one another, and recommend each other for future board openings. In fewer than twenty years, WCD has grown to 2,500 members and eighty chapters around the world.

In 2010, a new nonprofit in Boston called 2020 Women on Boards (2020WOB) arose as a public awareness and advocacy campaign to increase the number of women directors. Co-founders Stephanie Sonnabend and Malli Gero established the goal of having at least 20% of all public company board seats occupied by women by 2020.

As its core service to the public, 2020WOB provides annual research on its website, tracking how many women directors serve on every board of the three thousand largest public corporations in the U.S.

That research is important. Consider this: As of 2018, half the companies polled by 2020WOB had only one woman or no women directors. That means the road to achieving 20% is much longer than was generally understood. The discouraging news was no surprise to 2020WOB, however. The reality

[
Women held

9.2% of board seats

in **25 largest IPOs**

in 2017
]

is simply more evident when looking at 3000 companies rather than the Fortune 1000 or Fortune 500, where the companies were close to, or had surpassed 20%. Larger corporations understand the benefits of having women on their boards. Unfortunately, the news media tends to cite the Fortune 500 statistics—just 500 large companies—showing that women have surpassed the 20% goal on those boards. The real situation becomes evident only when getting the facts from six times that number of companies. The great disparity becomes clear. In an effort to accelerate more women to corporate boards, 2020WOB educates executive women about how to seek and secure seats, and it collaborates with companies and other organizations with a similar mission to raise awareness about this important business issue.

To announce how many seats in the Russell 3000 are held by women each year and to applaud those companies that have increased the number of women directors to 20% or more, 2020WOB holds the National Conversation on Board Diversity in dozens of cities across the country and internationally. Most of the city events are held on the same day in late November, bringing together 7,500 current and aspiring women board members, CEOs, and other experts to share their thoughts on advancing more women to corporate boards. Updated annually, the 2020WOB Gender Diversity Index (GDI) is available to the public at 2020WOB.com and is easily accessible to investors, advocates, and consumers.

Two invaluable resources are produced by 2020WOB: The online GDI Directory categorizes companies with a "W" for "Winning" with at least 20% women directors; "V" for "Very Close" meaning 18% to 19% women directors; "T" for "Transforming" with only one woman director; and "Z" for "Zero." Thanks to the 2020WOB Directory, aspiring board candidates can easily pinpoint boards that need more women. And, perhaps more significantly for the future of a company, armed with information about a board's gender diversity, shareholders and the public at large can decide whether that company gets their money.

The other resource is the GDI Report, covering in-depth analysis and trends, including the numbers of women directors by state as well as how many companies went public with no women on their boards. Pre-IPO companies are an ideal opportunity for women to find their first board seats through private-equity companies before those companies go public.

A much higher percentage of directors serving on large-cap boards (valued at $5 billion or more) are women compared to the boards of smaller companies in the Russell 3000. In fact, in 2018, more than one in five (21%) of the directors serving on large-cap company boards were women. However, only about one in nine (11%) of the directors serving on micro-cap company boards (valued at $300 million or less) are women. As you'll read later in this book, this dismal statistic offers good news: limitless opportunities for women willing to start their board service in smaller companies.

Senate Bill 826—Seven Years from Pipe Dream to Passage

The passage of California's SB 826 in 2018 was the result of groundwork that took seven years to come to fruition. First it took a resolution to prove that the law was needed. California companies had the chance to add women voluntarily, but the resolution demonstrated that boards would not add women directors unless there was a penalty. And the resolution had to come years before a law could be considered. The resolution "urged" the state's publicly traded companies to voluntarily increase the level of gender diversity among their board members. In 2013, after many conversations with elected officials, both houses in the California State legislature passed SCR 62, which has no enforcement mechanism—no fines, no public statements, and no acknowledgment required for non-compliance. But it was a warning to all publicly held corporations that their governing boards must have more women directors.

Although the resolution was neither binding nor ultimately effective, it encouraged discussion regarding board diversity among corporate directors and leaders and it supported institutional investors' initiatives targeting companies that lacked board diversity. California set the example, and other state legislatures followed with their own resolutions. By 2017, Illinois, Massachusetts, Colorado, and Pennsylvania had adopted resolutions to increase gender diversity on boards of directors.

When the resolution did not cause change, the groundwork was laid for State Senator Hannah-Beth Jackson to file SB 826 in January of 2018. Then came the yearlong struggle to win passage, an intense process that required six major committee hearings in Sacramento, visits and phone calls to state legislators, and hundreds of letters. The governor finally signed the bill into law September 30, 2018 and it took effect January 1, 2019.

In November of 2018, New Jersey State Assembly member Nancy Pinkin filed a bill that mirrored the California law and Massachusetts followed next with an abridged version. In 2019, Michigan filed a bill similar to the California law. Then Illinois passed a bill that was amended to simply require reporting of corporations' efforts to increase diversity on boards.

Europe Had Laws Long Before the U.S.

While the California law shook the rafters in boardrooms of public companies across the U.S., mandates for gender representation were nothing new in Europe. Norway was first to force the issue in 2006, mandating an unheard-of 40% quota for women directors on public company boards. And the penalty for non-compliance was delisting the company. Some companies went private to avoid the unthinkable: having to put a significant number of women directors on their boards. But most companies followed the law and not only did they live to talk about it, they thrived. Countries in Europe that do not have quotas are not meeting such targets, because they have no incentive, no requirement to do so.

The example set by Norway—the world's third most gender-equal country behind Iceland and Finland—helped push European countries to enact quotas. Spain adopted a similar target in 2007. Soon to follow were: Belgium (with a mandate for 33% women directors), France (40%), Italy (33%), and the Netherlands (30%) in 2011. Germany (30%) followed in 2016. These nations now have some of the highest proportions of women directors in the European Union (EU).

In addition to the targets of these specific countries, the European Commission, the legislative body of the EU, advocated for a gender quota throughout the EU that requires 40% of a company's non-executive directors to be women. On average, women currently hold about 22% of seats on boards across all EU countries.

Even in Europe, quotas still have fierce opponents. Critics argue that quotas encourage tokenism, which they say elevates underqualified women to boards, undercuts selections based on merit, and forces companies to dip into what some characterize as the same, shallow talent pool. In Norway, the quota prompted some firms to delist rather than comply; the same may have occurred in other markets. Regulators in France have highlighted circumvention

Norway was first to force the issue in 2006, mandating **an unheard-of 40%** quota for women directors on public company boards strategies used by some firms, such as decreasing the total number of board members so that fewer women must be added to meet the percentage required.

As in the United States, however, there is plenty of research in Europe that shows the positive effects of greater gender diversity on boards. Research says that companies with diverse boards are more likely to have strong financial performance and fewer instances of bribery, corruption, shareholder battles, and fraud.

Věra Jourová, the EU commissioner in charge of justice and gender equality, was quoted in *The Guardian* and sounded very much like American advocates:

> We have so much evidence that it is good for business to have diversity, to have women and men on boards. Women have a very good talent for long-term, sensible spending [and] for crisis-solving, because they can come up with proposals for negotiation and compromise. It is a necessary balance to the approach of men.

Béatrice Guillaume-Grabisch is responsible for global human resources and business services on the executive board of Nestlé S.A. and is former chief executive officer of Nestlé Deutschland AG in Germany. She is well versed in the international trends for women board members. She has been a director of L'Oréal S.A. since 2016 and a member of the supervisory board at Henkel AG & Co. She previously served as president of the German business unit at the Coca-Cola Company. She points out that the L'Oréal board now has 54% female directors, a majority. But she adds:

> The pace seems to be slowing down in Europe after the first push to meet quotas. Quotas have been extremely important in the initial push for parity, but I believe that companies must embrace the need for women members voluntarily and not be forced to do so.

If a company is willing and eager to add women to its board, she says, they must also commit to making the change successful. The women who join the board must be made to feel included, comfortable, and valued.

Guillaume-Grabisch says that women in European countries face the same challenges as American women in gaining board seats and being successful as directors. Many board members still believe that there are not enough capable women to fill the required seats, she notes. Sometimes the management at the company where a woman works is threatened by her desire to serve on another firm's board:

Her CEO might feel that she is not dedicated to her own executive job, if she is seeking an outside corporate board seat. Senior management might question the value of board activity versus the work needed by her company.

Guillaume-Grabisch also points out that following the devastating financial crisis in 2008, some very qualified women executives with solid business reputations chose not to join boards due to potential liability and fear of serving on a company that they might not know was financially unstable.

Guillaume-Grabisch urges women to be determined to achieve success on boards, as in many other social constructs, and to work to promote other women:

> In any constellation, women know it will be very difficult to make it through if there is only one woman. If the woman doesn't succeed, it is used as proof that having a woman director was a bad decision. So to make a significant difference, the goal should be to aim for more than one woman.

In Europe, that goal is realized at Paris-based luxury conglomerate Kering, whose brands include Brioni, Gucci, Stella McCartney, Girard-Perregaux, and Puma. Among Europe's two hundred largest public companies, Kering has the highest percentage of women on its board—64%—and 33% on its executive committee, according to the nonprofit organizations European Women on Boards and Ethics & Boards.

Great Britain's 30% Club

In the United Kingdom (UK), women have also gained more board seats over the last decade. Although the UK government has not legislated quotas, there has been significant progress, thanks to the 30% Club. Melanie Richards, deputy chairman and board member of KPMG UK, is a founding member of the 30% Club. It was established in Britain in 2010 by Dame Helena Morrissey, who is considered the UK guru of women on boards. The group committed to achieving a minimum of 30% women on FTSE 100 boards by 2015, a goal they surpassed. FTSE is Britain's Financial Times Stock Exchange 100 Index, listing companies with the highest market capitalization. The 30% Club initially focused on recruiting chairs to advocate for and make change. Additionally, large investment firms, including BlackRock, J.P. Morgan Asset Management, and Standard Life, have joined to form a powerful body of investors representing significant influence.

According to Richards, five factors have contributed to success for the 30% Club:

- A measurable goal with a defined timetable
- Supportive public policy that acknowledged that the status quo was unacceptable
- Change driven by those in power
- Openness to collaborate
- Concerted and consistent actions and programs

The launch of the 30% Club coincided with the publication in 2011 of the *Davies Review,* a report backed by Britain's Department for Business, Energy, and Industrial Strategy, calling for FTSE 350 companies to target 25% of seats on their boards and executive committees for women by the end of 2020.

According to Richards, "Until 2010–2011, the UK was going nowhere fast. In terms of women achieving board seats, we had just barely reached double digits. But the *Davies Review* created a real momentum and focus." Richards also credits many of Britain's leading corporate men in power with speaking up on behalf of gender parity.

25% of all US public companies had **no** women directors in 2018

The *Hampton-Alexander Review* is an independent review body in the UK which has built on the work of the *Davies Review.* Hampton-Alexander's October 2018 statistics indicated continued progress. According to the report, 30.2% of board roles in FTSE's top one hundred companies are held by women, dramatically up from 12.5% in 2011. In the second tier of 250 FTSE public companies, 24.9% of board roles are held by women and in the top 350 companies, the percentage is 26.7.

"The *Davies* and the *Hampton-Alexander Reviews* also provoked a very productive conversation beyond board seats," says Richards. The *Hampton-Alexander Review* has now been extended to report on the number of women in the executive ranks and their direct reports, setting a target of 33% women on all FTSE 350 Boards and 33% women in all FTSE 100 senior leadership teams by 2020. In addition, gender pay legislation was passed in 2017, shining a light on the disparity between what men typically earn at a company and what women earn, regardless of their role or seniority. The *Gender*

Pay Gap Report, now published annually by the British government, has provided needed transparency to assess progress for working women and ongoing media attention has kept a spotlight on companies. As Richards notes:

> The momentum was strong early on, but maintaining it remains a challenge. In the boardrooms, some companies suffer "one and done" syndrome, stalling the progress of adding multiple women on boards. There is much work to do so that people understand that having only one woman director is not only tokenism, but can stifle getting the best. We are making progress but there are plenty of highly talented women who are still not being considered for both board and executive roles.

In 2019 the U.S. number of women directors on Russell 3000 boards **hit 20% for the first time!**

This gives you a look at the global picture of women on boards. There is, indeed, a global imperative to advance women to corporate boards, not just in the U.S., but in other industrialized countries. American women may also seek to serve on corporate boards in other countries, as several of the women profiled in this book have done. Read about Elizabeth Bastoni, Dany St-Pierre, Patricia Lizarraga, Brenda McCabe, and Holly Van Deursen. Sometimes American women find their first boards in other countries which gives them "prior board experience," adds to their credentials, and creates a better chance that their second board seat will be with a U.S. company.

GO IMMEDIATELY TO

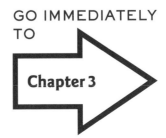

Chapter 3

3 The Inside Story About
B O A R D
Confidentiality,

SEARCHES —
Compensation, and Chemistry

I T'S IMPORTANT TO KNOW HOW BOARD SEARCHES WORK. HERE'S THE REALITY: a corporate board will rarely select total strangers as new directors—women *or* men. That means retained executive search firms are *not* likely to call you if you are not already known to someone on the board or to a member of the senior management of a company. It's critical that you understand this behind-the-scenes fact so you can proactively network with your own business contacts (or contacts of your contacts) who already serve on boards. There's the occasional stroke of luck out of the blue that lands you on a board, but barring such miracles, it is on your shoulders to be proactive and disciplined about seeking and winning your first corporate board seat.

Why is this? Because boards of directors are built on trusted relationships. A well-functioning board wants to maintain a collegial environment. Men are aware of this unspoken rule. Decade after decade, men have been courting their friends who serve on boards, lobbying them in hopes of being anointed when the more senior friend retires from his board seat. Once you know this fact of life, you can strategize to take advantage of your own network.

Opponents of the California law requiring more women on boards asked, "Why can't a woman just be included as one of the board candidates, rather than requiring that a woman be selected?" The answer is because corporate boards keep their succession planning process and candidate lists totally confidential. *There's no way to know if women were ever considered and, therefore, such a requirement could not be tracked.* The reality is that a woman may have outstanding credentials and experience and she may be "considered," but if she doesn't already know someone on that board, it is *not* likely she will be selected. The "Old Boys' Network" is too powerful.

Unfortunately, the only way to be certain that a woman will be selected is to make sure all candidates considered for a seat are women. And that's exactly what has been done in California since SB 826 was passed.

Another little-known fact is that new board members may be selected anytime during the year, regardless of when the shareholders' annual meeting is held. At the annual meeting for a corporation, shareholders vote their proxies and rarely object to a nominee. (Sometimes there's an activist shareholder who proposes his or her own personally nominated slate of potential candidates as an alternative to the slate recommended by the board.) The newly chosen director becomes official after the shareholders vote their proxies but he or she can occupy a seat and attend board meetings months before the annual meeting, though he or she cannot vote on issues at the board meeting until approved by shareholders.

In Europe, board searches are always handled by retained executive search firms. But in the U.S., only about 40% of board searches are conducted by retained executive search firms. Most are handled by boards without hiring a search firm and are focused on the board members' personal recommendations for a very short list of prospects. An executive search firm may be retained to check out the backgrounds of prospects on that short list who are already known and trusted by the board. Here's what happens:

During the succession planning process, nominating/governance committee members are seated around the boardroom table. The chairman of the committee states that the board should start the search for a successor to the director who is reaching the generally accepted board retirement age of seventy-five. Then, influenced by California's recent law or shareholder pressure, or to fend off an activist shareholder, the chairman of the board suggests that the new director should be a woman. (Let's give him credit that perhaps he is honestly acknowledging the advancing wave of qualified women who would bring new perspectives and career experience, as well as adding gender diversity to the board.) "So, does anyone know a woman qualified to serve on our board?" he asks the rest of the board, not kidding.

Before you laugh, understand that men on the board first bring up the fact that their spouses (the women they know best) are "outstanding executives," but cannot serve on the same board as their husbands. The C-suite women executives at their own company may be excellent, but conflicts of interest can arise when board members have personal, familial, or professional relationships outside the boardroom, perhaps with one having undue influence over the other, which would take away the "independent" status required for proper decision-making. So the women executives or business owners considered for boards are most often people men know and trust from their own past service on nonprofit boards, private company boards, industry trade associations, or commissions at state, county, or city levels. *That* is how women's names get on the candidate lists that are given to executive search firms to vet.

The search firm consultant might ask the nominating committee if the board would consider someone not on its list who fits the defined matrix of experience needed on the board—especially a woman or person of color who may not be known to the board. The answer is, of course, "yes." But the reality is that unless someone has heard of that potential candidate, odds are that he or she has a far lower chance than people already known to board members.

Recall that one of the primary duties of the public company board is to evaluate and hire or fire the chief executive officer (CEO). So, logically, the CEO does not want to bring on directors who have previously fired a CEO. The nominating/governance committee also wants to know how collegial—or disruptive—the prospective candidate has been as a director or as an executive elsewhere. So the search firm (and other board members) will confidentially contact members of the candidate's previous board(s) as references to find out what the person was like as a board member. Any potentially negative comments are reported verbally, rather than documented in writing.

The search firm will also check out the prospective candidate's calendar conflicts because attending all board meetings and committee meetings is mandatory. A calendar conflict is a non-starter.

The prospective candidate is not supposed to know which board is considering her or him. That's for two important reasons: 1) the board search is confidential; the company doesn't want the investment community to know

About 1/2 the boards in the country now experience some type of seat change **every year, which is an advantage to potential women candidates**

whom they are considering for the board since the stock price could be affected; and 2) a CEO does not want to disappoint any candidate who isn't selected, since this could be embarrassing to both the CEO and the prospect. So a professional search firm rarely reveals the name of the corporation looking for prospects until the board selects a candidate as a finalist, and the CEO then meets the candidate. Most often the CEO will have a personal interview with only one prospect (or at most two) as the final step of the process.

Age is also a significant factor. A successful candidate is expected to be able to serve for several years before retiring. Most publicly held corporations follow a generally accepted best practice that directors are expected to retire from the board at age seventy-five. So prospective candidates should secure their first board seats in their mid-fifties or sooner. This way the nominating/governance (Nom/Gov) committee has done its job—a new director in her fifties has a long runway to seventy-five. But not all boards have a retirement age. In the past, many directors thought they were appointed for life. So, even with age limits, board openings do not occur often on individual boards. However, because of greater pressure by shareholders who want to invest in companies with high-functioning boards, about half the boards in the country now experience some type of seat change every year, which is an advantage to potential women candidates.

Also, few companies have term limits for board members, because boards prefer stability rather than frequent turnover. However, there are no age limits or term limits on private company boards. So if you are in your late sixties or early seventies and still want to serve on a board, targeting private company boards is your best bet. Private equity investors seek board members for the companies in their portfolios. When portfolio companies go public, women who are already on the board often have a chance to stay on the board of the new public company. (Note: If the portfolio company is acquired rather than going public, the original board is disbanded and directors rarely move to the acquirer's board.)

For corporate board searches, people sometimes ask about the Rooney Rule. Why couldn't it apply to boards? The National Football League (NFL) created the Rooney Rule to require inclusion of at least one ethnic-minority candidate among those considered for very lucrative coaching positions in professional football. The NFL owners, including the late Dan Rooney, former owner of the Pittsburgh Steelers, agreed to this rule and to make public every list of potential candidates. So there's no way to hide whether or not a diverse candidate is on the list. But corporate board searches cannot be public and *should not* be public. It is up to the board members—and ultimately the shareholders—to approve the next director. There is no list that is made public, and there is no public scrutiny of the board search process. That's why the Rooney Rule will not work for corporate boards.

After the search firm vets the prospects on the list and gives its feedback to the Nom/Gov committee, the board members decide which *one,* or perhaps two, of the candidates they want to interview before recommending one or two finalists to meet with the CEO. There is no long list and no public knowledge of who is being considered. It's an inside decision. The shareholders do not compare backgrounds for a variety of potential candidates; they vote only their proxies—yes for one candidate selected by the Nom/Gov committee—or they can withhold their vote.

There are no ballots, there is no competition for choosing the best person, and the nominating committee generally chooses who will be the ONE person, or maybe two, who will meet the CEO for a "chemistry check." No one can "apply" or submit an "application" to be a board candidate. It's all about whom you know and who knows you. But don't be discouraged—now that you know the inside secrets, you can work your magic by networking to become known to board members. It may take time, but your discipline and persistence will pay off.

Board Compensation—and More

Fees paid to directors on boards include retainers for meetings, additional sums for committee meetings, and additional stipends for serving as chairs of committees and lead directors, board members who devote more time due to those leadership roles. Boards determine their own compensation, with approval by the shareholders at the annual meeting who vote their proxies. Compensation is generally half in cash and half in stock that is granted annually. Directors are not allowed to sell their stock until they retire or otherwise leave the board. The thinking behind this rule is: the stock remains in the company as an incentive, directors are motivated to guide the CEO well, and all investors are rewarded when the company does well or is sold.

Annual compensation can range from $50,000 for smaller public (or private) companies to $250,000 (or higher) for the largest public companies. In the U.S., compensation can be paid in both cash and stock. Companies in Europe pay less, and historically do not give stock to directors. In Europe, the practice of directors owning stock is thought to be a conflict of interest. In the U.S., it's considered an incentive for doing a good job on the board.

Because directors are compensated well, longtime board members are reluctant to give up their seats until they absolutely are required to leave.

Directors' friends hound current directors for years to be chosen as successors, because they want to earn significant compensation. But being a director has benefits beyond compensation. It means social and business connections, being among the elite of the business world, and travel to various locations for board meetings. For many, serving on boards is the ultimate business achievement—they have made it to the top, to the pinnacle of the business world. Directors are actually above CEOs, because the board of directors has the responsibility to hire, fire, and advise the CEO. In all public companies, the CEO reports to—and answers to—the board. Being a director is a powerful role.

But to many women directors, serving on the board means more than just money. It means making the difference. Board members help companies determine vision, strategy, and growth. Along the way, boards influence the environment around them. Boards affect the way employees are treated within the company. Women directors want to know their time is well-spent, bringing value to a company by serving on its board.

Chemistry—the Ultimate Selection Factor

Finally, board searches are determined by that all-elusive factor called "chemistry." That's why boards choose new members they already know; they already have chemistry in their relationships with them. However, chemistry should be seen from a larger perspective: the hard-to-describe connective tissue that helps a board be a *better* board. When a board selects a candidate, the decision often comes down to whom the board members and the CEO feel most comfortable with, and how they sense the person will interact with them in the boardroom. Unfortunately, sometimes a highly qualified woman candidate is not selected because the board feels the chemistry on the board (or the communication dynamics) would change if a woman were selected.

What does chemistry among board members have to do with making the difference? The women corporate directors profiled here unanimously agree that chemistry is the key to a well-functioning board that gets things done.

There is also agreement about what chemistry is *not*.

Chemistry is not simply collegiality, the ability to get along. It is not like-mindedness, finding a group of people who think alike and foresee the same outcomes. Nor is it commonality—where board members have similar backgrounds, status, education, and other biographical characteristics that bind them together—although this has been the principle behind the traditional makeup of most boards. As Lu Córdova puts it, chemistry should not be shorthand for finding "people like me."

Adding women to a corporate board actually enhances and strengthens board chemistry. Every woman profiled in this book brings unique qualities and distinct experience to her board service—whether as the first (and perhaps only) woman, or as a person of color, or as someone coming from a completely different background than the current members.

Beyond chemistry, the women you'll read about in this chapter all have made the difference on boards they serve because they call upon chemistry and empathy to bridge the communication gaps that may exist among members. They build trust based on listening, interacting, and reaching out to ask other directors for input and opinions.

Most of the women directors profiled here mentioned that women improve the board chemistry because women are such good communicators. They feel strongly that having women in the boardroom changes the conversation for the better.

Sheri Edison, Kathleen Holmgren, Gail Lione, and Lu Córdova all cite communication and the importance of board chemistry as primary ways they make the difference on their boards.

SHERI EDISON

❝ Chemistry is a two-way street: you are trying to get to know your fellow directors simultaneously while they are trying to get to know you. ❞

Chief Legal Officer Sheri Edison embarked on the path to corporate board membership over a decade before accepting her first director appointment to the board of AK Steel. She joined the National Association of Corporate Directors (NACD) to better understand governance from a practical, business-focused perspective.

SHERI EDISON
Green Bay, Wisconsin

Corporate Board:
AK Steel Holding Corporation

Career History:
Bemis Company, Inc.: SVP; Chief Legal Officer; Secretary
Hill-Rom Services, Inc.: SVP; Chief Administration Officer

Education:
JD, Northwestern University
BA, History and Journalism, University of Southern California

"I was trying to educate myself, but what I actually did there was serious networking with active board members. I developed relationships with the people who were doing what I wanted to eventually do—that was a major step in the right direction."

According to Edison, relationship building is key but also takes time and patience. In the process of attending NACD and DirectWomen gatherings, Edison became acquainted with three great mentors who would later open many corporate doors for her: Bonnie Hill (featured in *The Board Game Vol. I*), Paula Cholmondeley, and Reatha Clark King, past president of NACD.

"When you are looking to join a board, it is a tremendous help to be recommended. Those who endorse you, however, have to personally understand how you operate. And that doesn't happen overnight, or even in one year. So my best advice is to start navigating your pathway early."

In August of 2014, Edison received a direct call from AK Steel inviting her to participate in the search process to fill an upcoming vacancy on the board. Bonnie Hill was about to retire from the board, and she had recommended Edison to the position. As soon as Edison joined the AK Steel board, she felt she had chemistry with most board members. It was her intention, however, to better know all the board members. When one director extended the invitation for Edison to call whenever she felt like she needed a friend, Edison took him up on the offer.

"I called to ask his counsel after every single meeting. It was less about management and company performance, and more about the board dynamics and chemistry. He provided me with context and history, and he helped me process the unspoken words. After the first few meetings, I felt more and more comfortable contributing to the conversation."

At AK Steel, Edison sits on two committees: nominating and governance, and compensation. She says committee work is critical to board acclimation.

"You spend a lot of time listening and watching. Serving on a committee is an opportunity to understand the inner workings of the boardroom. Chemistry is a two-way street: you are trying to get to know your fellow directors simultaneously while they are trying to get to know you. It is helpful to open yourself up to the experience."

The purview of the nominating/governance committee includes succession planning and board refreshment. Members of the compensation committee also work closely with nominating and governance, tying executive performance to compensation.

"As SVP and CAO at my prior employer, Hill-Rom, I had far-reaching responsibility for the critical functions of the company, including IT, government affairs, and regulatory affairs. My work in that capacity shaped my perspective in evaluating talent, culture, and overall business dynamics."

Edison says experience in refreshing and implementing board evaluations has been extremely helpful on the AK Steel board. Board evaluations help to ensure whether each individual, regardless of term or age, is contributing in a valuable way to the board. While evaluations may initially cause tension among board members, Edison encourages active engagement.

"It's ultimately a performance review. Each director needs to contribute to the board at appropriate levels. If they're not, then there needs to be a conversation. But I've noticed, as board members become more confident and comfortable with the process, the feedback becomes more productive over time. It is truly an iterative process—you get better and better at it with time."

As an African American woman director, Edison says she brings the element of diversity to the entire board.

"My perspective helps drive richer and more robust conversations at the board and committee meetings."

To all women directors and executives, Edison emphasizes that diversity is the most important part of attracting, developing, and retaining talent.

"One way to proactively ensure that you are using a wide lens to seek opportunities in developing talent is to reach out to female executives who are coming up through the ranks. I try to really connect with women and make sure they feel they are supported—in every way I can."

Growing up as the youngest in her family, Edison was not always comfortable with the role of leader or mentor. College changed all that.

"I was elected president of my sorority. And then, I continued to be elected to positions of influence. As time went on, and I went to law school, I realized that people saw in me an ability to lead—something I had not seen in myself. I had also not considered how leading people and experiencing their growth can also be a true source of joy."

22%
of board seats were held by women in
Fortune 1000
in 2018

KATHLEEN HOLMGREN

> 66 *Critically important to board success is board chemistry.* 99

Strategic networking with other women executives who belong to the Executive Women's Alliance in the San Francisco Bay Area led Kathleen Holmgren to her first corporate board seat, at Group Delphi, a private company in Silicon Valley. Located where companies are notorious for lack of women directors on their boards, Holmgren tries to crack that brick wall whenever she sees an opportunity to do so. She was one of the charter members of the Stanford Women on Boards Initiative, designed to help MBA women from Stanford's business school find pathways to boards.

KATHLEEN HOLMGREN
Ventura, California

Corporate/Select Nonprofit Boards:
Calavo Growers, Inc.
Extreme Networks
Group Delphi
Automation Anywhere, Inc.
Fresh Realm, LLC
Silvercor, Inc.
Stanford Graduate School of Business, Advisory Board
California Polytechnic State University (Cal Poly) College of
    Engineering, Advisory Board
Alvesta Corporation
Mendocino Software, Inc.

Career History:
Sage Advice Partners/Holmgren Enterprises: Principal, Management
    Consulting
Automation Anywhere, Inc.: Chief Officer, Future Workforce; COO
Alliance of Chief Executives: Director
Mendocino Software, Inc.: President and CEO
Sun Microsystems, Inc.: SVP; GM, Disk Systems Business
Price Waterhouse (now PricewaterhouseCoopers): Senior Consultant

Education:
MBA, Stanford University
BS, Industrial Engineering, California Polytechnic State University

"Men are very good at using their own networks, and as women, we need to do the same. I also find that male executives who have daughters are more sensitized to the challenges of advancing women in technology."

Her mentor has been John Shoemaker (the proud father of two accomplished daughters, she notes). Shoemaker had been her boss at Sun Microsystems in San Jose, California. As Sun Microsystems senior vice president and general manager, Holmgren had grown Sun's storage business in three years to a $1.5 billion business, leading it to become a division of the company.

Over the years, Holmgren has had many conversations with Shoemaker about women in business—discussing topics such as differences in salaries and the lack of women in the top executive ranks, and especially on public corporate boards.

In 2015, Shoemaker recruited Holmgren to the Extreme Networks board. Two years earlier, he had secured a board interview for her at a public company that had been looking for a woman director. She wasn't selected for that board seat, but Shoemaker was able to introduce her to the board of Extreme Networks, Inc., a supplier of network solutions in eighty countries. Holmgren's experience—in technology business unit management, operations, and supply chain—worked out well. She says the Extreme board has great chemistry and is very productive.

Holmgren's two-year tenure on Extreme's board was so successful that, as board chairman, Shoemaker wanted to find another woman for the board. In 2018, Extreme found Maryam Alexandrian-Adams, also located in the Bay Area, with career experience in technology, sales, and mergers and acquisitions.

Serving on the audit committee at Extreme, Holmgren points out how important it is to have a well-run, professional board that works well with the company's executive team.

"As an example, I meet regularly with the internal management group that runs supply chain and operations. Bringing our respective talents to the senior leadership team, we can advise them and the CEO and make a positive difference when we bring our observations from an outside perspective.

"Having women directors also encourages female employees to approach us to ask questions about their career paths. They see us as role models and are anxious to ask us questions about how we got to this point in our careers.

"Extreme's management makes it a point for directors to participate in 'all-hands meetings' with the local employees, followed by a reception, whenever we visit a company location for our board meeting. On each occasion, I have been approached by women at all levels of the company to discuss topics ranging from career path to balancing work and family. It is a great practice, and employees feel connected to the board as a result."

Holmgren says that she was fortunate to have joined the board at one of the lowest points in that company's history and that she has enjoyed being part of the turnaround. When she accepted her seat, she and the other board members helped the CEO (who was a former board member) change the culture, reduce costs, acquire key products and technology, and turn around sales.

"Extreme acquired three networking divisions during my first year as a director that were being sold by other companies including Brocade and Avaya. These acquisitions were opportunistic to add volume, skilled workers, and new products to our existing business."

Thanks to an introduction by a retained search firm, Holmgren was invited to join the board of Calavo, a multichannel grower, manufacturer, and distributor of avocados and other fresh produce. She serves on both the audit and compensation committees at Calavo.

I'm not the required 'finance expert,' so it's good governance to have a CPA on the finance committee who is up to speed on audit and compliance implications." Holmgren has an MBA and was responsible for the profit and loss of Sun Storage Business Unit, but she does not have the credentials the SEC requires to be a designated "finance expert" on boards.

Calavo is also an investor in a prepped and prepared meal-kit company called Fresh Realm. Because of Holmgren's operations background, the CEO of Fresh Realm asked her to sit on his board. Because the firm is a start-up, Holmgren works closely with other board members and the CEO to help ensure that the operations of the company can scale to meet the rapid growth of their sales and geographic expansion.

Unlike technology companies, in the fresh-food industry, for both Calavo and Fresh Realm, there is no such thing as excess and obsolete inventory. If food sits on the shelf too long, it spoils, so the supply-demand process needs to be extremely fine-tuned.

"I love learning about this new industry. Many business problems extend across industry lines, so people should not be hesitant to try for board seats outside their industries. My advice to newcomers to any board is to take time to become acclimated. I took time to learn about each corporation and its issues, and spent time visiting with the executives to learn about their responsibilities and to develop relationships with them. Only then could I add real value when I had something to say at the board level.

"Critically important to board success is board chemistry. On one of my boards, there was disruption caused by one person, disruption that became more and more destructive to the board, the CEO, and the executive team. I approached other members of the board and brought forth my concerns that such negative disruption isn't right—our role as board members was to help the company, not tear it down.

"So as a board, we decided to ask that board member to resign. His departure completely changed the complexion of the board, our relationship with the CEO, and the way the executive team works with the board. That's one example where I've made a difference. Although everyone else was feeling the same way, I brought this issue to the forefront and asked why we were putting up with it. I was dreading going to board meetings at the time because of the destructive behavior; now I really look forward to going."

Holmgren has balanced family and career throughout her adult life, she says. She and her husband have three children.

"I have a great partnership with my husband—both of us work, and neither of us could have had successful careers and family life without the other partner. Doing homework with the kids, each of us has learned chemistry and physics three times over. As the children got older (and, of course, homework became more difficult), he left his job to start his own marketing consulting firm, so he could have a home office and be there for our teenagers. We are blessed with a beautiful family."

GAIL LIONE

> *A lot takes place in—and outside—the boardroom. I believe in informal mentoring and sponsorship.*

Gail Lione credits the YMCA for engendering leadership in her early years. She grew up swimming in the same YMCA pool where her mother learned to swim in Flushing, New York.

GAIL LIONE
Washington, D.C.

Corporate/Select Nonprofit Boards:
Badger Meter, Inc.
Sargento Foods, Inc.
The F. Dohmen Co.
Imperial Sugar Company
YMCA of Metropolitan Atlanta, Inc.
YMCA of Metropolitan Milwaukee
United Way of Greater Milwaukee & Waukesha County
University of Rochester Board of Trustees

Career History:
Dentons U.S., LLP: Senior Counsel
Georgetown University Law Center and Marquette University Law
    School: Adjunct Professor of Law
Harley-Davidson Foundation: President
Harley-Davidson, Inc.: EVP; General Counsel; Secretary; Chief
    Compliance Officer
U.S. News & World Report, LP; The Atlantic Monthly Group,
    Inc.; Applied Printing Technologies, LP; Applied Graphics
    Technologies, Inc.: General Counsel
Maryland National Bank: VP
Sun Life Group of America, Inc.: SVP; General Counsel; Secretary
The First National Bank of Atlanta (Wachovia): VP
Hansell, Post, Brandon & Dorsey: Attorney
Morgan Lewis & Bockius, LLP: Attorney

Education:
JD, University of Pennsylvania
BA, Political Science, University of Rochester

"I have the Y to thank for laying the foundation of my leadership training. I learned everything I know about how to organize groups and effectively communicate a goal when I was a child on the swim team. The leadership I've demonstrated on nonprofit and for-profit boards all stems from a similar place: passion. And I'm passionate about giving back to organizations like the Y that have given to so many for so long."

Lione began her career as an attorney, ascending the ranks to general counsel of companies including Harley-Davidson, U.S. News & World Report, and Sun

Life Group of America. She currently serves as a director on the board of Badger Meter, Inc., a publicly traded manufacturing company that is an innovator in flow measurement, control, and communications solutions serving water utilities, municipalities, and commercial and industrial customers worldwide. She is also on the board of Sargento Foods, Inc. and was previously on the board of The F. Dohmen Co. Sargento is the well-known, Wisconsin-based cheese company.

In 2006, her first seat on a board happened by way of relationships she developed when she was a senior officer at Harley-Davidson and on the YMCA board. Sargento was looking for a non-family-member director to succeed a director who was aging off the board. Two of the other directors on Sargento's board knew Lione.

"One was the CEO of one of Harley's largest suppliers, and we had worked together. The other was a prominent Milwaukee entrepreneur who co-chaired a YMCA annual fundraising campaign with me. They sponsored me for the board and, after I was interviewed by the family directors, I was elected to serve. It has been an incredible experience to work with such a remarkable company and family."

The second board Lione joined was in November of 2007—Imperial Sugar, a Texas-based NASDAQ company. The seat came through a less-conventional avenue.

"I was attending a good friend's wedding in Bermuda, and the chair of the board at Imperial was seated next to me at the rehearsal dinner. After a conversation over dinner, he gave my name to the search firm handling the open board seat for Imperial. The moral of that story is, you never know when or where you will meet a contact for a board seat, so always be curious, prepared, and willing to state your intention to serve on a board."

Lione says the best way to get on a board is to focus on your network in your own city.

"You know the resources. You know whom to call. You see the leadership at functions and at the grocery store. You know their spouses and their children. You know their ethics and how they conduct themselves when they don't think anyone is looking. That makes a huge difference."

For example, when Lione retired from Harley-Davidson in May of 2011, Richard A. Meeusen, the CEO of Badger Meter, called. This was not by coincidence, she said. Lione and Meeusen were both very active in the Greater Milwaukee business and charitable communities.

"I had chaired a United Performing Arts campaign, a counterpart to United Way for the arts in Milwaukee. Rich was the chair of the United Performing Arts board. My husband also knew him through his work on the Water Council. We knew each other from those nonprofits, as well as others like the YMCA and United Way. In fact, I also knew many of the other CEOs on the Badger Meter board the same way. These prior relationships were extremely helpful to me in understanding the company and ascertaining the chemistry of the board before making the decision to join the board."

Each board provides a unique experience, but Lione says she particularly enjoyed the boardroom dynamics at The F. Dohmen Co., the board she joined in March 2013 and served until the end of 2017, after which its largest division, Dohmen Life Science Services, was sold. The Dohmen board was led by a fifth-generation woman CEO. Its six-person board was evenly split—three women and three men.

"This company was not only strategically positioned to make great strides in the pharmaceutical industry, but also it had an incredibly innovative boardroom. The CEO transformed and strengthened the relationship between life-science companies and the patients they serve. Of course, the fact that the board was 50% female was a different and very positive experience for me."

In 2012, the *Milwaukee Business Times* named Lione as Woman Executive of the Year. She was the second woman to receive this honor; the first was Cynthia Dohmen LaConte.

"When I was given this honor, I looked up the previous winner and realized we had never met. For a city the size of Milwaukee, that is unusual, so I called her and asked her to lunch. We clicked immediately, and a number of productive conversations ensued, related to the strategic direction of her company. After a while, she asked me to join her board. It was fortuitous, but just goes to show where your own curiosity, interests, and initiative can take you."

Lione's experience in law and human resources, and that she worked at a large financial institution, makes her valuable to all board committees. At Dohmen, she served on the audit committee. At Sargento, she was on the audit committee and now serves on the compensation committee. And at Badger Meter, she is a member of the nominating/corporate governance committee and the compensation committee, and she just finished a two-year term as lead director.

"I would say that being on the audit committee is the best way to really understand the entire company. There is a natural tendency to have lawyers on the nominating/governance committee, especially if you are a general counsel, but audit is the ideal committee to join when you are new to a board.

"There are many ways you can make contributions on a board. A lot takes place in—and outside—the boardroom. I believe in informal mentoring and sponsorship. For example, I introduced a senior executive at Badger Meter to a group called Milwaukee Women Inc., where she later became an officer of the organization. Making connections for women (and men) at companies where you serve on the board is critically important and really helps to broaden their experience.

"Whenever possible, I counsel women who aspire to get on their first board that it's a two-way street. The board needs to be the right fit for you, too. It is not worth going on a board where there may be tension between directors and the CEO, or where members are not open to constructive dialogue. Chemistry is critical, and this is one of the biggest advantages of focusing on local companies to find your first board."

Lione also urges potential board members to think strategically and ask important questions:

- Ascertain whether the company and its board are moving in the right direction in the industry. Are they exercising best practices?
- Is there a clear corporate strategy? Are the directors and the CEO in alignment with this vision? Do the employees know and understand the vision?
- Is the board well versed in the industry's trends, technologies, other innovations, and potential threats, like cybersecurity?
- What is the tone at the top, and what are the company's compliance programs and track record of compliance?
- If the company does international business, how does management adhere to the Foreign Corrupt Practices Act and other compliance issues?
- During an interview with two or more board members, have your antenna up. Do the directors listen to each other? Or are they interrupting each other or already thinking about the next question?

Lione encourages women to listen intently once they join a board.

"Being in listening mode is a good thing—leadership on the board evolves over time. Listening allows new directors—both men and women—to pick up on subtle cues that will enable more effective participation in the future.

"Being able to persuade helps as well. Persuasion is truly an art form and takes longer to understand in a boardroom, even for lawyers who are used to advocating. You may have the best ideas and questions, but it's how you bring forth those ideas and how you ask those questions that will either make people feel comfortable enough to have open dialogue or make them wary. There is a real art to being heard."

Lione proved that from her early efforts to get a job in a congressional district office while growing up in Queens, New York.

"Every year I was in high school, I wrote my congressman a letter, asking for a job. Eventually, he hired me after I graduated. He always joked that it was my persistence that got me the job, and I believe that's partially true. I also was a legislative policy nerd. I loved politics and the political process. As long as you are passionate, learn how to motivate individuals, and yes, are persistent, you will achieve what you want in life—including serving on corporate boards."

Most recently, Lione was honored by DirectWomen, the nonprofit organization that trains women in the legal profession—general counsels and senior law partners—to become corporate board members.

Annually, DirectWomen awards the Sandra Day O'Connor Board Excellence Award to women lawyers who have served with distinction as independent directors of public companies and have worked to advance the value of diversity in board positions. An innovator and pioneer, Supreme Court Justice Sandra Day O'Connor was the first woman justice in the Supreme Court's history. Award winners exemplify paving new paths for women who come after them. DirectWomen honors the winners—and the companies on whose boards they serve—for promoting board diversity.

LU M. CÓRDOVA

> **I bring to the table a sense of the soft skills, but I focus on efforts that truly drive the business.**

From its pioneering days in the 1980s, technology set the stage for Lu Córdova's career, but it was her experience in business, mergers and acquisitions, finance, and economics that rounded out her qualifications for corporate boards. She served from 2000 to 2011 as an independent director on the board of the Federal Reserve Bank of Kansas City, where she gained regulatory knowledge for corporate governance and served a full term as its chairman.

LU M. CÓRDOVA
Denver, Colorado, and Baja California

Corporate/Select Nonprofit Boards:
Kansas City Southern Railway Company (now Kansas City Southern)
Colorado Venture Centers, Inc.
CTEK
Euronet Worldwide, Inc.
Federal Reserve Bank of Kansas City

Career History:
Almacen Storage Group (Mexico): CEO
Corlund Industries, LLC (U.S. and Mexico): CEO
Techstars Foundation: President
CTEK, CTEK Venture Centers, and CTEK Angels: CEO; Chairman of the Board
ACTEVA (previously TixToGo): CEO
Excite@Home: VP
McGraw-Hill's Standard & Poor's Information Group: SVP, Strategic Planning

Education:
PhD, ABD, Economics, University of California, Berkeley
BA, Political Science and Economics, University of California, Berkeley

Headquartered in Kansas City, the Tenth District of the Federal Reserve Bank is second only to the Federal Reserve Bank of San Francisco in size of geographic area served. It covers seven states: Colorado, western Missouri, Nebraska, Kansas, Oklahoma, Wyoming, and northern New Mexico, with 1,500 employees and branches in Denver, Oklahoma City, and Omaha. She served several terms, thanks to receiving a waiver from the Fed's Board of Governors to serve beyond its customary term limit to help recruit the current bank president. Prior to becoming a director, Córdova served for three years on the Fed's Economic Advisory Council.

From connections she made through the Federal Reserve and her work in Mexico, she was recommended in 2010 for the board of Kansas City Southern Railway Company, a firm with an $11.7 billion market cap and 7,000 employees in North America. She chairs its finance/strategic investments committee and is a member of the audit and the nominating/corporate governance committees.

As an American-born Latina, Córdova has dual U.S. and Mexican citizenship, which is very helpful for her work on this board. Along with her own company, which is headquartered in Mexico, dual citizenship allows her to see the operational and cultural differences between both countries. Córdova speaks conversational Spanish with business leaders and has met with the president of Mexico and several cabinet members.

"Railroads play an integral role in commerce and logistics in today's market, but it has historically been a male-dominated industry, so it is not surprising that I was the only woman on the board for many years. I was ecstatic when the board selected two more women directors in 2017. I submitted many candidates during the selection process. One of them has been chosen."

From her more than thirty years in local and global capital markets—from startup phase through initial public offerings and maturity—Córdova has developed a deep expertise in international finance. She has overseen structured finance, hedge strategies, and debt restructuring. She developed her technology experience, including cybersecurity and e-commerce, from her early career at the financial solutions company Standard & Poor's, part of McGraw-Hill.

From 2011 through 2015, Córdova was on the board of Euronet Worldwide, a provider of electronic payment services, including an international network of ATMs, electronic funds transfer (EFT) processing, prepaid phone and gift card processing, and money transfer, with a $5.1 billion market cap and 5,600 employees in more than sixty countries. She was an independent director and a member of the audit, compensation, and nominating/governance committees.

Córdova is careful to point out that board chemistry supersedes gender as a critical factor in selecting new board members, especially when adding women to a board that has historically been all men.

"'Chemistry' is their new euphemism for 'people like me.' To embrace inclusion and reap the well-known benefits of diversity, boards need to change the way they do recruitment and meet women candidates continuously—getting to know them, not just when the moment of succession comes to the fore. Succession planning is one of the greatest responsibilities of a board, and there are 'soft issues' around the interdynamics between personalities during the transition. It's an emotional time.

"I bring to the table a sense of the soft skills, but at the same time I focus on efforts that truly drive the business. To bring the gender diversity component, along with the skills needed to be effective, I think it is important to find a male ally who understands the value of having women on boards. Look for the board members who have daughters, and you will find ready allies."

17% of Russell 3000 companies had **no women** on their boards in 2018

GO IMMEDIATELY TO

Chapter 4

4

Cybersecurity, Marketing, Human Resources

BOARDS NEED

Women

EXPERTISE AND

Bring It

Board members should be trusted stewards of the company's long-term value; they should be viewed and respected as contemporary and up-to-date with the needs of the company. All company stakeholders—management, staff, customers, investors, and shareholders—put their faith in the leadership of the board and expect members to be as knowledgeable as possible about current issues and keep up with changing trends.

Boards that are "male, pale, and stale"—and have resisted adding women—are behind the times when it comes to the needs of a twenty-first century company. This chapter is devoted to women who have excelled in their careers through changing and dynamic times, and have proven their expertise in three areas that are critical to a corporation's success in the twenty-first century: cybersecurity, digital marketing, and human resources.

Cybersecurity

Many of the women featured in this book emphasize that cybersecurity—the protection of networks, programs, and data—is the Number One topic discussed in boardrooms today. In an era of cyber attacks, including hacking of sensitive information, boards must have members who are conversant and comfortable in the techniques used to protect the integrity of information technology systems.

Former Presidential Advisor Leslie Ireland, Major General Barbara Faulkenberry, and "First Lady of Defense" Linda Hudson each have a depth of knowledge and experience in cybersecurity issues, which is the value-added expertise that they brought to the boards of huge corporations.

LESLIE IRELAND

> *I find that many women in government don't fully understand that...their knowledge of how governments work is very much value-added for corporate boards.*

Leslie Ireland's remarkable three-decade-long career in the United States intelligence community brought her directly into the Oval Office, where she provided national security briefings for President Barack Obama. It also brought her to the attention of Citigroup, Inc., one of the world's largest banking institutions, where she has served on the board since October 2017.

LESLIE IRELAND
Washington, D.C.

Corporate/Select Nonprofit Boards:
Citigroup, Inc.
The Stimson Center

Career History:
U.S. Government:
Department of the Treasury: Assistant Secretary for Intelligence
  and Analysis; Director of National Intelligence (DNI); National
  Intelligence Manager for Threat Finance
Obama Administration: President's Daily Intelligence Briefer
Director of National Intelligence (DNI): Iran Mission Manager
Central Intelligence Agency (CIA): Executive Advisor to the Director
  of Central Intelligence; various leadership and staff and analytical
  positions (classified)

Education:
MA, Russian Studies, Georgetown University
BA, Government, concentration in International Relations, Franklin &
  Marshall College

Before retiring from the U.S. government, Ireland served as assistant secretary of the treasury for intelligence and analysis under President Obama from 2010 to 2016. In this role, she was the principal intelligence advisor to the secretary of the treasury. She also was responsible for leading the analysis of key financial vulnerabilities of foreign entities that pose threats to U.S. national security, as well as strengthening and expanding the infrastructure needed to protect the Treasury's national-security information.

Concurrently, Ireland served as the first national intelligence manager for threat finance under Director of National Intelligence James Clapper. She was responsible for overseeing the intelligence process regarding the use of financial information to combat threats to U.S. national security, including terrorism, weapons of mass destruction, narcotics trafficking, and transnational organized crime.

Before taking the presidential appointment in the Department of the Treasury, she spent twenty-five years at the Central Intelligence Agency (CIA). Ireland's assignments included giving President Obama's daily intelligence briefings during the transition and through his first year in office. She was also the first director of national intelligence: Iran mission manager, where she defined and directed intelligence-community priorities on Iran to give decision-advantage to U.S. policymakers including the president, national security advisor, cabinet secretaries, and warfighters such as the chairman of the joint chiefs of staff and combatant commanders.

She first met leaders from Citigroup as part of her work in national intelligence. It was her idea to establish a financial-sector advisory board to consult with Director of National Intelligence Clapper.

"There is a texture to the way money moves that the financial sector understands best. Money always moves for a reason and between people who know each other. Thus, the flow can tell you about networks, motives, and intentions. Like water in a river, money wants to move, and it will find a way to get around efforts to disrupt its flow. Our adversaries will always try to find ways to creatively move money around for their own benefit. We needed to tap into the expertise of the financial sector to stay abreast of the challenge.

"I invited people from a cross-section of the financial sector, including representatives of banks, to join that advisory board, and I ensured that they received appropriate security clearances. Having those private-sector connections was an innovative approach in the intelligence community, and I thought it was important to our ability to support U.S. policy efforts to help protect the financial sector."

When she was approaching retirement from government service, given the value she could provide on cyber issues, Ireland asked advisory board members for advice about how to pursue a corporate board, and she asked them to recommend her for future board seats they might hear about.

"At Treasury, our office was well-known for the analysis that was integral to sanctions programs and other U.S. and international policy priorities—for example, Iran's nuclear program, North Korean regime finance networks, and Syrian human-rights abuses. We also had an important cybersecurity role protecting Treasury IT systems from potential internal and external threats, and supporting Treasury's work to protect the financial sector and U.S. payment systems against cyber attacks.

"I draw on a lot of that experience for what I do on the Citi board."

Ireland was not only proactive in pursuing a board appointment, she also took important steps to prepare herself. Having spent her entire career in government service, she wanted to develop a greater understanding of corporate governance. She sought out a course that the National Association of Corporate Directors (NACD) was offering for flag-rank military officers called Battlefield to the Boardroom.

That course was designed to help prepare these officers for board service in retirement. Although she never served in the military, a former military officer with whom Ireland had worked endorsed her for the program. She was the first civilian to complete the course.

"I find that many women in government don't fully understand that they bring the kind of experience needed to qualify for corporate boards. However, their knowledge of how governments work is very much value-added for corporate boards. I know that my insights about cyber attacks, sanctions evasion, and money laundering are far different skills than what other directors bring to the board. All of these issues pose threats to the health and resiliency of the financial sector, which is a matter of national security.

"Because of this, I bring the same sense of urgency to the bank board that I brought to my government career. This is what I call my 'mission focus,' and it is central to my service for Citigroup.

"Cyber attacks and breaches are a matter of *when,* not *if.* This is true at all financial institutions and other corporations in America. Corporate boards play a valuable role in understanding and reviewing cyber-risk. It is not just the responsibility of IT; it presents enterprise-wide risk and requires enterprise-wide response. The loss of data, operational capabilities, and/or money likely means the loss of trust and confidence with customers, counterparties, and, in some industries, government regulators. This risk is particularly acute in the financial sector, which is integral to the major muscle movements of the U.S. and global economy. Directors are uniquely positioned to take an enterprise-wide look at an organization's cybersecurity defensive posture and to discuss what to do in the event of a breach, hopefully well in advance of one.

"As a woman on the board, I'm first an analyst who applies the critical-thinking skills I developed over years of government service. My instinct is to question things. I do think I have developed a way to ask direct questions without being confrontational that helps people think through a problem or an issue. I am also eager to learn about an industry that is relatively new to me. So, asking questions is a vital part of board work. On the flip side, management needs to be receptive to those questions. A good relationship between management and the board is critical to anticipating and addressing problems that could negatively impact shareholder value."

Ireland is clearly proud of the fact that Citigroup's board is 30% women. She is working hard to build capacity for other women to follow. She is part of a networking group in Washington, D.C. that is focused on helping women reach board seats and targeting appropriate boards.

"I tend to gravitate toward change, toward creating and starting something new. When I became the first Iran mission manager, I was responsible for overseeing the intelligence process on Iran for the entire U.S. government. The position was brand new, and a radical step, altering years of more 'stove-piped' intelligence efforts, with no one individual responsible and accountable for cross-communicating with other departments and stakeholders.

"I'll never forget a phone call I received two weeks after I took over. A colleague at another agency confided in me that they had seen this tried before and were just going to wait it out and see how fast it would fail. I thought, failure is not going to happen on my watch. I'm going to make it work. And I did."

BARBARA FAULKENBERRY

66 *In my first eighteen months, we dealt with activist investors, a CEO transition, and a strategy refresh.* 99

Major General Barbara Faulkenberry served with the United States Air Force for thirty-two years before retiring as one of the top one hundred leaders among the 330,000-person USAF in 2014. Over the course of her military career, she had been responsible for overseeing the global operations of 1,100 USAF mobility airplanes, conducting cargo/personnel movement, air refueling, and aeromedical evacuations. Her oversight spanned from flying the president of the United States on Air Force One, to airdropping people and supplies in combat operations across the Middle East, to bringing home wounded Americans in ICU-capable aircraft.

After such an exciting life of responsibility and public service, Faulkenberry says she asked herself a few years before her retirement from the Air Force, what she envisioned the next chapter of her life would look and feel like. From this self-reflection, she realized her high-level operations and logistics experience could be value-added for corporate boards in civilian life. It wasn't easy—and it took her fifteen months to find the right fit.

In January 2016, she was elected the first woman director on the board of USA Truck, based in Van Buren, Arkansas. A second woman, Susan Chambers, retired executive vice president and chief human resources officer for Walmart, was appointed a few months later.

"To prepare for someday serving on boards, I immediately started to educate myself on corporate governance—knowing that business is a lot different from the military. The more I learned, the more I became convinced that board service was what I wanted to do. I became very intentional about learning all I could learn, and meeting other people who serve on corporate boards. Of course, I knew the more traditional path to a corporate board seat would have been to build community networks by volunteering for local nonprofits, thus meeting people who could recommend me for board seats."

But her non-traditional career had relocated her eighteen times, every couple of years, to many different bases around the globe. She was never in one place long enough to develop deep local ties to business leaders who could nominate her for board seats. "I joined the National Association of Corporate Directors (NACD) and Women in the Boardroom (WIB) to take advantage of their board-training courses and webinars." Faulkenberry ultimately became a NACD board leadership fellow. She attended developmental NACD, WIB, and KPMG events held in various locations as she was traveling: New York, Chicago, Kansas City, Denver, and Washington, D.C.

BARBARA FAULKENBERRY
Colorado Springs, Colorado

Corporate/Select Nonprofit Boards:
Callon Petroleum Company
USA Truck, Inc.
National Association of Corporate Directors,
    Colorado Chapter
International Women's Forum Leadership
    Foundation
Women's Forum of Colorado, Inc.
Falcon Foundation, Board of Trustees

Career History:
U.S. Government:
U.S. Air Force: Major General
Eighteenth Air Force, Air Mobility Command: Vice Commander
U.S. Africa Command: Director of Logistics
U.S. Central Command: Director of Mobility Forces
15th Expeditionary Mobility Task Force: Commander
Requirements and Programs, Air Mobility Command: Deputy Director
    of Strategic Plans
Squadron Officers' College: Commandant
375th Airlift Wing: Wing Commander

Education:
MA, National Security Policy Studies, National Defense University
MA, Airpower Arts and Sciences, School of Advanced Airpower
    Studies
MBA, Georgia College and State University
BA, Operations Research, United States Air Force Academy

"My career also required long working hours and constant movement. So I had to create those connections a different way—by going to NACD-type events, not only to learn from their board development opportunities, but also to get to know other directors who serve on boards. Networking, education, and putting in the time and energy—that's what paid off for me."

She focused on this goal with the same high level of detailed organization, dedication, and enthusiasm that had been required by her global military missions. Faulkenberry honed her two-minute "high-impact sound-bite" to be explicit and cogent in citing her experience—including risk management, global logistics, strategic planning, and leadership development. At an NACD Summit cocktail party in October of 2015, her efforts were rewarded when she caught the interest of the chairman of the audit committee on the board of USA Truck.

"It all happened fairly quickly. After the NACD conference, the chairman of the board reached out. We met first in an airport while he was traveling through Denver. Soon thereafter, I met the nominating and governance chair, then the rest of that committee, but only by phone. By January, I was elected to the board."

The USA Truck board was seeking a member with technological expertise, so Faulkenberry was able to demonstrate how the technology she employed as part of the military's global logistics enterprise increased effectiveness and efficiency, as well as her significant operational experience with cybersecurity. Additionally, she had complementary experience including government affairs, planning, and negotiations—all things she had learned in the Air Force—which added up to a well-rounded candidate.

"Though I'm not a CIO or CTO, the Air Force incorporated cybersecurity in all our operations and exercises—and the military is constantly involved with both. I'm very familiar with cyber defenses, the tools needed, what to do in the event of a breach, and how to go about understanding and managing potential crises."

So the game plan is what it came down to for Faulkenberry. The United States trucking industry topped revenues at over $700 billion in 2015. At $507 million annual revenues, USA Truck fit neatly near the middle—smaller than behemoths like Knight, but in the top fifty trucking companies with operations in Mexico and Canada. After reviewing the firm's plans to increase revenue and profits and to revitalize the brand in order to compete with larger transportation players, Faulkenberry determined that her appointment to the USA Truck board was a perfect fit.

"This is right in my wheelhouse: transportation, the moving of things, international logistics. Except for the difference that trucks are on the ground and planes are in the air, many of the principles are the same that I dealt with in the Air Force."

With two women on a board that was completely refreshed in a short time, Faulkenberry says she has gotten great experience and been able to contribute in large ways.

"This is a very dynamic board. In my first eighteen months, we dealt with activist investors, a CEO transition, and a strategy refresh. I sit in on all the committees to be able to understand and contribute as much I can to the success of the company."

Faulkenberry was also asked to chair the technology committee within six months of joining the board, an unusually quick leadership role for someone new to corporate governance. In fact, USA Truck is innovative in even having a technology committee, as only twenty-three Fortune 500 companies had such a committee in 2016.

The only in-person interview Faulkenberry had before joining the board was with the chairman. Of course, she did her due diligence in terms of understanding the financial and legal status of the company, and visited in person to meet senior executives and assess the company's culture after being offered the board seat.

Despite a rapid introduction/interview/assessment/acceptance board process, Faulkenberry made the transition from major general to board member fairly easily.

"Maybe it's my background—diverse experiences in dynamic situations—I've been able to adapt and contribute to this high-performance team."

She attests to the supportive dynamic and overall openness of the board in terms of being able to embark on new initiatives and welcome fresh, new perspectives.

Faulkenberry's second corporate board came through a search firm. Through that conduit, Barbara is now the first woman on the board at Callon Petroleum, a $3 billion oil and gas company.

"You start your board reputation during your first board opportunity, be it in the profit or not-for-profit realm. I've heard it said that your first board is the hardest to land, but it's important to continue to develop your board expertise for future opportunities that might arise."

Her advice to other women seeking board positions?

"No matter what your expertise, there's much to learn. As a senior executive, your unique experiences and diverse perspective are valuable in developing strategies to create long-term value for a company. That said, it is up to you to broaden your understanding of all aspects of corporate governance. There are organizations and individuals to help in that journey, but you must put in the hard work to best prepare yourself. In my case, in addition to attaining NACD leadership fellow recognition, I earned the Carnegie Mellon University CERT certificate in cybersecurity oversight. I believe great leaders are a combination of natural and practical ability."

When Faulkenberry graduated from the Air Force Academy, hers was only the third class to accept women. She was able to apply her passion and her vision, and also develop her communication and leadership skills, in the Air Force, an organization that she believes is supportive of women.

"The military offers many opportunities for women; I think it is more enlightened than most other organizations. You absolutely must work hard and prove yourself, but when you do, the opportunities—and respect—are there."

Barbara Faulkenberry acknowledges that having been a major general in the Air Force inspires a level of respect among civilians—her board members included. But when asked if she'd ever wear her Air Force general's uniform to a meeting, she laughs: "Not the best outfit choice for board collaboration! That could be a bit *too* intimidating."

LINDA P. HUDSON

  ❝ *Cybersecurity, technology skills, and entrepreneurship are all qualities sought by boards today, and many women possess these skills.* ❞

Linda Hudson, a woman known in the highest echelon of the international engineering world as the "First Lady of Defense," zeroed in on her vast knowledge of cybersecurity as a way to make an important difference on corporate boards. Today's boards are rightfully focused on how to protect their corporations from cyber attacks. So Hudson was ready with knowledge and experience and a desire to serve. And that particular combination of skills was something few board candidates possess. And she's a woman.

LINDA P. HUDSON
Charlotte, North Carolina and Gainesville, Florida

Corporate/Select Nonprofit Boards:
Bank of America Corporation
Ingersoll Rand, PLC
Southern Company
BAE Systems, PLC
University of Florida Foundation
National Air and Space Museum, Smithsonian Institution
United Service Organizations (USO)
Center for a New American Security

Career History:
The Cardea Group: Founder, Chair, and CEO
BAE Systems, PLC: CEO and President
General Dynamics Corporation: President, Armament and Technical Products
Lockheed Martin Corporation: President, Lockheed Martin Ordnance Systems
Ford Aerospace and Communications Corporation
Harris Corporation

Education:
PhD (honorary), Engineering, Worcester Polytechnic Institute
PhD (honorary), Science, University of Florida
BS, Systems Engineering, University of Florida

Hudson's trailblazing career was filled with many firsts, culminating with becoming the first woman CEO of a major U.S. defense firm. Hudson began her engineering career at Harris Corporation and distinguished herself with leadership posts at Ford Aerospace and Communications Corporation, Lockheed Martin, and General Dynamics before becoming the president and CEO of BAE Systems, PLC. One year into her CEO role, search firms began approaching Hudson for potential board roles. Recognizing the need to improve diversity, boards were increasingly targeting female CEOs.

"There continues to be a huge demand for women CEOs of large public companies to serve on corporate boards, and as a woman, an engineer, and a CEO with a significant public profile, I was unique. I spent time reflecting on how my experiences could be of value to a company outside my industry.

"I decided my skills of interest were 1) cybersecurity expertise; 2) experience in a highly regulated industry; 3) significant global business experience; and 4) running a large, complex, multinational business. But I was taken aback when a search firm said they wanted to talk to me about Bank of America. My first question was, 'Why me?' I had no finance background. I knew absolutely nothing about banking."

But the recruiter fixated on Hudson's experience in cybersecurity, her work in a highly regulated industry, and the fact that she had worked on the global stage. The recruiter knew she was the perfect candidate.

After rigorous interviews, Bank of America, one of the largest corporations in the world, selected Hudson—even though this would be her first board seat.

"In hindsight, it was probably not the smartest thing in the world for me to accept my first board appointment with such a large company in an industry I did not know. I still had a full-time CEO job of my own, and it didn't occur to me to think about the workload demand. My company was supportive, but I didn't know what I was getting into as far as demands on my time."

But she knew how to evaluate and protect systems. All kinds of systems. That sealed the deal for her future as a corporate director.

Hudson's expertise and work ethic quickly made her a valuable board member for Bank of America. And just as quickly, she realized the value of her cybersecurity expertise, because no other director at that time had similar experiences.

Cybersecurity threats, and the tools and techniques to prevent, detect, deter, and remediate cyber attacks, have become important topics on all board agendas, as well as a top business risk. She next joined the board of Southern Company, where she chaired the business-security subcommittee, building on her physical and cybersecurity expertise. She also joined the board of Ingersoll Rand, a global industrial company, where she found her cybersecurity skills again to be a discriminator.

"The BofA board opened more doors than I could ever have imagined. It gave me instant credentials. Since then, dozens of different companies have approached me. But I am smarter about managing my time now."

Hudson notes wryly, "Too many recruiters are hung up on CEO titles. I was fortunate when I retired from my corporate career at BAE that I was a woman CEO. There aren't many of us, and there continues to be pressure on boards to increase their diversity. I was at the right place at the right time."

Hudson now encourages search firms and boards to look beyond the CEO position for talented women and minorities.

"I care deeply about diversity and have seen the benefit in my company and in the boardroom. Cybersecurity, technology skills, and entrepreneurship are all qualities sought by boards today, and many women possess these skills."

Hudson left BAE in 2014 to form her own consulting company, The Cardea Group, which advises businesses on leadership, communications, and business strategy. "Cardea is an obscure Greek goddess who embodies threshold and change. I new firsthand the importance of properly managing change, and all of our clients are experiencing some kind of career or business change."

As a consultant, Hudson also advises clients on improving their visibility, expanding their networks, and developing their own success stories to enhance their attractiveness to boards and search firms.

Growing up in the 1950s and 1960s, Hudson knows about change and crossing over thresholds.

"I was passionate about becoming an engineer, a thoroughly non-traditional goal for girls then. I was the first girl in high school to take an engineering drawing class."

Later, in the University of Florida's engineering program, she was one of only two women students.

"I became resilient and determined, and I had to excel in order to be accepted. Bottom line, though, I just wanted to be a good engineer. In the early days of my career, I experienced some pretty awful discrimination, but I've refused to be a victim. I always believe that success is the best revenge."

Women bring unique qualities to boards, as well as to the C-suite, says Hudson.

"We come with a much broader life perspective. From my generation, we had to fight harder to get where we wanted to go. Because of our experiences, women in business are more inclined to look for more diverse talent and be more sensitive to how people are viewed. We're making sure the business agenda focuses on the bigger strategic and cultural issues, and not solely on the financial numbers."

Hudson has observed board behavior change positively as more women are added to its ranks.

"Because of women's personal experiences in life—family, housework, money, and full-time jobs—we have a broader view of what defines success. We are multitaskers because we have had to balance more. Research indicates women tend to make balanced risk decisions because they have always juggled many variables when making these life decisions."

Marketing in a Digital World

"Every company operating today is a technology company—whether they realize it or not," says Shellye Archambeau, who is profiled in this chapter. Susan Thronson and Cynthia Cleveland are marketing experts with deep experience in customer acquisition and retention. Their expertise and knowledge of the digital marketing universe have paid off for their companies and customers. Using technology strategically comes naturally for these women. Their boards of directors have welcomed these three experts and the value-added that they bring.

Half of the 25 **IPOs in 2018** went public with **no women board members**

SHELLYE ARCHAMBEAU

❝ *Technology is disrupting every industry. An overall understanding of why and how, along with an insider perspective, is an important addition to boardroom conversations.* ❞

It is rare to find a woman digital director who has successfully built a software business in Silicon Valley, but that is exactly why MetricStream CEO Shellye Archambeau has been invited to sit on the boards of two big brand-name companies, telecommunications giant Verizon and fashion retailer Nordstrom. "I'm a planner. I was very firm in my goal of serving on a Fortune 500 company board by the time I turned fifty-five. I knew I needed to start on a smaller company board and work my way up."

SHELLYE ARCHAMBEAU
Palo Alto, California

Corporate/Select Nonprofit Boards:
Okta
Verizon
Roper Technologies, Inc.
Nordstrom, Inc.
The Arbitron Company

Career History:
MetricStream, Inc.: CEO
Zaplet, Inc.: CEO
LoudCloud LLC: CMO, EVP Sales
NorthPoint Communications Group, Inc.: CMO
Blockbuster, LLC: President, E-commerce
IBM: GM and VP of Public Sector for Asia Pacific

Education:
BS, Wharton School of Business, University of Pennsylvania

Archambeau joined the board of Arbitron, a media-research company focused on radio and outdoor advertising, in 2005. Since she was in the midst of building MetricStream, focused on governance, risk, and compliance software solutions, she says she had the bandwidth to serve on one outside board.

"I decided in 2004 I wanted to join a board, because I knew it was the right move for me, in terms of development and growth. So I told absolutely everybody I knew in business about what I thought I could contribute to a board."

Julie Daum, the head of executive search firm Spencer Stuart's board practice, was among the contacts Archambeau contacted during this networking phase, and Daum led to the Arbitron board opportunity.

"I advise everyone who is seeking their first board position to treat it like searching for a job. Let people know—executives, search firms, and private-equity investors. Do not leave any stone unturned."

Before the first Arbitron board meeting, Archambeau sought the counsel of more experienced board members. They advised her on the do's and don'ts of the room, advice that boiled down to one word: listen.

"The first meeting on the first board is the most intimidating. I'm a big believer in figuring out ways to improve your odds for success. So I *really* listened, trying to get a sense of the dynamics and the culture."

Nearly a decade later, Arbitron entered acquisition negotiations with Nielsen Holdings. Archambeau once again began her board search, but this time her eyes were set on much larger public boards. Marc Andreessen, founder of Netscape and co-founder of Andreessen Horowitz, had been chairman of the enterprise software company LoudCloud while Archambeau was chief marketing officer and executive vice president of sales. Andreessen knew that Lowell McAdam, the CEO of Verizon, was searching for a board candidate who was a well-regarded entrepreneur familiar with scale and telecommunications. Andreessen recommended Archambeau, who was offered the Verizon board position in December 2013, after a lengthy selection process that took almost a year.

"I fit the profile because I had the Silicon Valley experience, and I had run a multibillion-dollar global division at IBM. I had nearly a decade of corporate board experience, was CEO of a software company very comfortable with digital and technical issues, and was very good at turnaround transformations—also known as fixing things. That was my profile. That was what Verizon was looking for. And, although the Verizon board was already very diverse, I think it helped that I am a woman and African American, too."

Shortly after she joined the Verizon board, Nordstrom, Inc. invited Archambeau to serve on its board, because Nordstrom also wanted a digital director from Silicon Valley who understood the contemporary challenges of online marketing. She accepted. "Both Verizon and Nordstrom boards are comprised of high-quality, high-integrity people. An excellent culture and boardroom dynamics provide invaluable support—but you also have to contribute to creating a good environment. Part of that is learning the language."

During her board search, Archambeau also reached out to many of her mentors. One in particular advised her to join the audit committee.

"I was told that by serving on audit I will learn how a company really makes its money. This allows you to filter your opportunities and risks and contribute in valuable ways." That's why Archambeau has joined the audit committee on every board she has served. She's also on the nominating/governance committee at Verizon and the technology committee at Nordstrom.

Archambeau asserts that every company operating today is a technology company, whether they realize it or not: "Technology is disrupting every industry. An overall understanding of why and how, along with an insider perspective, is an important addition to boardroom conversations. For example, presenting opinions about how fast or slow to push digital capabilities, or the importance of having certain apps in the hands of your customers, can be critical. Due to my experience with cybersecurity awareness and social media communications and marketing, I am able to add weight to discussions and decisions, influencing focus and strategy. That is definitely how I am contributing the most value across all my boards."

Though she does not exactly blend in—"I'm a tall, black female. I stand out everywhere!"—Archambeau embraces her different perspective, both as an African-American woman and as a technology expert.

"It would be silly for me to go on the board and not mention technology or suppress my unique perspective. We bring our whole selves to the boardroom."

With a board of twelve directors—four are women, and five represent ethnic minorities—Verizon demonstrates its commitment to diversity at the highest levels, she points out.

Though she was the only woman on the Arbitron board for many years, she found a supportive voice in a fellow board member of Hispanic origin.

"It is important to find mentors and allies who will reinforce your voice. There is a reason you are on the board; make sure you filter your perspective through the appropriate lens, whether you are looking at pipelines, talking about improving diversity, or considering sponsorships. This may be intimidating, but women have to be more confident, more courageous."

Throughout her career, Archambeau says she has had more male mentors than female, but she is committed to changing this for future generations.

"I advocate for informal coaching and mentorship opportunities. I purposefully support women on senior executive teams and help advance their careers whenever I can. I believe it is more difficult for men to give women direct feedback—but without that feedback, how can you improve?"

As the eldest of four siblings, Archambeau noticed leadership qualities emerging early on in her life—"I always knew I wanted to run...*something.*" Always a planner, she set her sights on Wharton Business School at the University of Pennsylvania.

"I wanted to be a CEO, so I thought if I could get an undergraduate degree from the top business school in the country, that would be my best return on investment and resources. So I did it, and I encourage all women to set their sights on what they want early and go after it."

SUSAN THRONSON

> **Looking for the right board is very different from seeking a full-time professional job. It is a long-game, prospect-cultivating endeavor.**

It is a rare but a growing trend for corporate boards to seek candidates from a traditional marketing background. But Susan Thronson's career trajectory at Marriott International made her an attractive candidate for a corporate board looking for that needed expertise in digital commerce and what she calls "loyalty modeling." It was her marketing background that won her a seat on the board of Angie's List, the $400 million digital service offering more than ten million verified reviews in seven hundred service categories, providing members a resource for researching and comparing local service providers.

SUSAN THRONSON
La Quinta, California

Corporate/Select Nonprofit Boards:
Sonic Corporation, Inc.
PFLAG National
Angie's List

Career History:
Marriott International, Inc.: SVP, Global Marketing; SVP, International Marketing, International Lodging Division; VP, International Brand and Marketing Operations; Director, International Field Marketing, International Lodging Division;
Director, Regional Advertising, Western Pacific Region
McCann-Erickson Worldwide, Inc.: Account Supervisor

Education:
BA, Journalism, University of Nevada, Reno

Thronson spent twenty-four years of her career at Marriott, with headquarters in Bethesda, Maryland. She credits its sustainable performance environment with helping her build a career that prepared her for corporate boards.

"I feel fortunate to have been part of an organization that promoted business acumen. Though I have deep expertise in marketing, I was constantly challenged to work through the business rationale, and even at the early stages of my career, we were held accountable for financial performance. We were taught to understand the business levers and had accountability for creating profitable revenue at the hotels.

"I am a visionary marketer. I look at things through customer needs and solutions, and I'm very accountable for performance. One of the shifts we see in CMOs is to drive overall business strategy as opposed to simply customer strategy."

Thronson also credits Marriott with expanding quickly into digital commerce, as customers began to shop and book travel experiences much sooner than other categories such as retail or financial services. That's how her own experience skyrocketed.

"We were one of the first to add digital marketing to our traditional repertoire toolkit. In 1997, Marriott was taking reservations on a digital commerce channel."

Early in the 2000s, the Marriott Rewards platform evolved to become the Trojan horse for customer analytical insight, and its more than forty million members bought over half of all the rooms sold in Marriott's hotels in more than seventy countries. Thronson was Marriott's senior vice-president of global marketing in 2012 when she was approached to join the Angie's List board.

"It was complete serendipity. Angie's List had gone public and was looking for independent directors. One of Marriott's largest franchisees was on a university board with the board chair of Angie's List. The chair asked fellow trustees if they knew someone with experience in digital commerce and customer-relationship management."

Before that, Thronson hadn't thought about joining a corporate board. But Marriott was performing solidly at the time, and she felt that she had the time and bandwidth to do board work in addition to her day job.

"Busy professionals can juggle. I had good mentoring from colleagues at Marriott."

The CFO and the corporate secretary were both helpful, advising her about what she needed to do to learn about governance.

Thronson was also interested in what she could transport from Angie's List back to her own executive role.

"Angie's List was about $400 million in revenue, while Marriott was just under $30 billion. So I learned a lot from this nimble technology start-up."

Although Angie's List was her first corporate board seat, Thronson had solid credentials in work on large nonprofit boards, including a major hospitality association and the board of PFLAG National, where she serves on the executive committee and chairs the nominating committee. She served on the Angie's List board from 2012 to 2017.

When she transitioned from Marriott in 2013, she became more intentional about board memberships, choosing not to pursue another full-time C-suite position. She encourages women to be strategic in building their board profiles.

"When I made the decision to dedicate my post-Marriott career to corporate board service, I made a point to become the best board director I could be."

She went through the National Association of Corporate Directors (NACD) board governance fellowship program and also earned the NACD/Carnegie Mellon certificate in cybersecurity risk oversight for directors.

"Today, boards should be discussing cybersecurity risk. The best boards talk about it at almost every meeting. But although we discuss this emerging risk, most of us aren't experts in managing technology risks. I needed to understand the risk and be an informed contributor to the board's oversight of it.

"People expect you to have impact in the wheelhouse of your expertise, and mine was global marketing and digital transformation. Boards do turn to me for that. But over the past seven years of board service, I believe I've made an impact that is far broader than marketing."

Her second corporate board was Sonic Corporation, Inc., the nation's largest chain of drive-in restaurants with more than 3,500 locations serving more than three million customers daily. Sonic hired a search firm to help in its search. That firm identified Thronson because of her CMO qualifications and Angie's List work.

"Sonic was going through a comprehensive and intentional board-succession process, and a new director has joined the board each year since 2013."

Sonic's eleven-person board consists of four women members, while Thronson was the only independent female director on the Angie's List board. (Co-founder and CMO Angie Hicks held one of two management seats.)

"I really can't separate expertise from gender when it comes to women on boards. The difference is that with the four women Sonic has on its board, gender is off the table, and now the diversity issue is about various life experiences. We're all contributing something different. Women are not a voting bloc, but we are leaders on the board."

Thronson sees irony in the fact that women are some of Sonic's best customers, while its long-running advertising campaign features the ubiquitous "two guys." That has been recognized, and the latest version of the advertising campaign features two female comedians. Thronson is also championing discussions about the shift to digital customer interaction and social media.

While her own marketing career has ultimately led to impressive board work, Thronson cautions younger professionals to think more broadly.

"If mid-career marketers want to be effective C-suite leaders in the future, getting into general management with profit-and-loss responsibility is a smart move. Many women remain in supporting roles or on corporate staff, and with few exceptions such as finance and technology, those are not the experiences of people who are invited to join corporate boards."

She also recommends networking through organizations including WCD and NACD.

"Be very proactive in building your network when prospecting for a board placement. Looking for the right board is very different from seeking a full-time professional job. It is a long-game, prospect-cultivating endeavor."

CYNTHIA CLEVELAND

❝ Your role as a board member is not to manage the company; stay focused on maximizing shareholder value. ❞

A marketing background was rarely among the top criteria for corporate board searches in years past. Since brand marketing has become an increasingly sought-after expertise, women are afforded more opportunities and consideration, as they tend to do well in marketing careers. Now, corporations are clamoring for more marketing-related knowledge on the board, specifically in the digital realm. Cynthia Cleveland, a high-level executive who has been at the helm of product marketing divisions at the toy company Mattel, the media conglomerate Vivendi Universal, and the retail chain Imaginarium, can vouch for that.

CYNTHIA CLEVELAND
Los Angeles, California

Corporate/Select Nonprofit Boards:
Myers-Briggs Company (CPP, Inc.)
The Children's Nature Institute
Indiana University Board of Visitors

Career History:
Broadthink: Founder
BroadLit, Inc.: CEO
Vivendi Universal: Worldwide President, Consumer Products and
    Games
Imaginarium, S.A.: President
Teleflora LLC: President
Mattel, Inc.: VP, Marketing

Education:
MBA, University of Southern California
BS, MS, Education, Psychology, Indiana University Bloomington

Cleveland has used her marketing knowledge to good advantage as a director on the Myers-Briggs Company (CPP, Inc.) board, which produces the immensely popular Myers-Briggs Type Indicator psychological test, a well-known staple used by human resources professionals to assess employee talent and teamwork. Myers-Briggs also produces a suite of other online and on-site testing products. Cleveland notes that she was delighted to learn that the founders, Myers and Briggs, were actually mother and daughter, Isabel Myers and her mother, Katharine Cook Briggs, whose work was officially published and recognized in 1975.

When Cleveland was an executive at Mattel, the makers of Barbie dolls and Hot Wheels toy vehicles, in El Segundo, California, her boss Tom Kalinski gave her career-changing advice:

"Tom told me to join the Young Presidents Organization (YPO). He said it would be good for me and my family. I didn't fully realize until many years later, he was talking about the value of networking at YPO."

With characteristic zeal, Cleveland joined the nonprofit YPO organization, which convenes gatherings of global chief executives who counsel and help each other to create and run companies more effectively. Her involvement at YPO events and her volunteer service on committees led her to another contact who gave her the keys to building her career with corporate board service as a goal.

"One of my YPO friends was a very successful director on boards, and he showed me how becoming involved in industry associations and large nonprofits could give me the visibility and contacts who might invite me to serve on boards."

Additionally, Cleveland chaired the Women's YPO Network, which includes 1,800 women CEO members around the world, and she became active in 2020 Women on Boards.

"I would not have had a chance for the Myers-Briggs board if I didn't have personal connections with so many people whom I had worked with and who knew my expertise. It was a combination of luck and persistence."

It was also her work empowering women in various nonprofit and charitable organizations that got Cleveland the introduction to Myers-Briggs.

"The first phone call from Myers-Briggs was to ask me for my recommendations of women executive friends who might be candidates." Then when they described the requirements (direct-to-consumer marketing and branding), Cleveland decided to be straightforward and boldly say: "Hey, those are *my* qualifications!"

Her background was aligned perfectly with what Myers-Briggs was looking for, so they brought her in for interviews. Within six months, they offered her the seat on the board. Her consumer marketing background rounded out the "intellectually brilliant" board, which already included two other women, and more than half the company employees are women.

"This board is made up of very smart people. There are academics like the retired head of Stanford's psychology department and the current head of U.C. Berkeley's psychology department. I would never dare say to them, 'Here's how to improve the Myers-Briggs test,' but I feel very comfortable suggesting, 'Have you considered marketing in India?' They did not have a true marketing person among the board members, and I have taken brands worldwide, so my experience was greatly needed, and I am more than happy to add my talents to theirs."

Cleveland was selected to join the audit committee and help in the company's rebranding efforts.

"Since I have run companies, I felt comfortable on the committees. After a few years on the audit committee, I was elected chair. I have been integrally involved in rebranding and working to achieve benefit-corporation status (which the IRS recognizes as a company that provides good to the society). My colleagues were unaware of B-corps before. We also looked at different ways to market directly to consumers than the company had ever considered before."

Her advice to directors serving on boards?

"Your role as a board member is not to manage the company; stay focused on maximizing shareholder value."

Cleveland feels personal satisfaction helping lead a brand that enriches people's lives and enables them to pursue careers and relationships armed with scientific evidence.

"I am passionate about so many of our products, but particularly the Strong Assessment, which helps college students determine early on what their interests are and how those interests align with possible career paths."

One study measured Harvard students who had taken the Strong Assessment, and it found fifty years later that their interests had not changed and that the most successful people were those whose careers matched their interests.

"If you can figure out quickly who you are and where your interests are, that helps change lives. That gives me great satisfaction."

Of course, Cleveland has also taken the test herself. The results?

"It said I should be an entrepreneurial marketing person!" Her ENTJ ranking (which stands for Extroverted, Intuitive, Thinking, and Judging) also matches how driven Cleveland has been throughout her life.

"When I was in high school, my two girlfriends and I ran every single club by senior year. My brother always called me 'bossy,' and I must admit that was true—if I got involved in anything, I got involved on a deep level." As for her first spark of leadership? Cleveland says that came all thanks to the Myers-Briggs test. "I was in business school when I took the MBTI for the first time. When I got the assessment back, the results had only one word for me: Leader."

Human Resources and Compensation

Women executives who are chief human resource officers (CHRO) make crucial decisions on compensation: complex issues of salary, bonus, stock options and restricted stock units, long-term incentives, health benefits, and retirement programs. For boards, this knowledge is especially important when managing executive compensation packages. CHROs are additionally responsible for recruiting, hiring, motivating, and managing huge, diverse, and widely dispersed populations of employees. In recent years, the new strategic focus on "Diversity and Inclusion" (often a distinct department) generally is led by the CHRO and has become essential to public and private corporations. In this era of escalating sexual harassment issues, gender pay disparities, remote worksites, and diverse workforces, boards are wise to seek directors who bring hands-on experience to counsel management about these challenges.

Historically, departments like Human Resources (HR) have been considered part of the expense side rather than the revenue-generating side of any company. However, today HR executives are recognized for their expertise in handling compensation and benefits packages—both part of the profits equation. HR has been one of the most common areas in a corporation where women have risen to leadership roles.

One of the primary responsibilities of the board of directors is to determine the compensation packages of the CEO and senior managers and to make decisions regarding hiring and firing the CEO. That's why CHROs today are logical candidates for corporate boards. Most longtime board members do not have HR background, so many hesitate to get involved with the high compensation and benefits earned by CEOs. For global companies with employees in many countries, women HR executives have even more opportunities today to seek and secure board positions.

Robin Ferracone, a highly regarded executive compensation expert, formed her own company to counsel corporate boards on the complex issues of salary, stock, and incentive packages for CEOs, board members, and senior management. In her profile here, she also notes how strategic planning played a major role in her HR career and later in building her executive compensation business. She serves on company boards that value her HR and compensation knowledge and background.

Elizabeth Bastoni has international HR background which makes her a value-added board member for companies that do business around the world. Lynn Jolliffe urges HR professionals to expand their networks outside HR in order to maximize their connections to corporate boards. Eva Sage-Gavin strongly recommends that CHROs pursue a board seat while they are still in their professional roles. "Don't wait until retirement to seek and get ready for boards," she warns. "Unless you are a CEO or CFO, boards prefer to bring on new board members who are active, current, and relevant."

ELIZABETH BASTONI

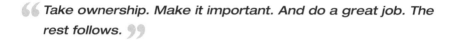

> *Take ownership. Make it important. And do a great job. The rest follows.*

Elizabeth Bastoni parlayed her global experience as a human resources executive, honed while based in the U.S. and France, into board positions in Europe. She lives in Seattle and sits on the boards of several family-controlled, publicly traded European companies that include global brand Bic (pens, razors, and lighters) and Jerónimo Martins, a Portuguese corporation that operates in the food-retail sector in Portugal, Poland, and Colombia.

ELIZABETH BASTONI
Seattle, Washington

Corporate/Select Nonprofit Boards:
BIC (FMCG), France
Jerónimo Martins
National Association of Corporate Directors—
    Northwest Chapter
Rezidor Hotel Group
Carlson Wagonlit Travel
WorldatWork

Career History:
BMGI: CHRO
Carlson: EVP, Human Resources and Communications
The Coca-Cola Company: Head of Global Compensation, Benefits,
    and Global Mobility
Thales Group: VP, Talent and Leadership Development; VP, HR
    Aerospace Division; VP, Global Compensation and Benefits
Lyonnaise des Eaux France S.A.: Head of Compensation and
    Benefits
KPMG International: Senior Manager, U.S. Tax

Education:
French Studies, University of Paris I: Panthéon-Sorbonne
Ecole du Louvre, Art History
BA, Accounting, Providence College, Rhode Island

Originally from Boston, Bastoni received her bachelor of arts degree in accounting from Providence College. The decision to take a gap year instead of immediately entering the accounting workforce would turn out to be emblematic of her non-linear career. She pushed herself beyond her comfort zone and traveled to a country—France—where she didn't speak the language and didn't know anyone.

In 1989, after eighteen months of learning French and studying art history at L'Ecole du Louvre, she accepted a position making photocopies in the international tax practice at KPMG. By 1998, she was slated to become the youngest female tax partner in the firm, and she decided that it was time, again, to move beyond her comfort zone.

Bastoni transitioned from KPMG into human resources roles in publicly traded and privately held companies, and along the way built a strong international reputation for her expertise as a seasoned HR leader. Her early decision to develop a career in Europe has paid off.

The Coca-Cola Company recognized her global experience and expertise and invited Bastoni to join them in Atlanta, Georgia, as global head of compensation, benefits, and global mobility. Her area of responsibility was considered a key element of the turnaround engineered by Chairman and CEO Neville Isdell.

Bastoni was present at all meetings of the compensation committee of The Coca-Cola Company, providing technical and regulatory content, facilitating discussion, and working closely with the board's compensation committee chair to provide in-depth analytical information to boardroom decision makers. She worked closely with the CEO and head of HR to reestablish trust and confidence between management and the committee.

"Coke was a breakthrough opportunity for me. My boss coached me and provided me the latitude to take the reins."

Frequent interactions with the board, a global mindset, and deep expertise in HR were the reasons Carlson, a Minneapolis-based, family-owned private company, recruited her to become executive vice president of human resources and communications. Carlson holds public entities across Europe, and her first board positions were with two of their portfolio companies: Rezidor Hotel Group (headquartered in Brussels and traded on the Swedish stock exchange) and

Carlson Wagonlit Travel (headquartered in Paris). In both cases, she was named chair of the compensation committees.

Bastoni believes the prime factor in her elevation to board member was her global experience combined with her HR expertise.

"I understood how to do business in Europe. I was seen as someone who could be a bridge between the European and U.S. cultures. In addition, I had expertise in areas that were complementary to the other board members. Finally, my network and my reputation were highly valued. In this case, my international experience and expertise were the deciding factors."

While joining two boards at the same time and working a full-time job may seem daunting, she got up to speed quickly by studying the separate businesses and understanding the different dynamics so she could add value in each situation.

Even before Bastoni left France to move back to the United States, she had cemented her reputation as one of the top global HR executives in Europe with expertise in compensation and benefits. It was this reputation that got her name on the list when the Bic board was ready to replace a director. Bic, a family-controlled company that is publicly traded on the Paris stock exchange, has four independent directors in addition to family board members. She is chair of the compensation committee and chair of nomination, governance, and environment/social responsibility.

Bastoni says majority ownership by a family adds a unique dynamic to governing companies, which is why she has chosen to specialize in this area.

"When the family name is on the product and above the door, it's not about just the quarterly results—it is much deeper than that. The quality and safety of the products, doing what is right for the long-term of the business and all its stakeholders, and proper governance run deep in the DNA of family-controlled organizations.

"I joined the board in May of 2013, as Bic was thinking about long-term evolution of the board and the business. The board was already thinking about the replacement of a member who would be terming out in 2018—five years out. Additionally, we knew the chairman would be aging out because of board restrictions and the CEO was likely to retire in the not-too-distant future.

"When I joined, the board was looking for a director with a specific set of HR experiences to help with these critical changes. They were extremely thoughtful about the challenges the board and company would be facing and what additional skills they needed at the board level."

Specific experience on a potential board member's resume can make all the difference, as it did for Bastoni. She advises women to focus on what sets them apart from other candidates, then develop and stay true to that unique identity.

"By being different, I've been able to make a difference. In the boardroom, this allows you to get the best from each director. The strengths and experience I bring complement those of other directors around the table."

For women seeking board seats, Bastoni reflects on the negative impact that doubt can have on advancing careers or accomplishing goals.

"Tenacity is key. A lot of times, I see potential women directors asking themselves questions that men never ask, such as: 'How am I going to make time for this? How will I be able to add value?' These questions should serve as motivation, not as a deterrent."

Bastoni has more than eighteen years of experience now serving boards in executive and director capacities on matters including governance, strategy and execution, CEO succession, and executive compensation. Her lasting impact on the boards she serves (and has served) stems from her tenacious, can-do attitude. She focuses on fostering dialogue and informed decision-making by using a combination of critical thinking, expert technical knowledge, and consulting skills.

"Oftentimes in my career—as an executive and in the boardroom—it has served me well to raise my hand to do the things that others didn't want to or didn't know how to do. Many times, the tasks were difficult and required a heavy dose of change management."

Bastoni advises women to use the work in the boardroom to get to know the other members of the board, the leadership team, and their challenges.

"Making a difference comes about from raising your hand, even if it's for a small project or something that seems less important. Take ownership, make it important, and do a great job. The rest follows."

ROBIN FERRACONE

> 66 *Regarding human resources executives on boards, their value often isn't perceived until later when the board says, 'We didn't realize you could bring so much strategy.'* 99

When she is not traveling the world advising Fortune 500 companies on executive and board compensation, Robin Ferracone enjoys relaxing at home with her two very special cats. How perfect that her current public board is Trupanion, a rapidly growing and innovative pet insurance company. Ferracone heads the compensation committee, of course.

ROBIN FERRACONE
New York and Los Angeles

Corporate/Select Nonprofit Boards:
Trupanion
Oaktree Capital Management, LP
Enlight Research, LLC
2020 Women on Boards
PayScale, Inc.

Career History:
Farient Advisors LLC: Founder and CEO
Mercer LLC: President, Human Capital Business
Marsh & McLennan Companies, Inc.: Chair, U.S. West Region
SCA Consulting: Founder, President, and Chair

Education:
MBA, Harvard Business School
BA, Management Science and Economics, Duke University

One of the best-known experts in executive compensation globally, Ferracone is founder and CEO of Farient Advisors, LLC, an executive-compensation firm based in New York City and Los Angeles that offers executive-compensation and performance-advisory services, including compensation-program design, board compensation, and investor communications. Because of her value-added experience in compensation and human resources consulting, when serving on boards, Ferracone is often tapped for membership on the compensation committee.

Based in Seattle, Trupanion went public in 2014. The pet insurance market may still be small in the United States—only about one percent of pet owners have insurance, compared to 25% in the United Kingdom—Ferracone says that growth possibilities are strong, and she is committed to taking a strategic approach to her board work, as she has done with her own company, Farient.

About making a difference:

"I'm pleased that I can contribute business knowledge that's wider and deeper than just compensation, which has been my career-long focus. I want to help differentiate Trupanion." She proactively sought a board seat through a retained search firm that identified Trupanion as a unique choice for Ferracone's capabilities and interests.

From March 2005 to March 2007, Ferracone was president of the human capital business of Mercer, a global talent and compensation consulting firm offering software and data services globally.

She is also the author of the book *Fair Pay, Fair Play: Aligning Executive Performance and Pay* and has written and been quoted in articles in national publications. Currently a regular contributor to *Forbes.com* and *Directorship Magazine,* Ferracone is a sought-after speaker and panelist on business issues, talent strategies, executive compensation, organization, value management, and performance measurement. She also sits on the national board of 2020 Women on Boards, a global campaign to achieve 20% women directors on corporate boards by the year 2020.

"The issue of executive compensation is critically important, and yet most corporate boards have little regard for human resources executives and the skills they bring to help boards with the complex issues of compensation today. The trends are showing a gradual uptick for chief human resources officers (CHRO) on boards."

Given that most CHROs are women, it's logical that boards will have more seats filled by women.

"The ascent of CHROs to boards should open more doors for women, although progress is slow."

About trends in board compensation:

"The average board compensation is increasing with inflation and is based on the size of the company. Smaller companies pay about $100,000 with 50% in stock. Larger corporations—in the $20 billion range—pay $250,000 to $350,000, with 40% stock and 60% cash. Startups and smaller companies generally pay more stock than cash... All board members are paid the same basic fees and stock, without regard to gender. Some committee chairs earn more for the additional time they are required to spend."

Whether in her board work or as a compensation consultant, Ferracone maps out the strategic front end of every engagement she works on.

"I understand all the elements it takes to run a business. However, the regard for human resources is still relatively low. When human resources executives are on boards, their value often isn't recognized as truly valuable until later, when the board realizes all the facets of business that HR strategists can influence positively—the workplace, the human factors of mergers and acquisitions, and of course the all-important compensation for the CEO and senior management. And today, when 'culture' is the byword in boardrooms and in the workplace, it's the HR professionals who can influence culture in meaningful ways."

LYNN JOLLIFFE

❝ *It's really important for HR leaders to find connections with people who are not just in HR. Get involved in other industries or trade associations.* ❞

A couple of years before her retirement from Ingram Micro (a Fortune 70 company), Lynn Jolliffe was paid the ultimate compliment and tribute for her years of service: the chairman and the CEO granted her the unique gift of a "reverse board search" as an entry to her first corporate board. This would pave the way for board service before and after she retired. It was considered a special benefit for her contribution, and Jolliffe says she welcomed this gift with gratitude. In a reverse board search, a company pays a search firm to proactively place its C-suite executive on an outside corporate board.

LYNN JOLLIFFE
Naples, Florida

Corporate/Select Nonprofit Boards:
KAR Auction Services, Inc.
Susan G. Komen
Sun Life Financial Trust, Inc. and Sun Life Savings
& Mortgage

Career History:
Jolliffe Solutions, Inc.: Founder & CEO
Ingram Micro, Inc.: EVP; Global CHRO
Ingram Micro European Coordination Center: Regional VP, Human Resources
White Rose Crafts & Nursery Sales Ltd.: VP; CFO; Corporate Secretary
Holt, Renfrew & Co., Limited: SVP and CFO

Education:
MBA, University of Toronto
BA, Sociology, Queen's University, Kingston

At the time, Jolliffe was EVP and global chief human resources officer at the worldwide distributor of computer peripherals and products. With her extensive HR and finance background, she was immediately qualified to serve on any public company's compensation committee. Being qualified for such an important committee from the outset is a huge advantage, almost a ticket to one's first board.

As for many CHROs, Jolliffe's challenge was finding a corporate board where the culture, as well as the product or service, would be a good fit for her. After an eighteen-month effort to find an appropriate board, Jolliffe was named to the board of an Indiana company, KAR Auction Services, a $5.7 billion publicly held company in the automotive industry with around forty auction locations across the country.

A personal recommendation actually led to Jolliffe's appointment as director of KAR, so her advice for other CHROs and human resources professionals is to "diligently work on expanding your network" to include executives and leaders in other vertical industries as well—from nonprofits to private-equity boards. "The Society for Human Resources Management is a great professional organization, but if you're only doing things within your industry, you may not meet people who will be able to help you get on boards."

Jolliffe's networking and visibility included chairing the Orange County chapter of the Susan G. Komen organization and completing various professional certifications while navigating her high-powered career—which would eventually garner her an award as one of the most powerful and influential women in California in 2012.

"It's really important for HR leaders to find connections with people who are not just in HR. Get involved in other industries or trade associations. Private-equity boards are helpful as well. When they buy companies, they look for independent board members. They are also in a position to recommend you when other businesses need directors."

Jolliffe was the second woman to join the KAR board, but considering the board had only recently gone through its initial public offering, the other directors were as new to the room as she was. "One benefit of a relatively new board is that everyone is getting to know each other, versus one new person getting to know nine seasoned members. We only meet four times a year, so it is very important to try to forge individual connections. KAR also did a wonderful job setting up orientation calls. We follow that with the occasional director-only dinner to get to know each other better, so that we can more comfortably speak up in the boardroom."

With experience on audit, compensation, and nominating/governance committees at KAR, Jolliffe says she has made the most impact on the compensation committee, where she has helped revamp the executive plan according to the company's desired results and helped set up succession planning and management-by-objective plans. "A good compensation committee is not necessarily trying to run the company, but it should be able to understand the SEC rules and know what potential hot buttons may be for ISS and Glass-Lewis. You must be able to say what you've done to drive the right behaviors—in business, there are certain pressures to finding the balance between all parties and making sure the CEO is happy, too."

According to Jolliffe, leadership is one's innate ability to motivate a team. "Leadership is being able to develop good qualities in people. To set expectations for them, challenge them, mentor them. It's also how willing you are to learn from the people you're leading. It's about surrounding yourself with more than just people who always say you are right."

345

Russell 3000 companies added seats to their boards in 2018 **to make room for new women directors.**

Naturally forthright, Jolliffe has learned how to achieve mutual respect on a board: "I could never keep just quiet, because I'm hired to ask questions and understand the business. But with a board, you are each leaders in your own right. You can't get into a situation with everyone trying to be *the* leader. So that's where mutual respect comes into play."

Jolliffe has always been a leader in her own right. "I'm the eldest of five, and I'm bossy. In high school, I ran for student council and came in second. That's when I realized I liked taking risks and trying things!"

EVA SAGE-GAVIN

> *My advice to women CHROs is to persist in your pursuit, because your unique workforce-centered perspective is a missing element most boards realize they need.*

Eva Sage-Gavin is a shining example of hope for corporate chief human resources officers who aspire to become corporate board directors. Sage-Gavin was chief human resources officer and EVP of corporate affairs at Gap, Inc. and networked successfully with her contacts and connections to win her first board seat. Her seats on the BroadSoft and TalentSky boards are paving the way for other CHROs.

EVA SAGE-GAVIN
San Francisco, California

Corporate/Select Nonprofit Boards:
BroadSoft
TalentSky, Inc.
Sapient Corporation (now Publicis Sapient)
The Aspen Institute
The Cornell Center for Advanced Human Resource
    Studies
HR Policy Association

Career History:
Accenture: Senior Managing Director, Talent Practice
Boston Consulting Group: Senior Advisor
G100 Network: Senior Advisor
The Aspen Institute: Vice Chair, Skills for America's Future Advisory
    Board
Gap, Inc.: EVP; CHRO
Sun Microsystems, Inc.: SVP
The Walt Disney Company: SVP
PepsiCo, Inc.: VP
Xerox Corporation: HR Leader

Education:
BS, Industrial and Labor Relations, Cornell University

With her consumer and tech-savvy background honed at companies including Gap, PepsiCo, The Walt Disney Company, Sun Microsystems, and Xerox, Sage-Gavin exemplifies the well-rounded human resources executive who brings diverse experience and strategic value to corporate boards. "My advice to women CHROs who aspire to serve on corporate boards is to persist in your pursuit, because your unique workforce-centered perspective is a missing element most boards realize they need, but may not have strategically valued in the past."

Sage-Gavin recalls a conversation from her one of her first board roles: "The chairman told me they initially brought me on to benefit from my knowledge of culture and global brand experience. A year later, he told me they realized how much more my background brought to the table, especially in terms of human-capital and consumer-growth strategies. He said he was pleasantly surprised, and had they known what they were missing, they would have put me on the board ten years ago."

Sage-Gavin began her board career in the nonprofit academic sector, serving as the chair of the Center for Advanced Human Resource Studies at Cornell University's School of Industrial and Labor Relations. She followed previous chairmen from GE, IBM, and Royal Dutch Shell and made strategic key contacts with Fortune 500 company executives. During her tenure, she partnered to launch the CHRO executive development program that is still successfully in place a decade later and prepares future CHROs in Fortune 500 companies.

For these contributions and her lifetime achievement in the field of human resources, Cornell's ILR School awarded her their highest alumni honor, the William B. Groat Award. As she advanced in her role as a chief human resources officer, specializing in companies at the intersection of the consumer and technology industries, Sage-Gavin started preparing for what was next for her. "I became very clear about the value I could bring to boards in key sectors, and I focused on those points whenever I encountered a corporate director—whether in business or nonprofit board discussions."

A critical piece of advice Sage-Gavin offers for women who seek board careers is, "Don't wait! Go for it, starting today. Women must get on their first board before they leave their role as senior officer of a corporation. Some women say they want to serve after they retire, when they think they will have more time. But from my experience, you can be even more effective in your current role today if you understand how boards work from the other side of the table. Unless you are a CEO or CFO, the chances of getting a first board seat after you retire are few. Boards value executives who are active, productive, and relevant."

While working at Gap, Inc., Sage-Gavin began her search for a board seat after gaining the approval of her CEO and board compensation-committee chair. Embarking on a less traditional path to her first board, she worked with executive recruiters to identify companies that would consider her as a board member. After turning down four opportunities, she eventually accepted a board position at Sapient Corporation, a global digital marketing and IT consulting company that was eventually acquired by the Publicis Groupe in France.

The core responsibilities of her board position included serving on the compensation committee and partnering on the successful global growth of the firm, as well as stewarding the strategic acquisition by Publicis. She participated in internal and external discussions featuring client perspectives. And partnering with the CEO, she participated in diversity and inclusion town-hall sessions globally. This leveraged her diverse experience from Gap, Inc., where she led the human resources, communications, government-affairs, and corporate-social-responsibility teams. Such well-rounded experience lifted her above other qualified candidates to win the seat. And she was also the first woman director at Sapient, so she was especially gratified to receive the highest shareholder approval of all directors for her first year serving on the board.

Sage-Gavin has also served on groundbreaking public-service advisory boards as a volunteer. She was the vice chair of skills for America's Future Advisory Board at The Aspen Institute and partnered with key public and private leaders in government and industry over a seven-year period. Under her direction, Sage-Gavin and her fellow board members were able to involve 20,000 people in partnerships to benefit skills development for job seekers, students, and mid-career professionals. This helped build her frame of reference for how to build strategic partnerships and work well with both public- and private-sector CEOs as well as White House administration leaders.

As happens to most CHROs who are elected to boards, Sage-Gavin serves on the compensation committee of both her current and past public-company boards. From CEO succession to culture strategy and executive development and compensation, she has brought her HR perspective to decisions and discussions, creating positive impact for companies as they navigate through ups—like double-digit growth per year; and downs—like a negative Institutional Shareholder Services (ISS) rating.

During her tenure as a board director, Sage-Gavin has learned, "You need to be ready to partner with management teams and CEOs on how to design for organization agility and proactively find new ways to operate in a constantly changing competitive landscape. The number-one skill needed for a CHRO and board member is the ability to make strategic shifts to remain competitive."

While the boards where she has served did not have women directors before she joined, they have since filled open board seats with other capable women directors.

During her HR career, Sage-Gavin navigated seventeen relocations across five global companies. Sage-Gavin says her career path has been challenging at times, but always interesting and rewarding. One of her life mottos, which she repeats often to encourage women to take on seemingly tough opportunities, is: "If you're not on the edge of terror a little bit each day, you're not growing."

GO IMMEDIATELY
TO

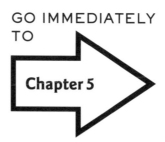

Chapter 5

5 Women Bring Financial Expertise,
G L O B A L
E X P E R I E N C E ,
Crisis

A N D

Management
Skills

I F THERE'S ONE THING THAT BOARD MEMBERS MUST UNDERSTAND, IT'S MONEY. That means every board needs a balance of expertise from directors who possess an understanding of how money is made, how it's paid, how it's lost, or how it works in countries around the world. Women with solid financial experience, global market perspective, and crisis management skills are always in demand when a new board seat becomes available.

Finance Experts

Since the Enron scandal of 2001 and the subsequent Sarbanes-Oxley accounting reform law, corporate boards are responsible for the financial health and accounting practices of companies. The law has been a door opener for more women who come from accounting backgrounds to serve on their first corporate boards.

After the regulations in Sarbanes-Oxley, the Dodd-Frank Wall Street Reform and Consumer Protection Act was signed into law in 2010 by President Obama. This law places strict regulations on lenders and banks to protect consumers and decrease risks in the U.S. financial system. It created several new agencies to oversee the regulatory process and, by extension, some aspects of the banking industry.

Both of these laws put additional responsibility on a corporate board's audit committee. Sarbanes-Oxley requires that an audit committee has a designated "financial expert" as defined by the Securities and Exchange Commission. According to the SEC, a financial expert must have an understanding of generally accepted accounting principles (GAAP) and financial statements, deep experience preparing and analyzing such statements, and a thorough knowledge of internal controls and procedures for financial reporting. The goal is to protect investors from the possibility of fraudulent corporate accounting. A board's audit committee must be vigilant in oversight of the company's financial matters. Says Molly Campbell, "'Audit' may not sound sexy, but it's important!"

Only 1% of Russell 3000 company boards **had reached gender parity by 2018**

Sheila Hooda, Jewell Hoover, Tracey Doi, Kapila Anand, Molly Campbell, and Leslie Heisz have all met those exacting standards by excelling in careers of ever-increasing responsibility and success in finance. They have all served on or chaired the audit/finance committees of their boards.

SHEILA HOODA

66 My advice is to start with your strength, then go further outward. 99

After nearly three decades in the finance industry, Sheila Hooda serves on the boards of Mutual of Omaha and Virtus Investment Partners. That's a long way from her childhood in India, where she learned to be self-reliant from an early age. After the death of her father, her homemaker mother was left alone to care for four children.

SHEILA HOODA
Westchester, New York

Corporate/Select Nonprofit Boards:
ProSight Global, Inc.
Virtus Investment Partners, Inc.
Mutual of Omaha Insurance Company
Pratham USA New York Tri-State
The University of Chicago Booth School of
    Business

Career History:
Alpha Advisory Partners Pte. Ltd.: CEO and Founder
Thomson Reuters: Global Head of Strategy and Business
    Development
TIAA-CREF: Senior Managing Director, Global Head, Mergers and
    Acquisitions, and Corporate Development
Credit Suisse Group AG: Managing Director, Global Head Client
    Relationship Management
Bankers Trust Company: VP, Management Consulting and VP, Private
    Banking and Wealth Management
McKinsey & Company, Andersen Consulting: Engagement Manager,
    Strategy Consulting
American Express, Banque Nationale de Paris (now BNP Paribas):
    Sales and Business Development Executive

Education:
MBA, Specialization Finance, The University of Chicago Booth
    School of Business
PGDM, Management, Indian Institute of Management, Ahmedabad
BS, Mathematics, University of Poona, India

Described as a bright spark with no trace of timidity, Hooda embraced challenges and risks early in her professional career. She started the entire customer service department for American Express India, having had very little guidance, then emigrated to the United States to head the global client relationship function at Credit Suisse Investment Bank and completed the first mergers-and-acquisitions deal for TIAA-CREF. Hooda has always taken on risks in a pioneering way, enthusiastically embarking on new, untested ventures.

"Very early in life, I learned if something had to be done, I would have to be the one to do it, often without direction. That propelled me to become self-sufficient. My philosophy is, the buck stops here. You can only depend on yourself. Push yourself, and make a go of it."

For three decades, she developed her financial expertise, first while consulting for McKinsey, then at Credit Suisse, then while working as senior managing director in the office of the CEO at TIAA-CREF, and ultimately moving up to global head of strategy and development at Thomson Reuters. Hooda believed she was at last ready for corporate board service.

"In my early fifties, I started thinking about the next logical step. This was around the time of the financial crisis, so board service very much appealed to me. I thought it would provide the perfect opportunity to bring together my experience in managing large global operations, leading mergers and acquisitions, and long-term strategy, including big B2B or B2C transformations. Driving vital technology—both digital refocusing and client-centric transformations—is a skill few people have."

From observing the boards of the various companies where she had worked, Hooda knew she had the critical skill set that financial companies highly desired. "I was very proactive in my outreach to find the right first board for me. I targeted the boards I was familiar with and started educating myself by joining organizations including the National Association of Corporate Directors (NACD) and WomenCorporateDirectors (WCD), and by participating in the many webinars offered by the big four accounting firms."

But her opportunity resulted from a chance conversation at a WCD event, when she happened to meet the chair of the audit committee at Mutual of Omaha. Though the conversation was brief, Hooda was well prepared with her previously rehearsed pitch and her paperwork. Six months later, the chair reached out to her, and the process moved swiftly, especially since Hooda was in the final states of being vetted for another board.

"The vetting process took only six weeks. There was a strong alignment of skills and needs...There were two other women on the board, and I was very pleased to see that the women definitely had a voice at the table. Chemistry was perhaps the most important factor—I watched for things like sense of humor and tried to get a feel for the camaraderie they shared. Even something simple like ordering a glass of wine at dinner showed they were relaxed and congenial. It was essentially love at first sight."

While Hooda had experience on nonprofit boards—Pratham and The University of Chicago Booth School of Business—this was her first corporate board. She developed three core tenets for a successful corporate board entry.

- Step back a bit. "I took a holistic view of the board and saw that the directors on the board got along well. I also made note that the women directors were chairing committees, which was very important to me."
- Stay calm. "For the first few meetings, keep a relatively low profile. I have been mindful about the preexisting dynamics, being careful to observe and just generally feeling my way around."
- Find a mentor. "It's really important once you're on the board to find a board 'buddy,' someone you can talk with about ideas, instincts, and issues. She will become an invaluable resource and sounding board."

At Mutual of Omaha, Hooda initially served on the investment and risk committees, which she says was a strategic and smart decision the chairperson made, considering her Wall Street, mergers-and-acquisitions, and finance background.

"I was also given the unusual but farsighted option of taking a few months to attend several committee meetings to see which I wanted to serve on. After a few months, I had a better sense of the board's needs and where I could best add value."

She subsequently served on the audit and compensation committees. From her vantage points, both on the Mutual of Omaha board and the WCD board, Hooda says she can promote greater diversity and empower more women to pursue C-level and director positions by enabling them and mentoring them through the process.

"I started immediately with financial services since I knew the industry very well, but now that I am an experienced director, I have demonstrated relevant skills that can transfer across industries to technology, energy, industrials, business, and professional services. My advice is to start with your strength, then go further outward, especially if you come from a corporate career."

JEWELL D. HOOVER

66 Know when to listen, and continue learning. Directors come from different business backgrounds, and there must be a healthy respect for diversity of opinions. 99

Jewell Hoover took a reverse approach to board service by earning a seat on a corporate board and then adding her first nonprofit—AARP, which is one of the largest nonprofit organizations in the United States.

JEWELL D. HOOVER
Charlotte, North Carolina

Corporate/Select Nonprofit Boards:
AARP: Audit/Finance Committee, Chair, Vice-Chair
Fifth Third Bank

Career History:
Hoover and Associates, LLC: President and
    Principal
United States Department of the Treasury: Office of the Comptroller
    of the Currency, District Deputy Comptroller, Western District

Education:
MA, Educational Administration and Supervision, West Virginia
    College of Graduate Studies (now Marshall University)
BS, Business Education, West Virginia State College

Huge and dynamic, AARP has nearly thirty-eight million members, revenues of over $1.6 billion, and offices in all fifty states; publishes a magazine that is the most widely read of any in the country, and recently funded $60 million for Alzheimer's research. Hoover serves as second vice chair and chairs the audit/finance committee, which oversees the balance sheet and enterprise risk.

"I believe in their social mission—to empower people to choose how they live as they age—and I wanted to help them execute the strategy." Hoover was recommended to the AARP board by a business contact and had a rigorous process in which she competed with hundreds of other candidates.

Hoover is a retired bank regulator and served at the Office of the Comptroller of the Currency (OCC) for twenty-eight years. The OCC charters, regulates, and supervises all national banks and federal savings associations as well as federal branches and agencies of foreign banks. It is an independent bureau of the U.S. Department of the Treasury, and it works to ensure that national banks and federal savings associations operate in a safe and sound manner, provide fair access to financial services, treat customers fairly, and comply with applicable laws and regulations.

She joined the OCC in 1975 as a national bank examiner, and her responsibilities increased steadily throughout her career. Her last position at the OCC was that of district deputy comptroller for the Western District, where she supervised 427 banks and eighteen credit-card companies located from Missouri, west to California and Arizona, and north to Alaska. Upon retirement, she was hopeful that her expertise in corporate governance would be valuable to a corporate board.

"I was shooting for the stars. I knew I had the skill sets to serve on a public company board, specifically a bank board. I contacted known acquaintances in the financial-services industry and the bank regulatory environment to let them know of my interest." It was a business contact that recommended Hoover for her first board position, at First Charter Corp.

"I believe that networking and having a sponsor are the key ingredients for earning a board seat. A sponsor is different than a mentor, in that a sponsor is an influential person in your business career who counsels and guides you to advantageous career moves and endorses you with other decision makers. Mentors are helpful for advice. But for achievement like a board position, you need to broaden your professional relationships to find someone of influence who already has a seat at the table."

Hoover grew up in poverty in southern West Virginia, during the period of segregation, which would seem unlikely to have prepared her for her illustrious career. She attended elementary school in a one-room African American school heated by a coal stove and later attended a segregated African American high school. Her first exposure to white students was in college, and the first time she was able to go to a non-segregated restaurant was her freshman year in college.

She worked twenty hours a week in college while carrying a class schedule of eighteen hours and graduated with a degree in business education. She taught school for five years. "To supplement my teacher's income of about $8,000 a year, I worked as a bank teller making five dollars an hour. I happened to meet the bank regulators when they visited the bank for a routine examination, and they asked if I would consider working for them. I kept their phone number around for a year before I finally called them."

Her challenging path to professional success was guided by three mottos she holds close. Two came from her grandmother, who was born in the 1800s and taught her to believe in yourself and always have good credit, never guessing that Hoover would someday have a career in banking. The other motto is from former U.S. Secretary of the Treasury James Baker, who emphasized the Five Ps: Prior Preparation Prevents Poor Performance.

Hoover has important advice for women (and men) seeking a board seat. "Be focused and intentional. Leverage your existing skill sets, understand your niche, and find your own unique voice. I was very aware of my important skill sets I hoped a board would value, such as audit, enterprise risk management, and corporate governance. These skill sets are transferable to many boards and committees."

Her commitment to "finding your unique voice" guides how she interacts with fellow board members.

"How you frame your remarks, questions, and opinions can result in respect from other members and bring added value to the governance process. One thing I've learned is you cannot participate in every board discussion. No one has a skill set that broad; but know when you can contribute in a meaningful way. Know when to listen, and continue learning. Other directors have diverse business backgrounds, so there must be a healthy respect for diversity of opinions."

She considers herself lucky to serve on boards with many women. "The AARP board has eleven members, and seven are highly accomplished women. All the women bring their own perspective based on their industry expertise and experiences.

"Understand that board culture is complex and differs among companies. Research the culture of the board you are considering. It's okay to say 'no' to an opportunity." Board and company complexity as well as cultures can change over time, and that's why she encourages term limits. "Having term limits allows the board to refresh thinking and governance practices. As industries and global economies change, boards must also evolve. Essential expertise for boards today includes cybersecurity and digital platforms, things boards weren't thinking about ten years ago."

Her final advice for achieving professional and board success:

"Increase your knowledge of current events and trends constantly so you are prepared to participate in deliberations and strategy."

Hoover's own path to professional leadership was daunting, but she strongly believes that having a vision for herself was the key to achieving her objectives.

"Even if your vision is not yet well defined, you should define long-term career objectives."

Early in her career at the OCC, she identified "deputy comptroller" as her ultimate career goal.

"The men co-workers dismissed my dream as unattainable, especially for an African American female. But over the years, I was promoted to various leadership positions, and when I retired, my title was deputy comptroller, which was one of the top executive positions. As my grandmother said, 'Believe in yourself.'"

TRACEY DOI

> ❝ ...Inviting line managers to make board presentations is a fantastic opportunity for women to gain recognition and visibility with board members... ❞

Tracey Doi, CFO of Toyota Motor North America and a director on the City National Bank board, says the relationships she's built and nurtured, while contributing her time and expertise to causes she's truly passionate about, have been instrumental to her professional development as a board member.

TRACEY DOI
Dallas, Texas

Corporate/Select Nonprofit Boards:
City National Bank
Emmaus Life Sciences, Inc.
Federal Reserve Bank of San Francisco
U.S.–Japan Council
March of Dimes California
Claremont University Consortium (now The Claremont Colleges, Inc.)
2020 Women on Boards

Career History:
Toyota Motor North America, Inc.: CFO; Group VP
Toyota Motor Sales, USA, Inc.: CFO; Group VP; VP; Controller
AT&T Wireless Services, Inc.: Director of Strategic Planning and
    Analysis
Los Angeles Telephone Company: Controller
L.A. Gear, Inc.: VP and Controller
Management Company Entertainment Group, Inc.: Director of
    Financial Reporting
Maxicare Health Plans, Inc.: Financial Reporting Manager
Arthur Andersen & Co.: Senior Auditor

Education:
BA, Business Economics, UCLA

There are four ways Doi prepared herself for corporate directorship so that she would be top of mind when an opening came up.
• Cultivating experience through nonprofits
• Being active in organizations like subsidiary boards to learn governance
• Receiving coaching from experienced board members and executive search consultants
• Making her interest known, being highly visible, and networking
Still, she knew it would take a long time to find a board seat.

After serving on a delegation of Japanese American leaders selected by the Ministry of Foreign Affairs to strengthen U.S.–Japan relations in various sectors from government to nonprofits, Doi joined the U.S.–Japan Council board. She kept in contact with fellow board member Dennis Teranishi, who introduced her to her first corporate board opportunity. Emmaus Medical is a startup that aims to develop and propagate cures for rare diseases including sickle cell anemia.

"The cause is heartwarming. My experience chairing the treasury and development committees of March of Dimes and the audit committee of the Claremont University Consortium positioned me as the financial expert they were looking for."

Chairing the audit committee at Emmaus, and serving on the compensation committee and the nominating/governance committee, provided excellent growth experience for Doi, who left the private board in 2015 to serve on the corporate board of City National Bank in Los Angeles. Serving on the Economic Advisory Council of the Federal Reserve Bank of San Francisco also provided invaluable experience that would prove useful for understanding the various economic drivers and policies that impact multiple industries drawing from the same resources. The Federal Reserve pulls representatives from different industries, including software, biotech, entertainment, hospitality, and retail.

"After the tsunami in Japan, there was a shortage of glass that impacted us heavily in automotive, but also those in the smartphone and construction businesses, as well. I learned a lot about connecting the dots. I apply what I've learned about the economy, and how it impacts industry, to my strategic and mid-term planning at both Toyota and City National Bank."

To support the community and augment her visibility, Doi speaks at events and participates in industry associations. She has been selected three consecutive times as one of the top 100 women in the automotive industry, as ranked by *Automotive News.* This has opened up opportunities for Doi to contribute to a newly formed women's initiative formed by Deloitte that aims to strengthen the pipeline from manufacturing to small business. She is also on the board of 2020 Women on Boards."

Doi has been quoted widely about finance when she has spoken at various CFO summits and events, and she has contributed several articles to magazines.

"It's always an honor to be asked to speak, but part of the benefit is also networking and learning from your peers."

Doi describes her experience on the board of City National Bank as a win-win.

"The City National culture is very similar to the culture at Toyota—there's a customer-first focus, plus value and respect for every colleague."

But the culture is only one factor to being successful on a board; the other is chemistry. Getting to know people first through orientations, informal meetings, or board dinners helps new members acclimate to how the established board dynamics work.

"I appreciated orientation meetings that the bank set up so I could meet the leaders of each pillar of the organization, get to know the people I'd be interacting with most often, and open up a dialogue about each other's strengths. That way, when the time came to partner on a project or tackle an issue, the right combinations of people would be selected."

One of Doi's passions that she honed during her time at Toyota is diversity, leveraging the strengths of all team members and ensuring representation from across the supply chain of vendors. Doi encourages the development of smaller businesses and suppliers, working with procurement and advocacy groups to provide mentoring and growth potential and ultimately, contracting.

At Toyota, Doi is active with its business partnering groups, cultivating the talent pipeline and providing leadership opportunities. One of the practices that helps ensure many voices are heard is to provide opportunities for leaders at all levels to make presentations or attend meetings.

"One of the best practices at City National Bank, too, is inviting line managers to make board presentations. That's a fantastic opportunity for women to gain recognition and visibility with board members, to demonstrate expertise, and to let them know about your interest in board service."

KAPILA ANAND

> *The head of the audit committee saw that I brought value-added expertise to the board, including cybersecurity, and was open to modifications to the established structure and agenda.*

Kapila Anand, CPA, began her career in accounting with KPMG three decades before retiring as a partner who specialized in the real estate/REIT, travel, leisure, and hospitality industries, which ultimately paved the way for her selection by the Extended Stay America board as an independent director. Long before her outstanding achievements in accounting, however, Anand discovered leadership was in her DNA during high school, when she ran her own business, working door-to-door selling Avon products as a teenager and later as an accounting intern at a state natural resources agency.

KAPILA ANAND
Chicago, Illinois

Corporate/Select Nonprofit Boards:
Elanco Animal Health, Inc.
Extended Stay America
ESH Hospitality, Inc.
Omega Healthcare Investors, Inc.
Rush University Medical Center
U.S. Fund for UNICEF
WomenCorporateDirectors
KPMG LLP
KPMG Foundation

Career History:
KPMG LLP: Partner, Segment Leader: Travel, Leisure, and Hospitality
Marriott International, Inc.: Advisor
Starwood Hotels & Resorts Worldwide, Inc.: Advisor
Hyatt Corporation: Advisor

Education:
MBA, Michigan State University
BA, Accounting and Finance, Michigan State University

"Before I ever held a full-time job, I learned lessons quite early in my life about the value of building relationships, cost accounting, repeat customers, customer engagement, and negotiated pricing in both the public and private sectors.

"I made enough money to get myself through college. I still fall back on those techniques today that I learned long ago. And you can be sure—good negotiating skills come in handy in the boardroom."

Years later, knowing she would soon retire from KPMG, Anand put that experience to good use as she sought to find corporate board seats.

"I took the time to make sure I had developed valuable strategy experience that would make me a good overall fit for a board—not just for the audit committee, which is the logical place for financial experts. I started my outreach a few months before retirement and sent out letters to my network expressing my interest in sitting on a board. Sometimes it's hard to sell yourself, but I learned many years ago that clearly articulating your value to your target customer is compelling."

Her network of strategic contacts was the key. Anand reached out to former KPMG partners who served as board directors and to her contacts from within the travel, leisure, and hospitality industries. Serving as lead director on the nonprofit boards of WomenCorporateDirectors (WCD) and the US Fund at UNICEF, she also made her intentions known to board members of those organizations. Ultimately, it was the general counsel at Extended Stay America, with whom Anand had previously worked as a client, who recommended her to the CEO. He knew a board seat would be opening up around the time Anand was retiring.

"Everyone told me not to take the first board opportunity that came along, however, because I had a lot of connections to this board, I had a very high level of comfort. The lead director of the Extended Stay America board was the former CEO of Hyatt Corporation, a former client and mentor. I had met the CEO at an industry event some years before and was impressed, and, of course, I knew the general counsel who introduced me to the board."

Anand was the first woman to join the Extended Stay America board, and she has served on both the audit committee and as chair of the nominating and governance committee. She was later named chair of the compensation committee. Extended Stay America's shares are traded with a sister organization that owns the real estate and is traded as a real estate investment trust (REIT). She subsequently joined the REIT board and chairs its audit committee.

"Due to the dynamic nature of the hospitality industry and the number of disparate forces disrupting the status quo, the board was really seeking an industry person who had experience with some of those disrupting influences, and I brought that experience. It was clear from the first few meetings that the board was focused on repositioning itself to address the changing business climate. The difference I've made is to add a strategic industry focus to the board, in addition to the experience brought by the lead director and now some of our newer directors."

Anand says she believes being the chair of the nominating and governance committee is a critical way to make a difference on boards. This role has an impact because Extended Stay America did not historically use search firms to source candidates.

"As the founding directors rolled off the board and departed the company, I have been able to make a difference by leading the nomination-and-selection process with a great search committee."

Anand relies on contacts through her many board connections with WCD as well as the National Association of Corporate Directors (NACD), whose members are all current directors.

To acclimate to the culture before her first board meeting, Anand scheduled one-on-one time with each of the directors.

"I asked about cultural dynamics and issues that the company was facing and communicated what value I could bring to the board. Outsiders had advised me to figure things out along the way, so I wanted to know what advice each director would share with me. I wanted to be productive from the very first meeting."

She says meeting with the chair of the audit committee was crucial to her smooth transition onto the board:

"Before I joined the board, he had established certain protocols. I shared with him my perspectives that I had learned from my previous experience, including attending WCD/NACD corporate director peer exchanges and KPMG's Audit Committee Institute. He saw that I brought value-added expertise to the board, including cybersecurity, and was open to modifications to the established structure and agenda."

Anand's recommendation for others joining a board—whether it's their first or tenth—is to establish trusted relationships with the existing directors through one-on-one interactions.

"The conversations that happen outside the boardroom are essential to making sure your voice is heard at the board meetings—you do however have to learn to pick your battles, and in my experience, that approach is appreciated in the long term."

MOLLY CAMPBELL

> 66 *I am the voice making sure process is carried out in a thoughtful way.* 99

"You never know where the recommendation might come from that leads to your first corporate board appointment. In my case, it was the wife of a senior executive at East West Bank, one of the largest publicly held banks in the U.S., bridging China and U.S. business relationships. He happened to mention to his wife in casual conversation that the board was frustrated looking to fill an empty seat on the East West board with a person who had international trade experience as well as finance and operations, and would bring immediate value to the board.

MOLLY CAMPBELL
New York, New York

Corporate/Select Nonprofit Boards:
Granite Construction, Inc.
East West Bancorp, Inc.
International Association of Ports and Harbors
American Association of Port Authorities
U.S. Maritime Transportation System National
    Advisory Committee
Planning Commission, City of Long Beach
Southern California Leadership Network

Career History:
The Port Authority of New York and New Jersey: Director, Port
    Department
Los Angeles World Airports: Director of Financial Management
    Systems
Port of Los Angeles: Deputy Executive Director; CFO
City of Los Angeles, Office of City Administrative Officer: Director,
    Public Finance
Disneyland: Manager, Business Planning

Education:
MA, Public Policy, Georgetown University
BA, Political Science, University of California, Los Angeles

"He wanted diversity and a woman if possible. His wife had met me at occasional business functions at the Port of Los Angeles, where I was Deputy Executive Director helping manage the nearly one-billion-dollar budget. And it was she who said to him, 'What about Molly Campbell?'"

Campbell's three best pieces of advice for joining a board are:

- Tell everyone you know about your goal to serve on corporate boards.
- Do your very best at your regular job.
- Gain experience through large nonprofit boards.

"Sometimes it may be women upon whom you've made an impression, even when you don't even realize you did, and they're in the position to influence boards."

The senior executive who nominated her became Campbell's greatest champion and advocate for gender and ethnic diversity on the board. Campbell's many years in an operations role at the Port of Los Angeles had given her the deep understanding of global trade that is required of directors on bank boards. Together, the Port of Long Beach and the Port of Los Angeles compose the world's largest port complex. This background impressed the senior executive, who quickly set up interviews for Campbell with the rest of the board.

"I was approved as soon as I had the approval of my own Port of L.A. Commission board chair. Being given the green light by your own CEO is always a hurdle—any potential conflicts of interest had to be cleared by the City of Los Angeles Ethics Commission. But the ethics commission determined there were no conflicts, and the pathway was clear."

Prior to her selection by East West Bancorp, Campbell had spent many months expressing her intention to serve on a board to a variety of her business contacts.

"I thought joining a board would be the ideal way to expand my learning and figure out how to transition into the next phase of my career. I spoke with some trusted women who were on corporate boards and asked, 'What's the secret?'"

Their general advice was to put yourself in situations where you will meet people who will vouch for your strengths. Nonprofit boards specifically are a great start, they agreed. So, when Campbell was offered a position on the board of Lakewood Community Hospital, a small regional hospital, she accepted with enthusiasm.

"I was casting a wide net. The hospital board was a great foray into healthcare, but I had made a list of many other companies I was interested in, where I thought I could help them grow if I were a director."

The East West Bancorp board position came about in 2014. Campbell spent several hours in a "good cop/bad cop" interview scenario with two East West Bancorp board members. At the end, they offered her the position.

"I said, 'Wow, you guys are tough.' And they said, 'All of us like each other on the board, and we want others who join to be a part of that collegial atmosphere.'

"I realized this bank valued much more than just knowledge or experience; it valued camaraderie. And that has paid off. We support each other. If anyone has an issue, we deal with it. Those two governance committee members became my mentors from the day I started on the board. In the beginning, I would sit next to them and whisper, 'What is that acronym?' And one would always educate me."

Campbell has a financial background, so she quickly was appointed to the audit committee, where she believes she has made the greatest contribution.

"We spend a lot of time going through interactions and discussions with government regulators for a variety of reasons. I'm absolutely grounded in process—it's not sexy, but it's important. How you do things matters, especially when you are making major decisions. The analysis is always important."

While the private sector is more nimble, highly regulated businesses such as banks require additional attention to detail. Campbell says she pays special care to the smallest detail.

"I am the voice making sure process is carried out in a thoughtful way."

Part of Campbell's thoughtfulness includes observing and learning before speaking. Calling herself a vocal and "bossy" child, Campbell has had to work on reframing her questions and positions so as not to come off as confrontational on boards.

"Recognize that others have come before you, and respect their expertise. I remind myself of that a lot. Especially in an environment with men."

The East West Bancorp board is not a typical board, which in turn affects the composition of the rest of the company. When Campbell joined, there was a woman president as well as a woman CFO and other women in top-level positions; the bank fosters a diverse environment. The board also has a second woman member, Iris Chan.

"We spent a lot of time getting to know each other. We are supportive of each other. We often share a car back to the airport, so that gives us one-on-one time to build a friendship. Building individual relationships is very valuable, and it helps to understand the business from all aspects."

Campbell calls herself an "all-in" executive.

"I went to school with the intention of providing service at the top. I wanted to be helpful to elected officials but not be a bureaucrat myself. I wanted to make a difference in people's lives. So when the City of Los Angeles offered me the opportunity to work as a civil servant, I applied. I took the employment test and scored only 95 out of 100 points, so I asked, 'What did I do wrong?' The interviewer told me 95 was their highest score. Guess I've always been an overachiever."

Campbell's "over-achieving" life includes her role as director at the Port Authority of New York and New Jersey, and serving on the board of East West Bancorp, plus being the mother of two high-achieving children: her daughter is following Molly's lead—she is a second-year law student. Her son is following directly in Molly's footsteps—he works as a budget analyst for the City of Los Angeles.

LESLIE STONE HEISZ

66 *There is no "I" in board—the board is a team.* 99

Leslie Stone Heisz is a former investment banker who has parlayed her financial acumen and business expertise into a successful corporate board career in diverse industries, including information systems, gaming technology, and healthcare. She currently sits on the boards of Edwards Lifesciences, Public Storage, and Kaiser Permanente. Heisz credits her considerable experience in mergers and acquisitions, and supporting each CEO's growth objectives, as key to her boardroom success.

LESLIE STONE HEISZ
Los Angeles, California

Corporate Boards:
Edwards Lifesciences Corporation
Public Storage
Kaiser Permanente
Ingram Micro, Inc.
Willis Towers Watson
HCC Insurance Holdings, Inc.
International Game Technology, PLC

Career History:
Lazard: Managing Director
Wasserstein Perella and Co., Inc.: Managing Director
Salomon Brothers, Inc.: VP
Price Waterhouse (now PricewaterhouseCoopers): Management
    Consultant

Education:
MBA, Finance and Accounting, UCLA Anderson School of
    Management
BS, Economics-systems Science, University of California,
    Los Angeles

When Heisz was just beginning her investment banking career, she partnered with a colleague to develop a new gaming industry financing effort in Las Vegas that would fulfill the gap left by the collapse of the junk-bond market and demise of scandal-ridden Drexel.

"The casino industry was on the verge of an historic expansion to about a dozen new states beyond traditional markets of Nevada and Atlantic City, but struggled with raising development capital. Many start-up companies secured real-estate and gaming licenses to launch riverboat casinos, and gradually gained enough success and profit to become public."

Heisz played a leadership role in structuring, negotiating, and financing the growth of dozens of these companies, which set the stage for her future board career.

"When I left Salomon Brothers and joined Wasserstein Perella, we did a lot of business consolidation in the gaming industry, which had mushroomed from a handful to more than fifty public companies."

Fifteen years after beginning her investment banking career, Heisz took a leave to tend to her family and reassess her career prospects. That's when the chairman of International Game Technology (IGT) called, offering Heisz her first corporate board seat. She remained on that board for five years but departed when a conflict of interest developed.

"IGT was simultaneously in the business of selling and leasing slot machines. By 2008, IGT had become the largest unsecured creditor of most of the casinos. Should any of my clients go into bankruptcy, it was a conflict of interest for me to both be their bankruptcy advisor and serve as a director of their major creditor, so I decided to resign from that board."

Almost accidentally, she explains, she was invited to the board of Ingram Micro, Inc., a global distributor of technology and computer peripherals and a longtime Fortune 500 company.

"I was on the golf course when I ran into a former client and the soon-to-be chairman of the Ingram Micro board. I was still working as a banker and sitting on a few boards, feeling schizophrenic. It was one of those chance meetings that came at a perfect time. This was the one and only time golf has ever helped me professionally!"

With a strong background in mergers and acquisitions, Heisz was an invaluable addition to the Ingram board, which successfully navigated CEO and other executive successions, as well as numerous acquisitions. During her long tenure on the Ingram board, she learned the advantages of a close partnership with the non-executive chairman and the CEO, and she advises directors to ensure that the CEO has a strong board mentor.

"As you look at CEOs where you might serve on the board, be clear about where the business is today versus where it's going. Sometimes executive skill sets may be different from what is needed to achieve those goals. Listen very attentively to different external touchpoints and to management, and make sure that the appropriate information is gathered and that complex decisions are made on a timely basis."

In 2016, Ingram Micro was acquired by the large Chinese conglomerate HNA Group, as an operating subsidiary of Tianjin Tianhai Investment Company. Soon after, the Ingram Micro board was disbanded due to new ownership, she was recruited by the board of Public Storage.

In the health industry, Heisz serves on two boards, Edwards Lifesciences and

Kaiser Permanente, and both seats came through search firms. She shares a personal story that when her parents died, she had experienced what she calls the dysfunction of the healthcare industry. That's when she decided she wanted to give back to society in a more meaningful and immediate way by serving on the board of a medical company. Not long after, a search firm representing Kaiser Permanente called, asking her to become the fifth woman on its board.

"It was complete serendipity, especially since I hadn't made my desire to serve on a medical board known to anyone. My background was different from all the doctors and representatives of the healthcare system, but my business experience was consistent with the moves they were making."

Having been a longtime chair of the audit committee as well as a member of the governance, risk, and nominating committees, Heisz has developed four core tenets of effective board leadership:

- Trust your instincts. Many women have really good instincts about complex or difficult issues. If you're uncomfortable, trust me, so are some others.
- Be courageous. Put your constituents, shareholders, customers, patients, employees first.
- Be flexible. You may be going down a particular path, however as you obtain new information, it's important to remain flexible in the course that you chart.
- Be a good listener. Don't assume you know all the answers and information; aim to increase your perspective of critical business issues by learning from your colleagues.

And most importantly: "There is no "I" in board—the board is a team with talent, curiosity, and experience, and should contribute through group discovery and engagement."

When it comes to issues that deal with an ethical element, Heisz has been described as "the conscience of the board." She says this is due to her ability to appropriately judge when to be proactive and when to let things settle, and her operational style, which is based more on influencing than forcing direction. The best way to do this is to be able to read the room.

"It's important how you present your ideas and opinions, particularly if you are the only woman director or one of few women on the board. I have three sons, and they only want to hear once whatever it is I have to say (and then, with economy of words). Women are more expressive—we like to share context and stories. But my philosophy is to be deliberate with your communication style, in order to have maximum impact. If you can't persuade people to your point of view, what's the point in expressing it?"

Global Market Experts

Today's boards of directors in every sector or industry must understand the impact and volatility of global markets, supply chains, and employment laws, as well as grasp the idiosyncrasies of doing business in other countries. Technology has spread American influence throughout the world, opening up unlimited markets for U.S. companies to sell products worldwide. Thanks to technology, even small companies are global.

10
Fortune 500 companies now have a **majority** of women on their boards

Anne Gates, Brenda McCabe, and Patricia Lizarraga honed their very different professional expertise in countries around the world. Gates spent much of her career in the entertainment and toy industry; McCabe's field is pharmaceuticals; and Lizarraga has a successful banking career. But what they have in common is an understanding of and appreciation for international markets and business that go beyond an American lens.

These women were able to seek out and secure board positions specifically because of their global finance experience and expansive worldview. They make a difference on boards because they understand and help their companies to be successful in other countries.

ANNE RABY GATES

Expertise is not gender-based.

Anne Gates spent much of her career in positions of increasing seniority at The Walt Disney Company, including the roles of Executive Vice President and CFO of The Disney Company's Consumer Products Division, with over $3 billion in revenues, and Managing Director for Disney Consumer Products Europe and

Emerging Markets. However, Disney was, and still is, a company that does not allow its executives to sit on corporate boards. Since leaving Disney and subsequently MGA Entertainment, she has more than made up for those years without board service by claiming seats on the boards of three large national and international companies: Kroger, Tapestry, and Raymond James.

ANNE RABY GATES
Los Angeles, California

Corporate/Select Nonprofit Boards:
The Kroger Co.
Raymond James Financial, Inc.
Tapestry, Inc.
PBS SoCal
CADRE
Salzburg Global Seminar
University of California, Berkeley Foundation
Board of Visitors of The Fu Foundation School of Engineering and
	Applied Science, Columbia Engineering

Career History:
MGA Entertainment, Inc.: President
The Walt Disney Company: EVP and CFO, Consumer Products; EVP
	and Managing Director, Consumer Products Europe and Emerging
	Markets; SVP, Planning and Analysis, Corporate
KFC Europe: Manager, Financial Planning
PepsiCo, Inc.: Manager, Business Development
Bear Stearns: VP, Public Finance
AT&T Bell Laboratories, Inc. (Now Bell Laboratories): Manager

Education:
Post-graduate work, Operations Research, Columbia University
MS, Operations Research, Columbia University
BA, Mathematics, University of California, Berkeley

Kroger is the retail food conglomerate with dozens of well-established brands. Raymond James Financial, Inc. is the well-known financial planning and investment firm, and Tapestry, Inc. is a leading New York-based house of modern luxury accessories and lifestyle brands that owns three major labels: Coach, Kate Spade, and Stuart Weitzman.

Gates's board appointments began when she was contacted by a search firm after leaving Disney to become president of MGA Entertainment, the largest privately held toy company in the United States, best known for its Little Tikes brand.

"Somehow, I was in the board recruiter's database, most likely through the recommendations of others."

Kroger was her first board, which she joined in 2015.

"Three women were on the Kroger board when I joined. The women on this board are very well respected, plus obviously incredibly talented and dynamic. Together, we have been active in driving discussions."

For Kroger, Gates chairs the audit committee and also sits on the public-responsibilities committee, which reviews Kroger's social and public responsibilities as a corporate citizen.

"Both gender groups on the Kroger board are attuned to grocery shopping. All of the Kroger board members make it a point to visit the stores, walk the aisles, and use Kroger's digital services. Expertise, passion, and commitment to the success of Kroger is a universal value shared by this board of directors."

Despite the fact that she did not have specific grocery industry experience, Gates says that Kroger was a natural fit for her. Being in consumer products for more than thirty years required strong understanding of both brands and retailers.

In 2017, one of the women on the Kroger board recommended Gates for the board of Tapestry, where she joined the human-resources committee, which oversees compensation. Gates says the diversity—gender, nationality, and ethnicity—among her Tapestry board colleagues is critically important for the company's growth.

"We have five remarkable foreign-born directors—one each from Italy, the U.K., and China, our board chair who emigrated from Nigeria, plus our CEO, who emigrated from Portugal. This is key, since the company is composed of global brands."

Gates's role on the Raymond James board came about through the same recruiting firm that placed her at Kroger. With Kroger based in Cincinnati, Raymond James in Tampa, and Tapestry in New York, she is amassing thousands of frequent-flyer miles.

"I really love my board responsibilities and the opportunity to work in different regions of the country."

On the board of Raymond James, she sits on the audit/risk committee.

"This board has such an impressive group of people. One of the twenty-three women CEOs in the S&P 500 is on the Raymond James board, and we have another female CEO whose company's market cap is over $1 billion. They have very impactful roles. Our Raymond James lead director, Susan Story, cares deeply about diversity and female representation. There is a great leadership style about her."

Gates's own leadership style was developed while working and living in international markets early in her career at PepsiCo, setting the tone for her successful career.

"I spent years working with international teams. There are key sets of leadership skills required to be successful internationally. Leading a team that is spread out globally means developing strong influencing skills. I went through a huge geographic restructuring and had to change multiple functions and processes to make sure we were all efficiently working together well worldwide. That required effective communication skills to explain why and how we were doing something, rather than trying to push change down with no discussion from the top. When you have staff six thousand miles away, it is very important for them to buy in. This takes lots of diplomacy."

Her early community service work is still reflected in her nonprofit board memberships. In addition to her three prestigious national and global public boards, Gates chairs the investment committee for PBS SoCal, Southern California's public broadcasting station; sits on the board of CADRE—a local community organization supporting education in poor neighborhoods—and joined the board of Salzburg Global Seminar, which challenges current and future leaders to discuss ways to shape a better world.

BRENDA A. MCCABE

" I always put myself in the shoes of end-users. "

Brenda McCabe is an accomplished international business consultant and an independent director with senior management experience in European as well as U.S. markets.

BRENDA A. MCCABE
Los Angeles, California

Corporate/Select Nonprofit Boards:
Versatrope Therapeutics
Jubel, LLC
Squire Systems, LLC
Natraceutical Group Reig Jofre
Lug Healthcare Technology
SolidQ
WomenCorporateDirectors, Spain

Career History:
Jubel, LLC: Advisor
Matchbook Services: Advisor
DBZ Arrow, SL: Managing Director
Infinia Corporation, Inc.: Managing Director
AstraZeneca: VP, Strategy Development & Customer Solutions
KA International: VP, Franchise Development
McKinsey & Company: Senior Consultant

Education:
MBA, The University of Chicago Booth School of Business
BS, Business Administration, Berea College
BA, Spanish, Berea College

"My career has led to corporate boards because of my diverse experience in key functions and sectors—from management consulting and retail to innovative pharmaceuticals and renewable/clean technology. I have been fortunate, because working in diverse areas provides different knowledge and skill sets—and the combination benefits board service."

Born and raised in Columbus, Ohio, McCabe was fascinated by languages and learned Spanish early in school. She went to Spain as an exchange student and fell in love with the country—and a young doctor, whom she married. She began her career as an auditor with a spin-off of PricewaterhouseCoopers and shortly after went to work for McKinsey in corporate consulting, where she developed her skills in international sales, business development, intellectual property, and company restructuring. After departing McKinsey, she advised and worked in retail, pharmaceutical, and technology companies throughout Europe. She lived for twenty-eight years in Spain and Italy.

Her first corporate board was a "listed"—or publicly held—company in Spain, introduced by her network from The University of Chicago Booth School of Business.

"I had established myself as an expert in pharmaceuticals, and a friend from Chicago knew about a company called Natraceutical Group. I later learned that Spain's securities-and-exchange government regulator for Spanish-listed companies had called out this company for not having an independent director chairing the audit committee. The company was given a time frame to bring on the board member."

McCabe says the timing turned out to be fortunate for her to have joined this board when she did—two years later, her mergers-and-acquisitions expertise was essential in a pivotal transaction for the company.

"I co-led the committee responsible for a large merger. The target company had a series of drugs in development for women's reproductive health. At the meeting, I was the only woman in a room full of men discussing the effectiveness of the drug on pre-labor contractions."

McCabe recounts that, by using humor, she was able to offer insights only a woman would know.

"I asked the men if they were fathers, and had any of them seen their wives suffer through these specific labor conditions."

When she explained the meaningful benefits of the product—only she could know as the only mother in the room, especially one who had given birth twice— she was able to bring substance and perspective with her pharma experience and real-life experience.

McCabe recalls that as a result of the meeting, the deal came together nicely as there was chemistry between the top executives of both acquirer and target company. It was a huge success awarded "best financial transaction for that year" by the International Association for Corporate Growth.

"I believe women make a difference on boards because they bring the perspective of half the population. Being an independent director, I represent the interests of the minority shareholders, so I always put myself in the shoes of end users and analyze how the board's actions make a difference."

McCabe has served on European private-equity portfolio companies and in two U.S. privately held companies. McCabe's committee work on her various boards has included audit, nominating and governance, and compensation.

"Most of us have been in senior positions in large corporations where financial reporting and hiring, firing, and compensation were part of the annual and quarterly planning. I would encourage candidates to package their executive experience in a manner that is seen through the lens of a board director—big picture."

For those joining audit committees, she recommends asking many questions along the lines of compensation comparisons to peers and competitors, and how the company addresses changes.

"You as a candidate must do your due diligence on the company before you join the board, so prepare accordingly."

Due diligence also includes investigating board chemistry, and McCabe says her pre-existing professional relationships with the chairman of each company led to her confidence that the chemistry would be good.

"Once on the board, my recommendation is always to ask permission from the chair of the board to seek time with the CEO and C-suite executives for their counsel on how to be most effective in board meetings."

McCabe says this strategy, along with seeking one-on-one conversations with individual board members, has never failed her.

"Even in potentially tense situations with dissenting voices, the underlying respect between board members that is developed outside the boardroom, along with the board chair's deftness in maintaining the chemistry among directors, keeps a positive balance and interaction.

"Ask probing questions—but do not be the bull in a china shop."

The fourth child of seven, McCabe says she suffered from "middle-child syndrome" until she hit her academic stride in high school, where she became class president.

"I owe much to McKinsey & Company as an institution. One of my mentors once said to me: 'The most exceptional growth is when a professional is put into a situation where they aren't yet ready and they are stretched. I was one of those who was stretched often.

"Perhaps my father has been the most influential person who pushed me beyond my boundaries academically and professionally. My mother was instrumental in teaching us by asking tough questions—she would drill all of us siblings often on why we were choosing a certain path versus another, personally and professionally.

"I believe leadership is a very lonely role to have—no one will ever tell you that. I don't believe leaders are born; they are made. What inspires me is the quality of a person with an intellectual curiosity and love for learning. But I also seek fun. If

I am not doing something meaningful—and for me, meaningful means learning and enjoying what I do—then I move on."

PATRICIA LIZARRAGA

> ❝ *I believe the world should have 50% women in the C-suite. Until we have such parity, society will be far less than it could be.* ❞

As Patricia Lizarraga worked her way through a successful international banking career in New York City, she became more and more certain that the business sector was shortchanged by not advancing qualified women to its senior-level ranks.

PATRICIA LIZARRAGA
New York, New York

Corporate/Select Nonprofit Boards:
Credicorp Ltd.
Banco de Crédito del Perú
Museo de Arte de Lima, Peru

Career History:
Hypatia Capital Group: Founder and Managing Partner
Credit Agricole Securities (USA), Inc., New York: Managing Director, Mergers and Acquisitions
Donaldson, Lufkin & Jenrette Securities Corporation: Associate
Grupo del Ande: Founder
Sigma SAFI—Sociedad Administradora de Fondos de Inversiones: Founding Investor

Education:
MBA, Harvard Business School
BA, Economics and Latin American Studies, Yale University

"I became more convinced that the world should have 50% women in the C-suite. Until we have such parity, society will be far less than it could be."

Her own success led to a board seat at Credicorp Ltd., the largest financial services holding company in Peru, and Banco de Credito del Peru, the country's largest bank and its leading supplier of integrated financial services.

Lizarraga founded Hypatia Capital in 2007 based on her belief that there should be more women at the helm of America's largest corporations.

"We strive to make this a reality by finding and partnering with top female executives to acquire businesses that they will lead to great success. We will carefully acquire businesses one by one, and we will not be satisfied until women are as well represented in the CEO suite as they are in the workforce overall."

Hypatia is aptly named for the ancient Greek philosopher, who was in her time the world's leading mathematician and astronomer, the only woman for whom such a statement can be made. Since New York-based Hypatia Capital began, it has made remarkable progress toward the goal of placing more women in control of America's wealth.

Lizarraga points to hedge funds, where data proves that women managers outperform men.

"There is ample evidence of women's investing and operating savvy in all industries and asset classes. But too few investors look to the diversity of the boards of companies they invest in. I am confident that is changing. Plenty of research tells me, as does my intuition, that adding women to your governing bodies will add to the performance of organizations."

In her native Lima, Peru, Lizarraga entered the banking world when she was twenty-two years old. Even in high school, her leadership abilities were evident. She held class and school-wide leadership roles. Talk about strategic networking early in one's career—the young people Lizarraga met in high school grew up to become her fellow board members of Banco de Credito del Peru!

These leadership roles built trust in her capabilities. She came to the U.S. to get her education at Yale and then Harvard Business School, yet she continued to travel regularly between the two countries. Today, comparing the two, she sees clear distinctions.

"Latin America is behind the U.S. in how far women have come. Most senior executives who are women are the exception to the rule. There are only three to four percent women in the C-suite. On the other hand, in Latin America, women are culturally more outspoken. I have definitely learned to be more vocal in my role on my boards.

"On the board level, Latin America is a very formal culture. The tone tends to be respectful and deferential. There is great respect accorded to all members' opinions."

Lizarraga recalls an honest, open, and non-confrontational conversation with the bank's senior leadership about the lack of women on the board and their concerted effort to change that.

"Like most women in the world, I didn't immediately think first of myself as the likely candidate. I wouldn't have suggested myself. I was typically thinking of experience versus potential."

However, the CEO and his directors thought she would bring the value the board needed. So she joined the board in 2017.

In her first year of service, Lizarraga felt it was too early to ascertain her impact. However, she appreciated being the second woman director, bringing the total to two women among its fourteen board members.

"To reinforce your value on the board, be sure to consider serving on the audit committee. It's more work and more risk, and it takes more time. But serving on the audit committee provides focus and gives you designation with the SEC as a financial expert, which opens up future opportunities."

Lizarraga suggests that initially it may seem riskier for a nominating committee to choose a woman, in many ways still an "unknown."

"But research shows that taking that risk of bringing on a woman director can increase the company's rewards and your own. Companies with gender balance outperform, and I have seen countless cases where that is true."

Crisis Management Experts

When large corporations struggle with a challenge, a turnaround, or a very public crisis, boards of directors must act quickly and competently. With today's 24/7 news cycle, troubling financial headlines or accusations against management require that all board members react with speed and with a unified voice.

Crisis management is a broad term that covers the prevention and response to a crisis in a business operation. Shareholders, employees, and customers are all affected by a corporate crisis. Remember the Tylenol recall decades ago that crystallized the need for advance planning, speedy response, ethical behavior, and leadership to pull the company together to resolve the crisis. Crisis management requires critical communications, targeted messaging, and top leaders pre-identified as spokespeople. Ultimately, it's the responsibility of board members and executive management to ensure the best outcomes, short-term and long-term, for all stakeholders and the greater public.

In their board profiles and resumes, executive women who have been involved in crisis management and crisis communications in their careers should emphasize the roles they have played in resolving crises. Such experience is definitely a "value-add" for corporate boards in today's volatile business climate. Business schools offer courses on crisis management and communications, but there's nothing like handling a real-world crisis to give you true depth and know-how for anticipating and responding to such situations.

Roxanne Austin, Irene Chang Britt, and Colleen Brown have each demonstrated this kind of board leadership during a company's challenging times. Their professional expertise made the difference as the companies they served navigated difficult waters.

Target experienced one of the first huge cybersecurity incidents, one that resulted in a mega breach of customer information. Board member Roxanne Austin moved to Minneapolis for several months and established her office in the company headquarters to lead it to recovery. Irene Chang Britt made a difference in the turnaround of Tailored Brands when its stock value plummeted. Colleen Brown made a difference on the board of American Apparel when it went through a painful and very public financial and reputational crisis.

These three women brought their professional leadership skills to companies, as well as empathy and sensitivity to the plight of employees. As Brown says, "There were ten thousand employees whose livelihoods were at stake; this was so much more than just a brand."

Boards are well advised to seek out and value the strong communication and listening skills that women bring to their board work, as these profiles demonstrate.

ROXANNE S. AUSTIN

Identify the strengths you would bring to a board in representing shareholder interests.

Roxanne Austin is known in business circles as the ultimate optimist. And she needed every bit of that optimism when Target was hit by a shocking data breach of its customer information records during the holiday season of 2013.

ROXANNE S. AUSTIN
Newport Coast, California

Corporate/Select Nonprofit Boards:
Target Corporation
Abbott Laboratories
AbbVie, Inc.
Teledyne Technologies, Inc.
Telefonaktiebolaget LM Ericsson
DIRECTV, LLC
PanAmSat Corporation (now Intelsat)

Career History:
Austin Investment Advisors: President and CEO
EQT AB: Chair, Investment Committee, U.S. Mid-Market Fund
Move Networks, Inc.: President and CEO
DIRECTV, LLC: President and COO
Hughes Electronics Corporation: EVP and CFO
Deloitte & Touche LLP: Partner

Education:
BBA, Accounting, University of Texas at San Antonio
Certified Public Accountant

Austin had been on the board since 2002 and remains on the board today. The Target customer data theft may have included more than seventy million customer records and made history as one of the largest corporate hacking operations ever, and at the time it was certainly the most visible.

"Because we were the first high-profile data breach, the media was relentless. Every day there was something negative in multiple media outlets. It was so heartbreaking for our 380,000 employees to see so much negativity about their company, especially when Target had always had a great reputation and was viewed as an iconic brand."

Then it seemed like everyone, including Congress, state attorneys general, the Security and Exchange Commission, etc., piled on Target to fix blame for the disaster.

Derivative lawsuits were filed by shareholders. Austin recalls the period:

"Adding to the turmoil was the Institutional Shareholder Services (ISS) recommendation to vote against all the current board members who served on the audit or risk committees. We mobilized outreach to as many shareholders as possible and won the vote, overcoming the ISS no-vote recommendation. Can you imagine destabilizing the board at a time of crisis? Winning the shareholder vote was the first big boost we had since the data breach was discovered. The board members received 70 to 90% shareholder approval that year, then all exceeded 90% just one year later. We all stayed on the board to help management through this challenging time. It was a huge crisis, but we survived, and the company became even stronger after the crisis."

After weathering the immediate crisis, the board determined it was time for a leadership change. Then-CEO Gregg Steinhafel exited the company, and the board named CFO John Mulligan as interim president and chief executive officer. Austin was asked to step in as interim chairman of the board of directors.

To be constantly available, Austin stayed in Minneapolis and took an office at corporate headquarters for three-and-a-half months while a search was underway to find the new CEO. She put her own business, Austin Investment Advisors, on hold indefinitely, so she could be there to work daily with Mulligan.

During those months, she worked with the management team to do a comprehensive deep dive into the Target business, creating a new strategic framework to focus on Target's strengths and its innovative multichannel retail opportunities, and to plan a stronger digital presence going forward. She wanted the team to be brutally honest in the assessment of the business, and to be prepared to present the results of the comprehensive study and to explain the new strategic framework to the CEO on his or her first day.

The motto for the team's work that summer, over 24,000 hours of combined effort, was, "The truth shall set you free!" Her goal was to leave the Target team in a stronger place, with a clear view of the business by the end of the summer, and to allow the new CEO to hit the ground running. She jokingly says her own mantra was, "CEO before the first snow!" Of course, she was there when Brian Cornell was named Target's new chairman and CEO in August of 2014, well in advance of the first snow. Mission accomplished!

"After serving as interim chair of the board, which had become literally a full-time job during the crisis, it was hard at first to transition back into simply occupying a seat on the board—which is only advisory. During the crisis recovery, I had become close to the management team and built strong relationships. It was like coming through a war together—fighting for our lives in the trenches. It was difficult to be a regular board member again, but it is what you have to do."

Before the crisis hit, she was named one of the fifty most influential people in boardrooms by the National Association of Corporate Directors. Her actions in a time of crisis made her worthy of such a distinction.

Having recovered from the crisis and forged a stronger company, Austin recommends four important action items so all board members are prepared for disaster—just in case the unexpected disaster befalls their companies:

- Know your emergency succession plan. Who will be chairman? CEO?
- Make sure your crisis management (including communication plan) is up-to-date and known to all directors.
- Regularly perform realistic war-game and desktop scenarios to practice the plan.
- Adjust your plan as necessary based on lessons learned.

Austin serves on four boards, including Target. She chairs the investment committee for the U.S. Mid Market Fund of EQT, a European private equity firm, in addition to running her own investment firm. Her professional life is typically dominated by her boards and their meeting calendars.

"I enjoy board service, and the responsibility that comes with it. For women who enjoy business, I recommend they become very strategic and focused if their goal is to serve on a board. The best way to share your intention is by telling people you know who currently serve on boards. Ask their advice. Identify the strengths you would bring to a board in terms of representing shareholder interests. Think in advance about committees to which you could add value. Getting invited to boards takes effort and time, but it's well worth it."

Abbott Labs was her first outside public board in 2000. She was called by a consultant at Egon Zehnder, an executive search firm, while she was EVP and CFO at Hughes. He told her that Abbott was looking for a board candidate with experience in mergers and acquisitions since Abbott's go-forward strategy would include significant acquisitions. He set up a meeting with Abbott Labs Chairman and CEO Miles White. After interviews with White and the lead director, she was selected. When Abbott split into two separate companies in 2013—Abbott Laboratories and AbbVie, each with over $20 billion in annual revenue—Austin was one of four board members asked to serve on both boards. She chairs the audit committee at AbbVie and the compensation committee at Abbott Laboratories.

In 2002, a call came out of the blue to her office at DirecTV, where Austin was president and COO. It was 7 p.m. on a Friday night before July 4th weekend. On the line was the former Target chief human resources officer who handled all board recruitment at the time (without a search firm).

"He said Target was interested in my experience, since I had led a recognized brand name (DirecTV), and in my financial background." Austin told him that she needed to do some research.

After that call, she drove to the nearest Target store on her way home from work and walked its aisles. She wound up with a basket full of very cool decor for her July 4th celebration, at a great price.

"I fell in love with Target and its style as a value proposition."

She spent the rest of the evening reading Target financial and analyst reports. The next morning, she called back and said she would be interested in pursuing a discussion about the Target board. Then-Chairman and CEO Bob Ulrich flew to Los Angeles the next day and offered her the board position over lunch.

When Austin joined Target, there were two other women on the board. Fast forward to 2018, and Target has four female directors out of twelve, making its board one of the most diverse in the country. In addition to Austin, serving on the Target board are Mary Minnick (partner, Lion Capital), Melanie Healey (former group president at Procter and Gamble, and a Verizon board member), and Monica Lozano (former chair, U.S. Hispanic Media, and a former member of the Disney board).

In 2006, she joined the board of Teledyne Technologies, a company providing enabling technologies for industrial growth markets. Teledyne is based in Thousand Oaks, California, with annual revenues of $2.4 billion and 9,800 employees. The corporation has evolved during Austin's tenure on the board from a company primarily focused on aerospace and defense to one that serves multiple markets requiring advanced technology and high reliability, including deepwater oil and gas exploration and production, oceanographic research, air and water quality monitoring, factory automation, and medical imaging.

"At first glance, that might seem unrelated to my background, but Hughes was an aerospace and defense, technology-based company, and my mergers-and-acquisition experience was a critical factor, since Teledyne has been very, very acquisitive."

The first call came from then-Teledyne General Counsel John Kuelbs, whom she knew from his time at Hughes Electronics. She also knew another director on the Teledyne board, Mike Smith, with whom she had previously worked as CFO when he was chairman and CEO at Hughes. Both men had witnessed her work performance. Lastly, calls came from Teledyne Chairman and CEO Robert Mehrabian, who convinced her to join the board. "Dr. Mehrabian is one of the smartest, yet most humble, CEOs I have ever met. His dedication to a performance-based culture at Teledyne and his growth agenda for the company is what really interested me in joining his board."

In 2008, Austin joined the board of Stockholm-based LM Ericsson, one of the world's largest telecommunications infrastructure companies with more than $30 billion in annual sales. Ericsson was her first experience with a European board. She recalls her time on the board fondly (she resigned in 2016). "I am really thankful for the time I spent on the Ericsson board. I learned so much from that experience. European boards operate and govern very differently than U.S. boards, but I learned that there are positive aspects you can learn from each model. I stepped outside my comfort zone and joined a board where I was the only U.S.-based board member when I arrived. I think I am a better board member on my other boards today because of this global experience."

She advises women that there will always be deep reference checks. "You may never know which director on the board called friends on other boards to learn more about how you performed as an executive or board member. Other directors will endorse you if they know your performance on other boards, know your performance as an executive, or know you as a visible leader in your industry." Perhaps because Abbott Laboratories would be her first public board, Abbott's CEO Miles White kept the high-level executive who was her reference on the phone for more than an hour. "Board members will work their networks to get off-the-record references from people with whom you have worked or served on boards. Frankly, it is these reference checks that typically carry the most weight."

About where she's made the most difference, Austin says that, above all, her most transformational contribution was on the Target board.

"During the summer of 2014, we were able to help the internal teams realize a different worldview. Target always felt it was on top of its industry, but in reality, Target had become too insular. We needed a more objective perspective on the business. As a result, we were so much further ahead bringing the new CEO on board. We had already figured out what could be improved and how the market forces were changing. We regained most of what we lost during the breach. Now, what we are working on is Target of the future—hopefully changing the face of experiential retail. Mobile is the new storefront—our goal now is to make

Target the top choice anytime and any way people want to shop."

Austin also recalls that when she first joined Abbott Labs, the board was preparing to quickly spin off a division. She was able to contribute her expertise, thanks to having gone through a similar spin-off earlier in her career at Hughes.

Designated a "financial expert," as defined by the SEC, Austin has chaired three audit committees, two compensation committees, and a recently formed infrastructure/investment committee at Target.

"Committees are where a lot of work gets done, and all are important to a public company. For women seeking their first boards, identify which committees you could bring greatest value to your first year. Simply identifying your value-added background for a specific committee can help you to get the attention of a nominating chair. And when there are strong women board members, that builds the case for more women on boards."

Austin's observations about board chemistry: "I have found it helps to get to know other board members outside the context of the boardroom—I've invited board members to lunch and spent time together before or after board meetings. Just making that extra effort to learn other directors' perspectives about the company really has allowed chemistry to evolve naturally. There was a situation where I thought I didn't have a good relationship with a board member, so I spent more time with that person one-on-one. It really helped when the company requested that board members fly on the same flights to board meetings whenever possible. So I made sure I was on the same flight with that member. On the flight home, we would digest, debrief, and analyze issues. Just this simple effort dramatically improved our relationship."

Austin believes her greatest strengths as a leader are her ability to inspire and encourage others to reach their full potential and her eternal optimism, which helps her to lead in tough times. "The management and employees just needed to know we would work our way through the crisis, that the company would survive, and that Target would come out on the other side better and stronger. I wanted the team to focus on what we could control—making Target a better retail experience for our customers, improving our performance, and working together as a cohesive team."

When one of the team members at Target told her, "You are one of the most optimistic people I've ever met. And your optimism is contagious," Austin says she considers that "a supreme compliment."

IRENE CHANG-BRITT

 Luck is merely preparation meeting opportunity.

Irene Chang-Britt, board member of Dunkin' Brands Group, Inc.; Tailored Brands, Inc.; Brighthouse Financial, Inc.; and BayBridge Senior Housing, Inc., started her first business while still an undergraduate student at the University of Toronto. Her entrepreneurial spirit led her to open up a high-end, European-style cycling store with her brother, where she recognized her first sparks of leadership. She discovered early on that she could motivate her team of employees toward success.

IRENE CHANG-BRITT
Sarasota, Florida

Corporate Boards:
Dunkin' Brands Group, Inc.
Tailored Brands, Inc.
Brighthouse Financial, Inc.
BayBridge Senior Housing, Inc.
Sunoco, Inc.
TerraVia Holdings, Inc.

Career History:
Campbell Soup Company: Pepperidge Farm, President and SVP
    Global Baking and Snacking; Global Chief Strategy Officer
Kraft Foods Group, Inc.: SVP and GM
Nabisco Brands Ltd.: VP

Education:
MBA, University of Western Ontario
BA, Anthropology, University of Toronto

"I wanted to run a company, not for glory or for the title, but because I believed in our mission and enjoyed doing my best to accomplish that vision. That has always been my core driver."

Throughout her later career in consumer packaged goods, Chang-Britt developed an excellent executive record in strategic transformations and company turnarounds. She further solidified her reputation as a leader in the snacking and baking industries by doing speaking engagements as a subject-matter expert at industry associations and forums.

"When people hear you speak, they get to know what you bring to the table. I put myself in the right milieu by attending WomenCorporateDirectors dinners and sessions at the National Association of Corporate Directors. Eventually, with a bit of serendipity, it was that networking that led to my first board position."

The first board Chang-Britt joined was Sunoco, Inc., in 2011. She started her own intentional board search while still working as a general manager at Campbell Soup Company after the CEO identified her as a top performer with high potential. A board seat provides an unparalleled development opportunity, which in turn benefits corporations like Campbell who invest in strong leaders and succession grooming.

"The approval and endorsement of the CEO is absolutely critical to a successful board-search journey. You still have to do all the legwork yourself, but when you are top of mind and your name is present in conversation, you get the attention of the right people."

Through visibility, she earned her position on the short list for board consideration, which enabled Chang-Britt to expand her network to include top leaders within her industry. When she met Lynn Elsenhans, CEO of Sunoco, Inc., they connected over their shared interest in corporate strategy. Elsenhans was one of the few public company women CEOs in the country at the time, and a big supporter of women in the boardroom. The timing was right, as Elsenhans was thinking of restructuring the organization. "Lynn said to me, 'I need someone with your skills, and you need your first corporate board seat.'"

One of Chang-Britt's favorite quotes is, "Luck is merely preparation meeting opportunity." Her top three tips for those seeking their first board position are:

- Be visible and prepared.
- Network everywhere. Board assignments often come from unlikely sources and places.
- Be generous with your time and your skills.

"Sunoco owned gas stations and convenience stores, so there was a confluence with my background in snack divisions at companies like Nabisco, Campbell's, Kraft Foods, and Pepperidge Farm. Soon after I joined, the Sunoco board embarked on a very exciting transformative strategy and within a year, sold the entire company to Energy Transfers Partners at a 20% premium to the stock price at the time."

The existing board rolled off after the Sunoco sale, and Chang-Britt decided not to take on any additional board assignments because of her all-consuming duties as president at Pepperidge Farm. Eighteen months later, she was contacted by a large executive search firm assisting Dunkin' Brands for an open director seat.

"I knew the ins and outs of fresh bakery and of widely dispersed independent distribution models, like franchising. It was highly complementary to my duties as president of Pepperidge Farm, and I also brought the knowledge of consumer packaged goods to them.

"I tried to contribute to the Dunkin' Brands board at a high level right away. There was an opportunity early on to help drive the development of a refreshed company strategy, and also to nurture the senior female leaders in the company, so I jumped into both roles enthusiastically."

After early retirement from Pepperidge, Chang-Britt added Tailored Brands, Inc. and TerraVia Holdings, Inc. to her board portfolio. She also began mentoring high-potential women executives at Dunkin', with encouragement by CEO Nigel Travis. "I've always stretched way beyond what was normally required from a board member. Once I retired, I had the time to engage in leadership discussions with women in upper management positions. I feel I have made a difference in a very deep way by working on strategic initiatives such as executive development—especially with women one step below the C-suite. I never push myself upon anyone, but if they call upon me, I do not hesitate to jump right in."

Chang-Britt credits CEO Travis with entrusting her to mentor the women executives. "Some CEOs keep their boards at arm's length from the executives. Nigel is very transparent, which I'm thankful for. You gain deeper insight and a better view when you can get down a layer or so in the organization. You must also maintain independence and objectivity as a board member."

Besides informal mentoring, Chang-Britt has also served on a wide variety of committees. While nominating and governance is one of the most powerful committees—and the one she chairs at Dunkin'—she recommends audit for all newcomers to a board. "On audit, you learn very quickly all there is to know about a business. It's a great place to be if you want to ramp up while also contributing in a positive way to the company."

Chang-Britt says that regardless of the committee assignment, it's best to position yourself based on your expertise. For example, she had been known for managing transformations throughout her career. So when she joined the board of Tailored Brands, which owns Men's Wearhouse and Jos A. Bank, they were going through a complicated integration.

"This was an iconic brand whose stock value had dropped precipitously and suddenly. I like those opportunities to take a company with a fabulous management team, a great fundamental business model, and help try to turn them around."

How to succeed when you first join a board? "The best thing you can do is to listen. A board is a wonderful, non-political, and non-hierarchical place to be. Your fellow members are your peers. It is critical to be intellectually curious, to be deeply, honestly interested in what fellow board members have to say. Especially if you disagree, listening with your heart and brain wide open will help you argue your point of view in a respectful way."

Chang-Britt says she has always subscribed to the servant-leadership model of gaining authoritative power with non-authoritative influence. According to her, sustainable leadership means leading by example. "As a leader, it's all about human dynamics. Who are your advocates? Who are your influencers? How do you rally people around an opinion or a cause? When you have the luxury of hiring smart people with smart thinking, you'll come up with a great plan. But if you don't act with determination and a goal, or you act without thinking, that's a travesty."

In the end, however, Chang-Britt says to never let failure stand in your way. "If you make a mistake, fail fast, pick yourself up, dust yourself off, and go at it again. Fear keeps people paralyzed. Add a little bit of levity, maybe grab a drink with other directors after the board dinner. Sometimes just hanging out goes a long way in building meaningful board relationships. Above all, don't take yourself too seriously!"

COLLEEN BROWN

> *Every aspect of business can be disrupted; the secret is to do it yourself before someone else does it for you.*

Few corporate upheavals leading to the separation of a contentious CEO and the downfall of a brand, have been as public, as loud, or as unfortunate as that of American Apparel. This upstart clothing design and manufacturing powerhouse was built by founder Dov Charney in Los Angeles. American

Apparel's *raison d'etre* was "Made in USA." The brand had a ubiquitous presence as the largest clothing manufacturing operation in the United States, where design, manufacturing, distribution, and marketing were all based at the famous pink warehouse headquarters in downtown L.A. The company was facing tremendous challenges: the retail industry headwinds, significant financial debt, and a reputation crisis.

As an experienced public company CEO and a high-performing strategic turnaround executive, Colleen Brown was invited to serve on the American Apparel board to help the ailing clothing retailer and manufacturer. When asked why she accepted this controversial board directorship, she answered with her typical directness:

"There were ten thousand employees whose livelihoods were at stake; this was so much more than just a brand. It was an iconic Los Angeles-based company that stood for 'Made in America.'"

She knew the company was in financial trouble, and it was well-known there were reputation challenges for the brand. However, what choice was there? Never one to back down from difficult challenges, she signed up to help save a part of "Americana" that stood for quality garments, LGBT rights, and authenticity.

She was confident in her experience and the expertise of other board members, so if American Apparel could be saved, they would find a way to do it. Shortly after joining the reconfigured board, she was asked to be the chair. Meanwhile, the company had fired the founder and CEO and had virtually no executive team left.

Though Brown and her cohorts were unable to stop the slide of the company and eventually filed for Chapter 11 reorganization, she looks at the situation with clarity:

"I wouldn't change anything about the relationships that were formed and the friendships that developed during my time at American Apparel. The complexity of the situation, the emotion surrounding the company, and the unrelenting disruption were extremely challenging. Ultimately, we had to make the best business decision we could by filing for reorganization with a plan to rebuild the company."

COLLEEN BROWN
Denver, Colorado

Corporate/Select Nonprofit Boards:
TrueBlue, Inc.
Spark Networks SE
Port Blakely
Delta Dental of Washington
DataSphere Technologies, Inc.
American Apparel, Inc.
Fisher Communications, Inc.
CareerBuilder, LLC
Classified Ventures, LLC
Young Americans Bank

Career History:
Marca Global LLC: Founder
Fisher Communications, Inc.: President and CEO; Executive Director
A.H. Belo Corporation: SVP
Lee Enterprises: President, Broadcast
Gannett Co., Inc.: KPNX, Phoenix: President and GM; WFMY,
  Greensboro, North Carolina: President and GM; KUSA, Denver:
  VP, Station Manager

Education:
MBA, University of Colorado, Boulder
BS, Business Administration and Political Science, University of
  Dubuque

The company was ultimately sold to a Canadian-based company.

Brown has been a problem solver from the earliest days of her career. She completed her MBA at just twenty years old and entered the fast track to success as one of the first MBAs at Gannett, a growing media company that was the largest newspaper company in the world at the time, as well as owning television and radio stations and an outdoor billboard company. During her time at Gannett, *USA Today* was established along with CareerBuilder and Cars.com.

"Gannett hired me before I finished my MBA. Our team at the University of Colorado had just won the national marketing competition sponsored by General

Motors. I was the youngest person on the team and the only one in graduate school—imagine being seated at dinner between former CEO Roger Smith and then-Chairman Tom Murphy. It was quite a career-starter."

She honed her financial expertise, exercised her technological curiosity, and became the first woman promoted from the rank-and-file to become president and general manager at a Gannett television station. That was after getting noticed for her ability to identify and write software to save money and accelerate growth for the company.

"I became known as a strategic player who could tackle tough problems. At that time, we did not have companies such as Salesforce or Concur to help us perform better. If we needed something, we were creating it ourselves. That became a sweet spot for me during that phase of my career."

That different approach led Brown to take on a growing list of challenges, or "opportunities" (as she calls them), at the company. Besides running television stations, she eventually headed up strategic planning for the broadcast division, forging skills that would serve her well later in her board career.

Brown was selected for her first corporate board while she was twenty-eight years old and volunteering for the nonprofit Mi Casa, Mi Carrera, which helps Hispanic women find fulfilling careers. "Every board I've been recruited onto has been a result of my volunteering and serving on boards of nonprofits." It was this early experience that opened the door for Brown to interview for an open board position on the Young Americans Bank board.

Though she was still building her own professional career, her experience on the Young Americans Bank board, and learning the ropes from a "phenomenal" board leader, set the foundation for Brown to gain invaluable knowledge for her future work on boards. As a friend and Microsoft board member once told her, "You can't fix the system when you're not in the system. We don't just make up the board rules—but once you're in, you have a seat at the table to change things."

So Brown's best advice for any woman joining a corporate board is to be patient, committed, and active until you get that first board seat. Then, you can make a difference on that board. She recommends that building strong working relationships results in more and more opportunities, as evidenced by the many boards Brown has joined since she was in her late twenties.

"Technology has played a big role in my development, both in my career and as a board member. The role it played in media was one of constant disruption—for me, it was a matter of embracing it rather than fighting it. Every aspect of business can be disrupted; the trick is to do it yourself before someone else does it for you. With that in the back of my mind, it's a lot easier to get comfortable with disruption, anticipate change, and look around the corner to the future."

In 2014, Brown was inducted into the GAMCO Management Hall of Fame alongside well-known activist investor Carl Icahn. The annual selection was made for outstanding creation of shareholder value. This recognition followed a somewhat famous debate with an activist shareholder held at the Harvard Club in New York. In this standing-room-only, adversarial situation, she gained respect and recognition for her abilities and turned a few heads at the same time. Turns out a high-profile executive was in the audience. He introduced himself to her there, and they became friends. "He later called me about joining the American Apparel board. That's how it began."

"The best thing you can do on a board is immerse yourself in the business. It helps you understand your company and your competitors as well. In timber, I became familiar with family-owned companies, operating in a regulated industry, and the type of competition faced by organizations with inventory to distribute globally."

"I'm also very action-oriented. The shift from CEO to board member takes a lot of internal conversation. It's my job to be curious and look for ways to offer advice without creating 'gotcha' situations with senior executives. Board members are meant to counsel the CEO, not be the management. But as a former CEO, it takes great discipline to avoid overstepping those boundaries to learn more about the company."

Coming from a family of six brothers and three sisters, Brown learned early how to convey her opinions.

"My older brothers always called me the curious one; the younger siblings just called me bossy. Now I've come to learn their labels simply meant CEO material!"

GO IMMEDIATELY TO

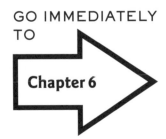

Chapter 6

SIX IMPORTANT
6 to Securing

STEPS
a Board Seat

LONG-TERM PLANNING AND STRATEGIZING IS ESPECIALLY IMPORTANT WHEN YOU WANT TO SECURE A BOARD SEAT. If you don't know where you are going, it's hard to get there. The women profiled in this chapter knew where they wanted to go, and they are excellent examples of women who learned the value of planning ahead, making smart strategic choices, and taking advantage of opportunities to build a roadmap to corporate board service.

Don't be discouraged along the way—it's all part of your plan. There's no instant solution, even though you hear stories about how some women got lucky and landed their first board seats soon after they started looking. But "luck" is no substitute for careful planning and diligence. How many times have I said to myself, the harder I work, the luckier I get? It can sometimes take four to five years with disciplined, methodical forward actions to get your seat on a corporate board. So starting now in your career, at whatever stage you are, will be critical to achieving your first board seat.

Plan Ahead

To plan and pursue her path to get on boards, Susanne Meline was thinking far down the line and making smart and strategic choices early in her career. It took her several years to secure her first board seat. Meline thoughtfully evaluated her career strengths, her achievements, and the not-necessarily-logical variety of positions she held. Many women make the mistake of thinking they will only serve on big, brand-name company boards. But realistically, it is smaller corporations (the lower half of the Russell 3000) that don't have women on their boards. Meline's greatest interest and strengths are in the new FinTech category of technology for financial services. So she pursued board positions on small-cap and micro-cap companies. She knew she could make a difference by helping those companies grow. Every micro-cap is in business to become a large-cap company someday. Her motto became "Think small and help them grow."

545

Russell 3000 companies **added women in 2018**

SUSANNE MELINE

66 *Small is beautiful. Often micro-cap or small-cap corporations provide a great first board for women, where you can really add value to help them grow.* 99

Many women think they only want to serve on well-known, brand-name corporate boards, which can be challenging because there are so few of them. Susanne Meline shows why initially serving on boards of small private companies, then publicly traded small, micro-cap ($250 million to $2 billion) or nano-cap (smaller than $250 million) companies, can be a smart, enjoyable, and profitable way to climb the ladder. But it still takes a long time to secure the first one.

SUSANNE MELINE
Los Angeles, California

Corporate/Select Nonprofit Boards:
Aqua Metals, Inc.
ClearSign Combustion Corporation
Finomial Corporation
The Blue Ribbon of the Music Center of Los
     Angeles
Craft and Folk Art Museum

Career History:
Francis Capital Management, LLC: Co-founder; Investment Analyst;
     General Counsel
Houlihan Lokey: Investment Banker
Jones Day: Corporate Bankruptcy and Restructuring Attorney

Education:
Board of Directors Certification, Anderson School of Management,
     UCLA
JD, Hastings College of Law, University of California, Berkeley
BA, Political Science, UCLA

"To find a first board seat, smaller companies are ideal, but you still need to articulate and carve out your specialized area of expertise—something no one else can do."

Even with deep experience in investment banking, focused on technology and finance companies, it took Meline five years of consistent effort to win her first public-company board seat.

"There was no clear pathway. So I tried everything to learn all I could, then started with small, private, and mostly unknown public companies.

"I read Betsy Berkhemer-Credaire's first book, *The Board Game*. I went to the UCLA Anderson School and took the course over several days to become a certified director. I became a dues-paying member of the National Association of Corporate Directors (NACD), attended its conferences, listened to various webinars, and am in the process of becoming an NACD fellow. I used all of those resources to stay current on the hot topics related to board governance and increase my confidence that I was a great board candidate. I spent a lot of time and money self-educating. And it all paid off.

"During this long process to find my first board, it dawned on me that I really had to figure out what value I would offer that is unique, that others don't have. So now, I advise women to match their experience with a board where that need exists. I also realized that micro-cap and small-cap companies may need my expertise more than large companies. Yes, I found out small is beautiful."

After five years of preparation and networking, Meline was named to her first corporate board, Finomial Corporation in Boston, a private regulation technology company that provides automated regulatory support to the "back-office" of hedge funds and their administrators. Her background suited the board's needs since she set up the back-office operational and compliance infrastructure of the hedge fund she co-founded. Previously, she was an investment banker at Houlihan Lokey and specialized in mergers and acquisitions for companies that were experiencing challenges raising additional capital on reasonable terms. She also practiced corporate law at Jones Day with an emphasis on restructuring transactions.

Meline's long track record of dealing with institutions at financial crossroads—from new entities raising money to mature companies dealing with cash-flow problems—made her uniquely qualified to help small companies raise money.

"There is an art to accessing capital when a company needs money to grow or execute a turnaround. Having sat at the table as an attorney, an investment banker, and an investor of such securities, I'm in the unique position to understand the mindset of all participants—as well as the long-term negative consequences to the company and its shareholders if the company doesn't get it right. I understood how to do this for micro-cap companies, so that's the unique value I bring."

To find the right small company for her first board, Meline actively began looking into start-ups, because that is where new boards are being created or changed all the time. In addition, Meline began focusing on the financial technology start-ups, which help financial institutions comply with the growing regulatory burden, as this is where Meline has experience as an operator. She had read dozens of articles noting that boards often seek candidates with operating expertise in the same industry.

"But the actual connection to Finomial was an unexpected surprise! I met a woman over coffee who invests in women-led businesses through an angel investment fund called Belle Capital. As an early-stage investor, Belle Capital often had the right to designate a board member for its portfolio companies. I invested my own money into this fund and told its leaders that I was interested in serving on the board of one of the portfolio companies.

"When a transition happened at one of the companies in the FinTech space, I was very proactive about letting them know about my experience, qualifications, and desire to help Finomial. I was determined to reach my goal as well as support this company."

When board members of Finomial learned of her experience in hedge funds and investment banking, as well as her legal training, they wanted to add her specific experience to their board.

"With my unique blend of experience, I can immediately help guide a capital-raising process, so that's one big value I bring. I'm an investor, I'm a lawyer with a strong understanding of fiduciary responsibility, and I have credibility and expertise that boards value.

"Whenever new companies are created, public venture capitalists are required to raise capital.

"I had read in Betsy's book that private companies were a place to start. It's hard work, and the board compensation is much lower, or in stock—or none at all if you are representing a venture fund—but you get very close to the business. But if you are an independent director, you can remain on the board when they go public."

Meline stresses that women should get to know angel investors and venture capitalists, because many handpick their own representatives for boards of companies where they invest.

"Many candidates don't think about publicly traded micro-cap boards, because they don't generate much attention and often aren't as strong on corporate governance."

But to Meline, this spells opportunity.

"There are many more board opportunities for women in start-up or micro-cap companies than with larger-cap companies. Because this is where women have the best odds of getting their first assignment, it's a great place to start. Small-caps and micro-caps rarely use retained search firms to find board members, because small companies don't have the cash to pay the fees."

Meline also recommends serving on the toughest board committees—specifically audit.

"The best opportunities can be in areas where everybody else doesn't want to go because they are difficult."

In order to make sure that she is highly knowledgeable about the area, Meline reinvested some of her first board fees by taking a class at Harvard Business School specifically designed to improve directors' knowledge about serving on audit committees.

Meline's second board seat was ClearSign Combustion, an emerging-growth, micro-cap company that makes low-emission burners and other "cleantech" solutions for the combustion industry. Because the company currently consumes cash and needed to sell stock to fund ongoing operations, a group of shareholders suggested that the company round out its board, which was composed of industry experts, by adding someone with micro-cap capital markets experience to guide the company through the process.

Even though all the seats on the board were filled at the time, the company was able to create a new seat so Meline could serve. Boards can add or remove a seat anytime they choose. Shareholders are asked in their annual proxy votes to approve any change in the number of board seats, but that can be after the addition is already made.

ClearSign subsequently raised two rounds of additional capital, and she volunteered to help with both of them.

"I know I added value, because I was able to ensure that the company raised capital on good terms while preserving future flexibility. Now I have a track record of raising money, which will benefit me later when future boards consider me as a candidate."

Like many other women executives, Meline has served on several nonprofit boards, which provided important governance insight, as well as hands-on impact. She joined the board of the Craft and Folk Art Museum in Los Angeles at a time of financial challenges.

"While I was there, we worked hard to support the director, who was orchestrating a turnaround after facing fundraising difficulties post-financial crisis. It was an operational board, so I realized it was going to be hard work and time-consuming. It was a rewarding experience, which also confirmed that I have an aptitude for board service."

Meline serves on the endowment committee and is a former board member of The Blue Ribbon, the long-established and revered fundraising nonprofit support group of the Music Center of Los Angeles. This committee of powerful Los Angeles women has raised more than $75 million over the years.

"I want to spend my time where I'm going to have the most impact. Board service provides that satisfaction, and I would like to do more of it. Looking at the corporation from the perspective of an investor helps me be a smarter and more effective board member."

Her advice for women seeking a board seat is straightforward.

"Care deeply, educate yourself, go the extra mile, be vocal about your interest and qualifications, and don't envy the big brand names—starting small can lead to big steps forward!"

Your Networks

Strategically building your network of contacts and colleagues is vitally important. I have spent my entire career cultivating friendships and relationships in the business world by attending luncheons, dinner panels, speeches, receptions, business programs, and other events where I not only make new connections, but strengthen relationships that can have mutual business benefits. I've made many true and lasting friendships this way, too.

The *Board-Smart Networking Chart* (see Chapter 8) is a great tool for systematically figuring out who knows whom within your network. This chart will help you map the contacts you need that will lead to wider and wider circles of influence as you systematically work toward your goal of being selected for boards.

It's often more difficult for women to carve out extra time for all-important networking due to balancing the responsibilities of a busy career, home, and family. But developing collegial relationships is critical. You must get out of your office and be seen and be recognized by others inside and outside your industry. Building a network of professional colleagues pays long-term dividends. These are the people who observe your competencies, witness your professional growth, and see how you interact in many circumstances. When you are ready to pursue a seat on a corporate board, it will be people from your network who will recommend and endorse you. Holly Van Deursen is eloquent on the subject of networking.

HOLLY VAN DEURSEN

66 When selecting new directors, you shape the way the board works together, the issues they will address, and how the CEO and the executive team are motivated. 99

Based in Norway, the Petroleum Geo-Services board is composed of more than 40% women—as mandated by Norwegian law. And Holly Van Deursen says the system is working.

HOLLY VAN DEURSEN
Chicago, Illinois

Corporate/Select Nonprofit Boards:
Synthomer, PLC
Capstone Turbine Corporation
Actuant Corporation
Bemis Company, Inc.
Petroleum Geo-Services ASA (based in Norway)
Anson Industries, Inc.

Career History:
British Petroleum (BP), PLC: Group VP, Petrochemicals and Strategy
Amoco Corporation
Dow Corning Corporation (now The Dow Chemical Company)

Education:
MBA, University of Michigan
BS, Chemical Engineering, University of Kansas

"Norway was the first country to require a quota for 40% women on public-company boards—back in 2005. Norway is a very egalitarian country. There are quite a few female CEOs and government officials. Norwegians, as a culture, are not troubled by age, gender, or race, so I have never felt like a token diversity candidate."

Van Deursen was still working as a senior-level executive at British Petroleum (BP), a $350 billion company, when she began thinking about future board service. As she contemplated retirement, she created a relationship map charting all the

C-suite and senior-level executives she had previously worked with, who could vouch for her as an effective and results-oriented executive. Then, she began scheduling face-to-face meetings.

"My intentions were to serve on a corporate board, so I mapped my networks and strategically contacted them. I'm a great believer that face-to-face is a much more effective way to connect or reconnect with people, versus phone or email. I was willing to travel. I booked flights across the country. And that paid off."

It was one such face-to-face meeting with a former coworker that led to Van Deursen's first appointment to the board of the privately held Anson Industries, a construction-services company. Within three weeks, she was interviewed for the open board position. While Van Deursen acknowledges this may sound fast, the process required nearly nine months of behind-the-scenes work to bring about that board appointment.

Then just two months later, her second board appointment came from the Norwegian seismic-mapping company Petroleum Geo-Services, by way of recruiters and search firms she had previously worked with to bring employees into BP. By making her intentions of serving on corporate boards in the industrial space known to many recruiters, Van Deursen broadened her network.

"I always advise people to meet with board recruiters in their given industry or space. My top two tips are: 1) connect with your existing network, and 2) create a new network of recruiters who specialize in your industry as well as in board searches."

Van Deursen prepared in advance to recount key points from her high-impact statement. She identified her most valuable expertise and experience, and highlighted those in her conversations.

"Think about your personal presentation—what you have accomplished that you want to put forth. For me, my strengths are global operating experience, strategy, corporate governance, and a strong chemical and technical background."

Respected for her industrial experience, with both engineering and business backgrounds, Van Deursen has become an expert in operations, governance, and strategy in the chemical, oil, and gas industries, expertise that has fueled her rise to being named chair of the board of Capstone Turbine Corporation. A global executive who lived and worked half a decade each in Europe and Asia, Van Deursen is also a subject-matter expert with a highly coveted skill set in international operations and board governance.

"When you are looking for that first board seat, market yourself to appropriate companies. I looked at companies where I believed I would be a good fit. My chemical-engineering degree and international exposure set me apart from many people who sit on boards of technology or industrial companies. I knew my background was valued in the industrial space just as a finance background is valued in audit."

Having worked in oil and chemical industries for many years, Van Deursen was deliberate in planning her board service.

"I had decided I wanted to be on one NYSE company board and one listed on a foreign exchange. I also wanted to be on a privately held company board, along with a green company. Although I wanted some knowledge link to my personal experience, I also had a strong desire to diversify, to keep things interesting."

While at BP, Van Deursen spearheaded creating a book of corporate strategy that outlined resource allocation, environmental factors, predictions on where technology and oil were headed, major division business strategies, upstream-operation methodology, and refining the company's statement on refineries, gasoline stations, chemicals, gas, and renewables.

"This wasn't about how the board operated but rather, about how the company operated. There are very explicit rules of separation in the U.K., guidelines around who communicates with whom, and what is communicated. Having a book allowed for clarity of direction and efficiency, along with adherence to legal policy."

Van Deursen joined the boards of two NYSE companies in 2008. Actuant Corporation is a major player selling components that benefit the energy, agriculture, and mining industries. Bemis Corporation is a high-end, high-margin manufacturer of niche packaging, including zipper pouches used for Sargento cheese or Oscar Mayer bacon.

"These are all companies that make our lives work. I come from a chemical-engineering background, and engineers like to make things work—and that's where I like to think I fit."

Throughout her board career, Van Deusen has been a part of four CEO searches and eleven director searches. While she believes the audit committee is the best way to quickly understand what makes a company tick, and that compensation committee service gives great insight into what motivates company employees, she says one of the most impactful ways to shape a company is to be on the nominating/governance committee. She has served on four such committees and has chaired three of them.

"When selecting the CEO, you're responsible for choosing the person who is going to run the organization and have an enormous influence on shareholders and the community. When selecting new directors, you shape the way the board works together, the issues they will address, and how the CEO and the executive team are motivated."

The most attractive attributes that the nominating/governance committee looks for are candidates who have C-level experience at a corporation. Van Deursen suggests that women executives attend National Association of Corporate Directors (NACD) conferences or webinars to stay current and topical as well.

Her primary focus in building a board is bringing on a diverse set of candidates who have the expertise and relevant knowledge to steer the company toward success.

"I have been able to get at least one woman director added to the board of most companies, if not more. Diversity is a requirement for every search I have led."

The Bemis Corporation has two women on its board, and Van Deursen recently succeeded in bringing another woman to the Capstone board. She rotated off the Petroleum Geo-Services board in 2018 after twelve years of service and was soon after appointed to the board of Synthomer, PLC, a specialty-chemicals company headquartered in London.

Van Deursen stresses that it is important to feel that you are respected within a board—that is where board chemistry comes into play.

"On one board, we have designated a mentor to new individuals. If that practice is not in place, I would suggest finding one or two mentors on any new board. Identify those colleagues you think you would work well with, and take advantage of that soft time between meetings."

Van Deursen will frequently contact colleagues if she is passing through their hometown and request face-to-face time, a quick coffee at home, dinner, or even a full-blown day of sightseeing.

"This makes a huge difference in getting involved and building relationships on the board, especially if you're the new person on the block."

She also says that board evaluations are essential to board refreshment. When Van Deursen initially joined her boards, there were few peer assessments in place. She worked with her colleagues to develop evaluation protocols, and these have been instituted across each of her boards.

"There has to be a strategic approach to bringing new directors on and rolling off long-term directors. If a long-tenured board member is no longer at the top of his or her craft, it is helpful to have structure around the process, to be able to point to where the company is headed and make the shift strategically, citing skills or experiences that may be missing on the board."

Find a Mentor and Be a Mentor

Throughout your career, you are going to meet outstanding and successful women who are prepared to advocate for you. It is your job to cultivate them and impress them with your professional credentials, your determination, and eagerness to serve. No longer are women closing the door behind them, proud to be the only woman on a board. That's what we used to call "The Queen Bee Syndrome." Now women realize the advantage of having other women on the board with them: together they can really make *the* difference.

I have found that the truly great and inspiring women who have made it to the top are always eager to help other women become viable board candidates. The women who are already there want a voice that represents more than just themselves; they want support for their ideas.

There's a generally accepted maxim that one woman on a board is often considered a token (even if she has an influential voice); two women back each other up; and three women actually make *the* difference—they get things done. Jacqueline Kosecoff, Kristina Leslie, Kathleen Ligocki, and Billie Williamson are all outstanding examples of women who benefited from the advice and counsel of women mentors, and each of them now enjoys helping others who are following a path to the boardroom.

JACQUELINE KOSECOFF, PhD

If you want to help women, be the best director possible— without regard to gender.

"If you want to help women, be the best director possible—without regard to gender," asserts Jacqueline B. Kosecoff, PhD, former founder and CEO of public companies, including Value Health. And she should know. As a director on the boards of Athenahealth, STERIS Corporation, Houlihan Lokey, and Sealed Air Corporation, Kosecoff is an exemplary executive with a wealth of experience in innovation, health services, and life sciences, as well as the mentorship of other women.

JACQUELINE KOSECOFF, PhD
Los Angeles, California

Corporate/Select Nonprofit Boards:
Athenahealth, Inc.
Houlihan Lokey
Sealed Air Corporation
STERIS Corporation
ALARIS Medical Systems, Inc.
CareFusion Corporation
DJO Global, Inc.

Career History:
Moriah Partners, LLC: Managing Partner
Warburg Pincus, LLC: Senior Advisor
UnitedHealth Group: CEO, OptumRx
PacifiCare Health Systems, LLC (now UnitedHealth Group, Inc.): EVP
Protocare, Inc.: President
Value Health Sciences: Co-CEO & President
Chassin & Kosecoff Medical Systems, Inc.: CEO
Fink & Kosecoff Associates: CEO

Education:
PhD, University of California, Los Angeles
MS, Applied Mathematics, Brown University
BA, Mathematics, University of California, Los Angeles

"It helps to sit on the nominating/governance committee when you are on the board, so you can ensure diversity will be considered when the board evaluates candidates for new directors."

Kosecoff has a history of pioneering change. She was one of the first to incorporate information technology into the medical-science world with her own company Value Health Sciences, and she has taken on various board seats despite being the only woman in the boardroom in most cases.

While most people navigate their nonprofit networks for corporate board recommendations, Kosecoff was recommended for her first board, ALARIS Medical Systems, by attending the Center for Corporate Innovation and meeting then-CEO Dave Schlotterbeck at an industry roundtable. Cardinal Health acquired ALARIS while Kosecoff served on the board.

Kosecoff made sure her performance on the ALARIS board was strong, which opened the door to other opportunities, including STERIS and Sealed Air.

"Exceptional performance on one board leads to being recommended for another board."

Kosecoff's experience while a CEO in the highly regulated health-services and life-sciences industries gave her a perspective about what a board needed. At STERIS, Kosecoff chaired the compliance committee during a period when the company was confronted with a host of regulatory actions from the Federal Drug Administration.

"There was an issue that could have turned our best product topsy-turvy, but as a board member with related knowledge, I hope I was able to help mitigate a very serious situation. My previous experience with the FDA, paired with my experience dealing with many different regulators in the life-sciences and health-services environment, helped create a smooth and effective working relationship between the committee and the rest of the board."

On the Sealed Air Corporation board, Kosecoff chairs the organization/compensation committee and sits on the nominating/corporate governance committee. From Sealed Air, Kosecoff has gone on to become a member of the board of directors at CareFusion, where she sat on the audit committee; Athenahealth, where she chairs the compensation committee and sits on the nominating/governance committee; as well as Houlihan Lokey, where she sits on the audit and governance committees.

Though she's been the lone woman on several boards, Kosecoff says she believes that diversity begins with attention to cultural indicators. She volunteers to mentor women as they seek roles in upper management. When Kosecoff speaks at events or in committees, she advises women to make decisions by collecting evidence and basing conclusions on objective facts and experience.

"What you see is what you get with me. Often, especially when I am the only woman, I try very hard not to be characterized as aggressive or emotional. When I was CEO, I brought potentially controversial matters to the board, only after first talking to individual board members. You never know when you may discover additional information that enables you to present the issue in a way that allows people to take appropriate action—rather than feel blindsided."

Besides sitting on the boards of four publicly traded companies, Kosecoff has embarked on a career in private equity that affords her the opportunity to sit on the boards of portfolio companies in various stages of development.

"A proven way to get recommended to sit on private-equity boards, whether big or small, is when you have skill sets that can help take portfolio companies to the next level. For example, if a retail-health company needs financial and e-commerce expertise, they might seek a chief financial officer of a complementary company who has excelled in engaging with customers online."

Kosecoff notes that whether one is born with leadership tendencies or not, there is a path to developing those skill sets through work experience and directed efforts.

"As a board member, you are a steward responsible for ensuring that management sets actionable and appropriately aggressive goals consistent with the company's strategy and vision. A great company serves its customers well, is a good citizen in the communities in which it resides, and treats its employees well."

To help women attain director positions, Kosecoff keeps an ongoing list of about ten qualified women on hand, so that when she's recommended for a position she cannot take on, she suggests alternate candidates from her list. There's one simple piece of advice Kosecoff has for everyone:

"Be the very best professional you can throughout your career. If you become a successful business leader, you will be considered for boards."

KRISTINA M. LESLIE

Wherever I've been, I've advocated for women who are the best candidates for the job.

Former CFO of DreamWorks Animation, Kristina M. "Kris" Leslie served on the boards of a local hospital and her children's private high schools before being recruited to Bare Escentuals, her first corporate board, in 2009. Since then, she has served on several boards simultaneously, currently Glassdoor, Inc.; CVB Financial Corporation (Citizens Business Bank); and Blue Shield of California.

KRISTINA M. LESLIE
Los Angeles, California

Corporate/Select Nonprofit Boards:
Glassdoor, Inc.
CVB Financial Corp.(Citizens Business Bank)
Blue Shield of California
PICO Holdings, Inc.
Orbitz Worldwide, Inc.
Obagi Medical Products, Inc.
Bare Escentuals, Inc.

Career History:
DreamWorks Animation SKG, Inc.: CFO
DreamWorks, LLC.: CFO
Viacom, Inc.: Director, Financial Planning and Analysis
Paramount Communications, Inc.: Director

Education:
MBA, Finance, Columbia University
BA, Economics, Bucknell University

Leslie was with DreamWorks, LLC for eleven years, running strategic planning and corporate finance before being promoted to CFO. The company split, and Leslie stayed on for three years as CFO when DreamWorks Animation went through its initial public offering.

"Being CFO in a public market is challenging, and the entertainment industry is a volatile business, so I decided after a decade, it was time for a change."

With three sons at home, Leslie decided to take a six-month break before resuming her search for a new CFO position.

"Six months became a year, and I realized I didn't want to go back to a full-time job. I was enjoying my time with my sons.

"I didn't have a grand plan for board service. Almost coincidentally, I was approached for the Bare Escentuals board. My friend Jaynie Studenmund, who serves on several corporate boards, was on the Flintridge Preparatory School board with me. Jaynie helped me think through an intentional strategy to serve on corporate boards. She explained that board service is a great way to stay engaged, stay current in business, while generating income through board compensation and stock."

Leslie was approached for her first board, Bare Escentuals, by a mutual connection from Goldman Sachs, who had worked with her through the DreamWorks IPO. Bare Escentuals had recently gone public, and the board was looking for an entrepreneurial financial expert to sit on the audit committee. Leslie accepted and served on the board for two years before the company was acquired by the Japanese cosmetics giant Shiseido.

With a woman CEO and several women on the leadership team, Bare Escentuals was a great first board to join.

"I very much enjoyed counseling the management team along with the other board members. Learning about the beauty industry, which was new to me, was great. It's still the only board I've been on where mascara is passed around at the meetings—even to the male directors!"

She was recommended for the Citizens Business Bank board by a fellow director on her nonprofit hospital board who introduced her to the search firm handling the board search. In stark contrast to the Bare Escentuals board, Leslie became the first woman director at Citizens, serving with all men who wanted to bring diversity to the board.

"I was the first diversity candidate. When I was interviewing, somebody asked: 'What do you think it will be like to be the only woman on the board?' I said, 'Well, probably fairly similar to being the only woman in my house with my husband and three sons.'"

Since then, the Citizens Business Bank board has changed, and she has been helpful in finding additional diverse members, including Anna Kan.

"Every board needs at least one financial expert. My dream is to join a board and not have to sit on the audit committee, which often requires the biggest time commitment."

Leslie joined the board at PICO Holdings, a value-play organization with undervalued holdings across several industries, from water rights to canola. PICO had never had women directors until Leslie joined, alongside another woman. Soon after she joined, the chairman of the board decided to step down for personal reasons, and Leslie was asked to serve as his successor. In order to help Leslie acclimate to the board and company, the CEO gave her one year as chair of the audit committee before elevating her to chair of the board.

"I think the reason the founder approached me as the replacement was because he looked at the landscape, and he realized more than half the current directors would be retiring soon, and the other newer board member had just been elevated to university president, so when I became chair she took over audit. Even though it's not technically more responsibility or liability, being board chair felt very different—the biggest difference was that I spent about 70% of my board time interfacing with the CEO."

Leslie stayed on the PICO board until company performance prompted activist shareholder attention. Feeling as though change was in the best interest of the PICO shareholders, Leslie stepped off the board. Two additional directors also stepped off the board during that time. It was a difficult decision, Leslie acknowledges, but she says she hoped it would be a catalyst for further change.

Chemistry is one of the most important elements Leslie emphasizes when it comes to evaluating whether or not a board is the right fit.

"When companies are doing well, you don't see issues. But when tough decisions have to be made—and something difficult almost always comes up—that's when camaraderie and chemistry are even more important. That's also why personal references about candidates for the board are so necessary. Sitting on a board is hard work, and it's not always pleasant. You really want to be in the room with people you like, who are respectful of each other and have high integrity, and you can work well with them."

Leslie was a director on the Orbitz board until Expedia purchased the travel-booking company in 2015. She recalls enjoying the board dynamics immensely and learning invaluable lessons that she applies to her current boards.

From 2017-2018, **men lost 382 board seats** in Russell 3000 corporations

"We went through a lot of growth challenges on the Orbitz board, trying to remain competitive in an industry with two very large players in Expedia and Priceline. In the end, given the challenges around executing our long-term strategy, Expedia's offer to purchase the company was in the best interest of all the Orbitz shareholders."

The Orbitz board had three women directors—including Leslie's friend Studenmund and another woman with a banking background. Leslie recalls a particular lunch event where they brought together the top women executives and employees in the company for a moderated discussion.

"This panel was a great opportunity for the women in the company to learn about the inner workings of the boardroom, which can seem somewhat mysterious from the outside. We also discussed having families and careers before pursuing service on boards, and balancing work/life commitments. It was very gratifying how many women thanked us for sharing our stories with them."

Throughout her board career, Leslie has taken advantage of her leadership roles to help women further their own careers.

"I reach down into the finance organizations to get to know the people, and more often than not, the result is that the women will contact me later for follow-up advice. More senior women will approach me saying they're looking forward to the next five to ten years and ask me how I went about it, and I try to help. I try to make myself accessible, which makes a big difference for those women to be able to see a path to their own board careers. Wherever I've been, I've advocated for women who are the best candidates for the job, and that helps a lot."

After Orbitz, Leslie joined the Glassdoor board as the first independent director. She was referred to Glassdoor CEO Robert Hohman and Board Chair Rich Barton (founder of Expedia and Zillow) through mutual colleagues with whom she had served on the Orbitz board.

Leslie advises women who are joining a new board to take time to fully understand the board dynamics at work—both inside and outside the boardroom. Getting a good sense of the culture of both the organization and the board allows for more effective contributions down the line. She also recommends pairing new board members with existing members as mentors in a deliberate yet informal way.

"There are many aspects to joining a new board, from how the conversations and discussions work to what the culture and management are like. These are all questions a mentor can help answer for new directors. When you intentionally have a mentor program on the board, it makes it easier for the new member to have someone to reach out to, and creates a comfortable transition."

She recognized her first spark of interest in being in a leadership role when she was elected president of her sorority in college.

"It was the first time I understood what having a seat at the table meant. I was able to bring change to the organization, and that caught my attention. I learned how to get people to come to a consensus and how to make difficult decisions. That was the first time I realized what leading an organization was all about. I liked the feeling of being able to accomplish something as a woman heading a team."

KATHLEEN LIGOCKI

❝ *There is so much untapped talent out there. I keep my list of five outstanding women for whom I advocate to place them on boards.* ❞

A Midwestern native, Kathleen Ligocki literally grew up in the automotive business. She started at General Motors in her early career, later joined Ford Motor Company, and worked her way up the ladder to become president of Ford Mexico, based in Mexico City.

KATHLEEN LIGOCKI
Costa Mesa, California

Corporate Boards:
Agility Fuel Solutions, LLC
Lear Corporation
Ashland, LLC
Tower Automotive, Inc.

Career History:
Agility Fuel Solutions, LLC: CEO
Harvest Power, Inc.: President/CEO
Next Autoworks Company: President/CEO
GS Motors (Mexico City-based auto retailer owned by Grupo
    Salinas): CEO
Tower Automotive, Inc., Detroit: CEO
Kleiner Perkins Caufield & Byers: Partner
Ford Motor Company: President, Ford Mexico
General Motors

Education:
Honorary doctorates: Indiana University Kokomo; Central Michigan
    University
MBA, The Wharton School, The University of Pennsylvania
BA, Liberal Studies, Indiana University Kokomo

Not surprisingly, Ligocki previously served on several automotive-related corporate boards, including Ashland, LLC (which owned Valvoline at that time), and is currently on the board of Lear, a Fortune 200 automotive supplier. She is currently the CEO of Agility Fuel Solutions, based in Costa Mesa, California, an innovator of natural-gas solutions for medium and heavy vehicles, whose mission is to transform transportation through the global adoption of clean fuels. Ligocki served on the Ashland board for ten years and was offered the position after she reached out to the board members of Tower Automotive, where she was the sitting CEO, her first CEO position.

"At Ashland, I learned how board members treated each other with mutual respect and, through a process of disagreeing and agreeing, would reach better outcomes. Through networking, I was asked to join the Lear board because they wanted a woman with C-suite automotive industry experience—and there were not many of us around. I believe in augmenting the use of executive recruiters for board searches—too often they seem to circulate the same list of people who are already on several other boards. Yet there is so much untapped talent out there. I keep my list of five outstanding women for whom I advocate to place them on boards."

The prior chairman and CEO of Ashland advocated for diversity on the board, and as a result of Ligocki's presence on the board, he was convinced diversity leads to better outcomes. Ligocki was one of the early champions of establishing women's resource groups at both Ashland (AWIN—Ashland Women's International Network) and Lear (GROW).

"This became a great way for female board members to connect with women… and men…throughout the organization. I have spoken to the groups, provided mentoring, and certainly served as one of the most enthusiastic cheerleaders as both these resource organizations have grown to be influential platforms for women's leadership and networking. The Lear women's group hosts one of the hottest speaker series at the company, bringing in top leaders from both inside and outside the industry. I believe women in board positions can serve as role models and sounding boards even more effectively when they are accessible to senior leaders at the companies they serve.

Previously, Ligocki led four other companies as the president and CEO: Harvest Power, a large organics management company focused on transforming organic wastes into bioenergy and soil amendment products; Next Autoworks, an auto company with a unique low-cost business model; GS Motors, a Mexico City-based auto retailer owned by Grupo Salinas, a large Mexican conglomerate; and Tower Automotive, in Detroit, a Fortune 1,000 global automotive supplier. From 2012 to 2014, she worked as an operating partner at Kleiner Perkins Caufield & Byers, well-known venture-capital providers in Silicon Valley, sponsoring greentech ventures, scaling operations and commercialization. Ligocki also founded her own firm, Pine Lake Partners, consultants to start-ups and turnarounds. Prior to her entrepreneurial life, Ligocki held executive positions at Ford and United Technologies, where she led operations in the Americas, Europe, Africa, the Middle East, and Russia. She has travelled to more than 186 countries and has broad and deep expertise in automotive supplies. She is also a fiduciary board member at the Indiana University Foundation.

One of her fellow board members was Bernadine Healy, who died at only sixty-one in 2011 of cancer. Dr. Healy had been the first woman director of the National Institutes of Health (NIH) and past president of the American Heart Association and the American Red Cross. A respected cardiologist, Dr. Healy had launched the Women's Health Initiative at the NIH, a $500 million, ten-year study of diseases that affect women at midlife and beyond, which for the first time revealed the risks of heart attacks and strokes in post-menopausal women. Board chemistry?

"To succeed in the boardroom, I use humor. That especially helps when you are the only woman director. Don't be afraid to contribute to the conversation. Ask questions as you gain legitimacy on the board. Women must balance between assertiveness, diplomacy, and listening. Showing respect is critical, but I have seen men 'talk over' women in the boardroom, as if they weren't there. When it happens, you simply must hold your own.

"At Lear, the board members are huge golfers. My fourth year on the board, I didn't want to go on the annual golf outing for senior executives and board members, so I suggested there should be an alternative event for non-golfers. In jest, I threatened to launch a poker tournament, but ultimately a Detroit river cruise was arranged, so even non-golfers, which included a very diverse group of U.S. and international executives, could benefit from the camaraderie of spending a casual afternoon together. A huge hit.

"To acclimate to the board culture, I recommend finding a mentor who is an 'insider' for advice. And be attentive—be aware of the human element on the board. Don't be afraid to ask another board member for counsel."

Where did she learn leadership? Ligocki was the oldest of five children: a brother, now a retired partner of a construction firm; and three sisters—who grew up to become a school superintendent, a teacher, and chief of staff for the attorney general of Indiana. The siblings still get together one weekend a year. Her mother had great influence over Ligocki.

"Mother, in addition to having five kids in under five years, was a medical technologist, a student of various religions, and an ardent social revolutionary who came home from a church bake sale with Czechoslovakian refugees who lived with us for a year...without calling my father beforehand. Her view of life was, 'Scoot over, there is always room for more,' and, 'If you believe in it, live it and fight for it...it's the only way to change the world.'" Lessons she tries to follow still today.

BILLIE IDA WILLIAMSON

> *Sometimes when a woman puts forth an idea, it is overlooked until a man offers it. But I never care about who gets credit for an idea...as long as there is a robust discussion.*

Billie Williamson has been the personification of a champion for women throughout her career. She is known for promoting women's professional careers and now works hard to make sure that women also have the opportunities to attain corporate board seats, as she did. Her own personal path was characterized by dogged persistence and single-minded focus.

BILLIE IDA WILLIAMSON, CPA
Dallas, Texas

Corporate/Select Nonprofit Boards:
Annie's Homegrown, Inc.
The Beneficient Company Group, L.P.
CSRA, Inc. (now General Dynamics Information
　Technology, Inc.)
Cushman & Wakefield
Energy Future Holdings Corporation
Exelis, Inc.
Janus Capital Group, Inc. (now Janus Henderson Group, PLC)
Kraton Corporation
Pentair, PLC
Pharos Capital BDC, Inc
XL Group, Ltd.

Career History:
Ernst & Young, LLP: Senior Global Client-Serving Partner and
　Americas Inclusiveness Officer
Marriott International, Inc.: SVP, Finance; Corporate Controller
AMX Corp.: CFO

Education:
BBA, Business Administration and Accounting, Southern Methodist
　University

Williamson enjoyed a career as one of the first women partners at Ernst & Young, the multinational professional-services accounting firm. She served on Ernst & Young's Americas executive board, which functions as the firm's board of directors for strategic and operational matters, so in her professional capacity, Williamson was gaining valuable board experience. As she approached the company's mandatory retirement age of sixty, she determined that she wanted to serve on corporate boards. So she started planning ahead and began aggressively looking for her first board seat.

Her path to her first board membership was hampered by the same conundrum facing all women without board experience: How can you get on a board if you don't have prior board experience?

"I did not make the cut on my first board search because I didn't have public board experience. So I called a friend and colleague, the chairman of a large defense contractor who had been one of my clients. I told him about my struggle. To help me, my friend called the CEO of the global aerospace, defense, information, and services company where I was interviewing.

"He explained how many audit committees and board meetings I had been in front of and presented to throughout my CPA career. Then the CEO viewed me as a candidate."

Once she was named to her first public board, Exelis, Inc., additional board opportunities came up swiftly. Williamson was asked to join the board of Annie's Homegrown, Inc., the California-based producer of natural and organic foods. That invitation came through a personal contact in private equity that she had made while working in her many women's initiatives. For her next board, Pentair, PLC, a multinational diversified industrial company, she was sought out by a search firm.

Her appointment to the board of Energy Futures also came through someone she had called in her network.

"Building a network early on is very important, and you have to stay in contact with those people. I value those relationships a great deal."

"I reached out to my professional network to say I was interested in board service. And I was specific. 'What do you look for in a board assignment?' 'Can you introduce me?' 'How many boards are appropriate?'"

With that kind of intensity and clarity, Williamson had secured her first public corporate board seat by the time she retired. Now she spends her time opening doors for other women seeking their first seats. She is known for recommending women candidates for boards when she hears about openings, and she speaks at many professional women's events on the topic of board membership. A popular speaker at the 2020 Women on Boards National Conversation, she is also co-chairperson of WomenCorporateDirectors in Dallas and is a very active member of the National Association of Corporate Directors (NACD).

Williamson's efforts as a mentor for women who aspire to advance in their careers, and eventually serve on corporate boards, includes participating in programs for high-potential employees.

"On the Exelis board, for instance, every board member was asked to mentor high-potential individuals to coach and guide them. That made me a better board member.

"A CEO once said to me, 'You ask a lot of questions, but I learn from everything you ask me.' What makes women different is that we are more curious. Women board members want to understand the business we are governing. I think we hold ourselves to high standards. What that CEO told me was a lovely compliment."

Williamson's extensive technical, financial, and client-services background has given her solid expertise in matters critical to boards. During her time at Ernst & Young, her impressive client list included Texas Instruments, Lockheed Martin, Fluor Corporation, and Neiman Marcus. Her background working in mergers and acquisitions has been a huge asset for Williamson's boards. Her resume, plus her natural curiosity about business, has been an asset to her boards.

She has chaired audit committees and served on the executive committee of some of her boards, meeting monthly with the management teams to make sure nothing was being missed.

"Women tend to want to understand the interactions of people. For instance, when a corporation is buying a company, there is lots of focus on numbers, then a reasonable focus on products, but then it gets harder when you look at culture and what kind of leadership team is in place. What are their skills? How will they mix with your company? Women are looking at those kind of things. We want to make sure that we understand all of the aspects of a transaction before making a decision.

"You must find the right way to advance your ideas. When they secure their first board, I always advise women to attend at least two meetings where they are observing, listening, and learning, before they start diving right in and talking.

"Sometimes when a woman puts forth an idea, it is overlooked until a man mentions it. But I never care about who gets credit for an idea. You can't care about that sort of stuff. It doesn't matter who brings up an idea, as long as there is a robust discussion and the board makes a good decision."

Leadership started in high school for Williamson, where she was active in many student groups. That led to her roles in student government in college.

"You can learn leadership skills, but not everyone has the motivation and inner drive to be a leader. I always had a keen interest in leadership, and when I started at Ernst & Young, I loved challenges and have always been committed to achieving a partnership with clients and the companies that I serve as a board member. That's just who I am!"

Be Visible

You can network, prepare, learn, and do your professional best—but you also need to be visible. That means being seen, heard, and recognized as an expert in your industry.

There are many ways to get in front of different audiences to spotlight yourself and your credentials. Start by joining one of your industry's associations. Once involved, you can help organize industry events, volunteer to host and chaperone important guests, and offer to participate on panels. When you're ready, run for elected office in your association and take on more responsibilities to raise your profile. Make yourself available to the media for interviews on your particular subject area (but make sure you have cleared this with your employer if it involves your day job). As you expand your profile in your industry, you can branch out to join advisory groups or clubs where your expertise can be tapped. Accept speaking engagements whenever they are offered, and strategically use those speeches to market yourself on your social media platforms. Develop opportunities where you can make presentations to your company's board of directors. This will not only build your profile with company leadership, it will also give you the hands-on experience of participating in board interactions.

Aida Alvarez, Christine Jacobs, Ilyanne Morden Kichaven, and Ronna Romney approached their board seats from very different directions, but all of them worked on building a public profile that made their qualifications impossible to ignore.

AIDA ALVAREZ

> 66 *During my time in Washington, I created an agency from scratch, making a lasting contribution.* 99

Aida Alvarez, the first Latina to be appointed to a U.S. president's cabinet, enjoyed a long and pioneering career in media, banking, and public service before serving on corporate boards. From New York, to Washington, D.C., to Silicon Valley, her goal has never wavered.

AIDA ALVAREZ
San Francisco, California

Corporate/Select Nonprofit Boards:
K12, Inc.
HP, Inc.
Oportun, Inc.
Zoosk, Inc.
The Cisneros Center for New Americans
Walmart, Inc.
Union Bank (now MUFG Union Bank, N.A.)
PacifiCare Health Systems, LLC (now UnitedHealth Group, Inc.)

Career History:
U.S. Small Business Administration: Administrator
Office of Federal Housing Enterprise Oversight: Director
First Boston Corporation: VP, Public Finance
Bear Stearns: VP, Public Finance
NYCity Health and Hospitals Corporation: VP, Public Affairs
Metromedia Television: Anchor, Reporter
New York Post: Reporter

Education:
Honorary Doctorates: Iona College; Bethany College; Mercy College; Inter-American University, Puerto Rico
BA, Harvard University

"I work extremely hard to support the inclusion of women at the top ranks of companies."

For Alvarez, serving on the boards of Hewlett-Packard Inc. and K12, as well as Oportun and Zoosk, presents great balance. Oportun, a financial technology company, and Zoosk, an online dating company, are both privately held companies headquartered in the San Francisco Bay Area.

"For women, getting on their first board takes intentional focus and many cups of coffee with people who currently serve on boards. Women are not usually afforded the traditional leadership path that men enjoy. That means we need to get creative and recognize that leadership comes in many different forms."

Regardless of the enterprise, she says the single most important factor in receiving an invitation to a board is recognition by industry insiders or influencers.

"Any woman who is interested in being on a board should decide what her strength is and play a leadership role, especially in the finance and business arena. Visibility and strategic planning will get you the call."

Alvarez honed her own leadership and business skills while working for the government, first as a founding director of the Office of Federal Housing Enterprise Oversight, and later as administrator of the U.S. Small Business Administration (SBA) under President Bill Clinton.

"During my time in Washington, I created an agency from scratch, making a lasting contribution."

As head of the SBA, Alvarez increased financial support for small businesses and oversaw the distribution of nearly $11 billion to stimulate growth. Government-guaranteed loans to minorities doubled; loans to women-owned businesses tripled.

"People who own small businesses are the ultimate optimists. They face a lot of challenges, but they stay focused on their work."

Alvarez says she admires the determination and perseverance of small business owners.

"I moved back to the Bay Area after my cabinet term ended. There I received a call from an executive search firm recruiter, with whom I'd had breakfast in D.C. He asked me about my interest in an open board position at PacifiCare."

She hadn't been seeking a corporate board seat, but she took the interview and was recruited to the board of directors. Alvarez served on the board until 2005, when PacifiCare was acquired by UnitedHealth Group Inc., a multibillion-dollar healthcare insurer. The same search firm called again, this time about a board position with Union Bank of California (now MUFG

Union Bank). Her experience leading the SBA in Washington, D.C., made her an attractive candidate. Alvarez spent ten years on the Union Bank board of directors.

On all of her boards, Alvarez has taken it upon herself to coordinate meetings with new board members, which she says is especially important for new women directors who are most likely to be outnumbered by men on the board. These meetings are an opportunity to inform new directors about board dynamics in a comfortable and transparent way.

"Once on the board, women directors should assume that their opinions will be heard and respected. In the end, vibrant discussion will lead the board and company to better, more constructive, and perhaps more creative, decisions."

The Walmart board opportunity came through a friend who happened to be the board's lead director. He knew of the leadership role Alvarez had played in the Clinton administration, and he said her experience would be a good fit for a global company like Walmart. Alvarez served on a range of committees there, including strategic planning and finance, compensation, nominations, and governance.

"At Walmart, I coached and met with women executives. I put together the first Latino forum, which connected Hispanic associates from the U.S. and globally for a two-day conference with the CEO, board members, and heads of business. The focus was on the role Hispanic leaders and associates can play to advance the interests of the company.

"Change does not happen easily, but I was pleased that Walmart recognized the need for giving women and Latinos a pathway to the top, and that the CEO was personally involved in the implementation."

After completing her ten-year board term at Walmart, Alvarez went on to serve on the Hewlett-Packard board of directors, chaired by Meg Whitman.

"Like Walmart, HP is an iconic company, a legacy company looking to reinvent itself by forming two new companies—HP Inc. and HP Enterprise." (Alvarez serves on the board of HP Inc., best known for its printers, ink, and personal computers.)

The path to boards for some women is sometimes through leadership in governmental and academic institutions, though more and more women are pursuing business careers that expand their opportunities to serve on corporate boards. Alvarez advises women with a finance background to seek out board seats on pre-IPO companies.

"Many pre-IPO boards are primarily male—they benefit from having women on the board and are actively seeking to diversify. Pre-IPO companies provide a fantastic growth experience. And the best part is, many board members stay on after the company goes public."

The theme of carving one's own path has been present throughout Alvarez's life. Despite being a straight-A student in grammar school, Alvarez was told by her school principal that she was "not college material." The principal insisted Alvarez attend a commercial high school to become a secretary. Alvarez had different ideas in mind.

"I was determined to get a college education. I started applying for National Science Foundation grants offered to high-school students. I got the grants and attended Columbia University on weekends, as well as other colleges. I constructed my own profile. Not only was I accepted at all my colleges, I was accepted at Harvard!"

Reflecting on her early traits of leadership, Alvarez says that school principal with low expectations actually did her a favor.

"It was the first time I realized I had to be in charge of my own destiny. I was not crushed, merely challenged to rise above. When you go through life, you need to have a sense of self. No matter what obstacles are put in your way, don't let that get you down, because you can overcome!"

CHRISTINE JACOBS

> *I always advise women to gain visibility for being the best at what you do.*

When Chris Jacobs rang the NYSE opening bell in 1986, she became the first woman chairman and CEO to switch her company from the NASDAQ to the New York Stock Exchange—that company was Theragenics Corporation. Now a longtime director on the board of McKesson, Jacobs began her remarkable corporate career in a very non-corporate setting—working as an emergency-room trauma technician in an Ohio hospital.

CHRISTINE JACOBS
Moultonborough, New Hampshire

Corporate Boards:
McKesson Corporation
HBO & Company (HBOC)
Theragenics Corporation
Landauer Inc.

Career History:
Theragenics Corporation: Chairman, CEO, and President
Theragenics Corporation: COO and VP, Sales and Marketing
NeedleTech Products, Inc.: CEO

Education:
MBA, Georgia State University
BS, Medical Technology, Daemen College

"I did not enter the corporate world until I was thirty-four years old. I worked in the trauma trenches and was an expert in the lab and blood bank. When I was twenty-eight, I applied to medical school but was rejected."

Undaunted, she found a sales job at a British company and discovered she liked sales.

"As soon as I entered the corporate world, I found it almost sublime. Nothing that ever happens to me in corporate ever comes close to the life-and-death pressure I felt when I managed a trauma center at 2:30 in the morning."

Jacobs went back to Georgia State to get her MBA. She took a part-time job at a medical start-up at Georgia Tech that was doing uncharted research and manufacturing of radioactive palladium for prostate cancer. That start-up grew to become Theragenics, where she built her career. After tripling the sales revenue, she was offered the promotion to president—four times.

"I turned the job down—over and over again. No one had ever done what we were trying to do, and we were struggling with production. Manufacturing issues can challenge the viability of a company. If I accepted the job, I would be responsible for building the largest cyclotron-particle facility in the Western Hemisphere. I was confident in the science, but that mountain seemed so impossible to climb."

But she took on the challenge and accomplished what seemed impossible to her at one time.

"I *did* build that factory. I *did* pull off everything that had previously scared me to death."

Theragenics placed her on the board as a director, and that would be her first executive-director role.

To applaud Jacobs for her achievements, a local magazine ran a cover story about her and Theragenics. As a result, the CEO of Atlanta-based HBOC, a healthcare software company, invited her to join her first outside board.

"I always advise women to gain visibility for being the best at what you do. It was my public persona that caught the attention of the CEO, who thought I would be a good fit."

Within seven months of joining the board, HBOC entered discussions to merge with McKesson, a huge and well-known logistics company in San Francisco with strategic diversification plans. HBOC was doing nearly $5 billion in revenue, while McKesson had surpassed $25 billion.

"That merger was the largest transaction for either company. When McKesson absorbed HBOC, the proper governance required that the chair of both companies elect director candidates for the newly combined board. I felt my board tenure had been so short, that the better part of valor was not to campaign for myself to stay on. I proffered my resignation, which was accepted, and graciously stepped down."

Four months later, she received a phone call from the new CEO asking her to join the newly combined McKesson board, after all. The decision had been made to unilaterally increase the board by one director from each company, and Jacobs was the invited candidate.

"My first question was: Why? I wanted to hear what the board thought I could do."

Among the qualifications the CEO said Jacobs brought to the McKesson board were her scientific background in healthcare, her positive reputation both inside the industry and out, and her familiarity with governance and running a corporate board.

That governance expertise came in particularly handy when McKesson uncovered fraudulent profit reporting by HBOC, which no one on its previous board had known about.

"What ensued was a significant crisis for McKesson, its shareholders, employees, and customers. There may be very few corporate boards that can say they made the right decisions and moves under a crisis of that magnitude—I will forever be proud that I was part of a team of directors who put McKesson back on track and created wealth beyond measure for all who stuck with us during that time."

Having survived setting the company back on track, Jacobs says it all came down to moral fortitude and standards.

"Everyone who served on that board was a talented and ethically grounded individual. Together, we created the fiber by which the company now governs itself."

On the McKesson board, Jacobs has served on both the compensation and nominating/governance committees. She believes her prior experience at Theragenics helped her make a difference on the latter. "From my previous public-company background, I understood all the critical elements of governance—from the Dodd-Frank Wall Street Reform and Consumer Protection Act to Glass Lewis and Institutional Shareholder Services (ISS), and how to handle shareholder activism and awareness. I have always studied hard to keep up with all new laws and regulations. It's time-consuming, but such advance study has contributed to my expertise."

Advice to women: "When you have earned the opportunity to chair a committee, the best way to make an impact is to simply act as if you own it. Don't feel you must prove yourself to be the chair. Just be the chair. It's no different than walking in your first day of the hardest organic chemistry class—simply sit back and let the room unfold. You were selected. You belong.

"Even with that attitude, and despite having been the longest-seated woman CEO of a NYSE company, whenever I walked into a room full of men, there was still at least one of them who made me prove I belonged there."

Her best advice for women who face similar situations is to be extra aware of diction and participation.

"Don't make anything the men have heard about us women directors or executives come true. After you prepare, take notes, and organize your thoughts, then blow them away with your succinct position, statement, or opinion at the optimum time in the conversation."

Reflecting on her early career working in hospitals, Jacobs was responsible for handling some of the worst trauma cases.

"Imagine everything from gunshots to train wrecks to malaria and PTSD. When you are faced with blood and guts and gore, you cannot fall apart in front of a patient. You can afterward, but not on the job."

Changing careers to corporate America required finesse on Jacobs's part.

"I was used to moving fast, shooting first, and asking questions later. In the corporate world, I had to learn to holster the gun. Once I took a step back, I started seeing how I could contribute on a leadership level."

Jacobs defines leadership as something more than simply the ability to inspire.

"I realized I wanted to make others believe they could achieve anything. My job is to make others believe in what they can achieve. My message to all women is, "Believe in yourself." If you can believe in what you are capable of doing, you will be able to achieve the impossible."

Jacobs herself has accomplished the seemingly impossible: from working late nights in the trauma center to being one of the most respected and highly regarded women CEOs in the country. She has pursued a non-traditional path that led to her success.

There's one more unusual world where Jacobs has found success. In 2004, she began buying and training bucking bulls for rodeo competition. To date, she owns seven prize-winning bulls—one of which she co-owns with fellow McKesson board member Marie Knowles and Yahoo board member Jane Shaw.

"I've never done anything for the money, per se. But I sure have worked hard for the cause. I've had a twisted path, but that just goes to show you—if you're passionate about something, anything, the world is yours to take."

ILYANNE MORDEN KICHAVEN

> **I am the one bringing the "every-person" voice, speaking the viewpoint of regular working people.**

Reading the book *The Board Game: How Smart Women Become Corporate Directors* and speaking with its author, Betsy Berkhemer-Credaire, sparked Ilyanne Morden Kichaven's curiosity.

ILYANNE MORDEN KICHAVEN
Los Angeles, California

Corporate/Select Nonprofit Boards:
Federal Reserve Bank of San Francisco, Los
    Angeles Branch
Hollywood Chamber of Commerce
FilmL.A., Inc.: Vice Chair
Motion Picture & Television Fund Governing Body
The Actors Fund, Western Council

Career History:
Screen Actors Guild/American Federation of Television and Radio
    Artists: Executive Director, Los Angeles
Screen Actors Guild: Executive Director, Hollywood
Screen Actors Guild: National Director, Communications and
    Marketing

Education:
BFA, Theater Arts, UCLA

"Before that, it never crossed my mind to join a corporate board. What influence could I have in the corporate world? I have always been involved in boards outside the C-suite, and it never occurred to me that I could make a difference in the corporate world. I never thought about using my advocacy and executive skills to impact a company to improve business practices."

Morden Kichaven is the executive director, Los Angeles, of SAG-AFTRA, the combined Screen Actors Guild (SAG) and American Federation of Television and Radio Artists (AFTRA), the country's preeminent union representing famous— and many more not-so-famous—actors, singers, dancers, stunt persons, broadcasters, and recording artists. Combined, the unions have approximately 160,000 members nationwide and 80,000 in Los Angeles. She is responsible for supporting all aspects of collective bargaining, contract enforcement, organizing, governance, operations, and member concerns, as well as union activities, industry, public and government relations, and outreach. She supports the forty-six-person SAG-AFTRA Los Angeles local board.

For three consecutive years, she was named one of the 500 Most Influential People in Los Angeles by the *Los Angeles Business Journal*. Her work affords her interaction with not only celebrities, but leaders from all different industries, dignitaries, and political leaders. But she says she "was blown away" by an email from the Federal Reserve Bank board when they formally invited her to join the Los Angeles branch board.

"I was surprised because I'm not an expert in finance, nor do I have an economic background. After the conversation, it became apparent that what was lacking on the Federal Reserve's board was the narrative to accompany their data findings. They had plenty of C-suite and institutionalized banking representation, but no one with a "boots-on-the-ground" perspective of the daily struggles of working people, especially unionized labor."

But she still felt unsure about the invitation from the Federal Reserve board's regional branch.

"I didn't know much about the Federal Reserve at the time. I had to do a lot of homework and faced a huge learning curve. So I reached out to other Federal Reserve Bank board members and asked about their experience. I read everything I could to make informed decisions."

That homework proved invaluable. The Federal Reserve Bank's mission is to promote a safe, sound, and stable banking and financial system that supports the growth and stability of the U.S. economy and fair and transparent consumer financial services. As a non-partisan entity, the Federal Reserve performs key functions in the public interest to promote the health of the U.S. economy and the stability of the U.S. financial system.

With the knowledge she gained from asking questions and researching the Fed, she says she felt more self-confident and compelled to accept the seat. Although she knew she would be just one of many, she jumped at the chance to represent workers and bring their concerns to the table. Morden Kichaven now sits on the board of the Federal Reserve Bank of San Francisco, Los Angeles branch, which reports to the Twelfth District San Francisco Board. San Francisco is the headquarters of the Twelfth Federal Reserve District, which includes the nine western states—Alaska, Arizona, California, Hawaii, Idaho, Nevada, Oregon, Utah, and Washington—plus American Samoa, Guam, and the Commonwealth of the Northern Mariana Islands. Of the twelve Federal Reserve Districts, the Twelfth District is the largest by geography and the size of its economy.

The Fed's twelve districts around the country report into the Federal Open Market Committee, commonly referred to as the FOMC. Each board member is requested, almost monthly, to submit observations on trends in employment and the economy, all of which are relayed to the San Francisco main office. In turn, all remarks are compiled and sent to Washington, D.C., to the FOMC governors, who affect the interest rates in the national economy. Additionally, she often provides commentary to the "beige book," which goes directly to the head office in D.C.

"I take my seat seriously and feel a responsibility to point out real-world scenarios about wages and employment with the hope of bringing a different perspective. In 2016, Janet Yellen, the previous chair of the Federal Reserve, gave a speech about how the loss of the Affordable Care Act might impact the national economy and individual spending habits and patterns. I had previously provided multiple reports on this topic and gathered a fair amount of substantiation to my belief. I like to think that perhaps I had a tiny influence on Chairman Yellen bringing that concern to the spotlight."

Referencing the Federal Reserve board, "I have no hesitation adding my voice to information and opinions presented by economists. While it is important to rely on data, it is equally important to have the real-life narrative accompanying the numbers. Other members of the board bring large- and small-business views to the table. I knew I could be the much-needed voice of the everyday worker." She says she is not shy to call out those corporations, including Walmart and McDonald's, whose wage and employment policies continue to prove unsustainable for workers while, at the same time, forcing an unreasonable burden on taxpayers and crucial social and emergency services.

Morden Kichaven joined SAG in 2000, just as the union began a strike, one of the longest in history. She then became the first woman executive director of the Hollywood Division in 2006 and transitioned to executive director of the Los Angeles Local when SAG merged with AFTRA in 2012. Active in both entertainment and labor, she is a primary delegate to the Los Angeles County Federation of Labor, California Federation of Labor, Los Angeles Citywide Film Task Force, and Los Angeles Public Affairs and Arts Coalition, and serves as the liaison to many of the union's essential partners.

Morden Kichaven is actively pursuing a future seat on a public corporate board. She has reached out to search-firm executives and women holding board seats to garner knowledge and advice on how to prepare. One suggestion was to get involved in boards outside the entertainment industry. That advice prompted her to accept the invitation of a seat on the Hollywood Chamber of Commerce (HCC) board of directors.

Although the HCC has a large entertainment focus, its board is composed of local business owners and stakeholders and is influential in City decisions. She knew she could expand her knowledge of business and community as well as legislation.

"I am continuously challenging myself, getting involved in new ways, both to learn things for my organization's benefit but also to maximize my opportunities and prepare myself for the future. Women need to be part of any equation and conversation."

Morden Kichaven makes a practice of always looking ahead, first exhibiting her independence and leadership qualities at an early age. She started in the film business in pre-production, then post-production, and then worked in publicity and marketing for many years. But when she was fired by an award-winning independent film company while on maternity leave, she stepped up and created her own business formulating and executing publicity-strategic alliances for independent feature films, making a name for her clients (one of which was SAG) and herself. Transitioning to SAG as a full-time employee was the next logical career move.

"The self-confidence needed for seeking board positions happens when rebounding from unexpected downturns. I should know—I have had to reinvent myself many times during my career! The low statistics of women holding seats on boards is shocking, especially in California. It's surprising that my home state, which typically leads in forward-thinking concepts, is woefully behind the curve. I am working to change that."

RONNA ROMNEY

A smart woman brings a little extra something to the boardroom. Women are able to read faces and body language, assess situations a little differently, seeking signals.

The first thing board member and political fundraiser Ronna Romney says when asked about corporate board service is:

"It's a lot of work, so you better be interested in the business."

RONNA ROMNEY
Northville, Michigan

Corporate/Select Nonprofit Boards:
Molina Healthcare, Inc.
Park-Ohio Holdings Corporation

Career History:
Momentum (1988) and *Giving Time a Chance*
(1983): Author
The Ronna Romney Show: Host
Back to Back: Co-host
President's Commission on White House Fellowships: Chair
White House Commission on Presidential Scholars: Chair
President's National Advisory Council on Adult Education:
Commissioner

Education:
BA, Education, Michigan State University

The one-time Republican nominee for the U.S. Senate from Michigan is adept at many skills critical to becoming a successful director, such as public speaking, strategy, fundraising, and consensus building. This was not always the case, however. Romney rose from humble beginnings, a first-generation college student. She had a fear of failing and avoided classes that required oral presentations, generally kept quiet—despite being well-read and confident in her smarts. When she married into the prominent Romney family, which included her father-in-law, former governor of Michigan and presidential candidate George Romney, and her brother-in-law Mitt, who would eventually become governor of Massachusetts and a presidential nominee, her life was forever changed.

"I kept quiet early on because I was hesitant about saying something incorrect and looking foolish—of failing. But I was thrown into this family that had rigorous, robust conversations around the dinner table each night, and gradually I found my voice. Losing my fear of failure has been one of my greatest lessons in life. I have come to know that failing is just part of the road to success. And I try to share that knowledge with other women in the workplace and where I serve on boards."

Romney's political career began somewhat accidentally.

"When you have a well-known name, people ask you for all sorts of things, but they don't expect that you'll actually deliver or contribute on a high level. Any time I was asked to chair a nonprofit campaign, I took on greater and greater responsibility. I wanted to learn how to run the whole thing. I wanted to understand where the money was coming from and where it was going."

With more than a decade spent in various roles at the Republican National Committee, becoming a U.S. Senate candidate, chairing two presidential commissions, hosting her own radio and television shows, and being the author of two best-selling books as credentials, Romney built an attractive profile for companies seeking to find women directors.

In 1999, Romney was contacted by an executive search firm specializing in family-owned businesses who was seeking a board member with political experience. The then-private Molina Healthcare, based in Long Beach, California, was preparing to purchase a smaller company in Michigan, and Romney seemed the ideal candidate to facilitate the transition, especially since health insurance is highly regulated by the federal government.

"Not only did I have the professional background, but, with five children, I was also a family person. I first interviewed with the two Molina brothers who ran the company, which was started by their father. To them, business was all business. But they wouldn't sign off on my joining the board until their mother approved. With Mary, the business was about family values. She also had five children, and they were all co-owners. I understood that, fundamentally."

Molina was preparing to go public when Romney joined the board. With a presence in California and Michigan, along with impressive expansion plans, the company afforded Romney the ability to grow within her role as board member.

"I had never sat on a publicly traded company board before. But my political background had prepared me for the organization and leadership required of a director. We all learned a great deal as we took the company public in 2003. That's when I became lead director."

Within a few months of joining the Molina board, Romney received another call from an Ohio-based businessman who had been following her political career.

"My previous political campaigns and fundraising missions had taken me to Ohio over the years. I caught the attention of a man who liked my direct attitude and ability to swim with the sharks. After I lost the U.S. Senate race, he asked me to join his Park-Ohio board—where I was the first and only woman."

Park-Ohio is a global, publicly traded holding company that specializes in supply-chain management for diversified manufacturing and engineered products.

"When I think: How did this happen? I can point to two extraordinary male mentors. Mario Molina of Molina Healthcare and Edward Crawford of Park-Ohio both believed in me, completely unconscious of gender or age. Each thought I would be a valuable asset to their boards. Once they opened the door for me, it was up to me to step in and follow through. Don't let fear of failure stop you. Once the door is open, take the opportunity. You will find the ability and talent within yourself to accomplish what is needed of you."

Having served on both boards for nearly twenty years, Romney says she has become quite skilled at identifying the "it" factor successful directors have. NACD named Romney to the list of the Top 100 Directors in America.

"Being a board member is not just about your skill set. There is a need for collegiality and an inherent understanding of strategy. We are always careful when selecting new board members—it's easy to get married but hard to get divorced."

She finds that women more frequently demonstrate a certain *je ne sais quoi* quality.

"I think a smart woman brings a little extra something to the boardroom. Women are able to read faces and body language, assess situations a little differently, seeking signals. When my kids came home from school, I could immediately tell whether it was a good day or a bad day, or if something was on their minds. I use that intuition today in the boardroom, because every board member is a human being who has a real life outside the boardroom—which may sometimes impact how they deal with issues.

"Frequently, I discuss human qualities with the chair or the CEO. Because I was lead director, they came to rely on my counsel. Other board members know they can give me a look during a meeting, and I immediately understand whether they agree or disagree, or whether they have something to say. I always go around the table asking everyone their thoughts."

One of the most important actions Romney has instituted is making interim phone calls between board meetings.

"Communication of information is key. When I'm on a committee, I do not like surprises. Nor do I like to surprise the board, other committee members, or upper management. Whenever we need to deal with a difficult situation, I prep the CEO in advance, and we strategize together. I make sure everyone is informed and up-to-date. Transparency and preparedness ensure success.

"I believe in preparing way in advance. That can include setting the agenda for the next meeting six weeks out, and putting practices in place that will help future business. Molina was a *tabula rasa* pre-IPO. We were very thoughtful and deliberate about forming good habits before going public. We conformed to the rules of the SEC and NYSE pre-IPO, and brought on consultants to guarantee we would hit the ground running once we went public."

Since having a solid board is consistent with building a strong company, Romney advises patience throughout the board-member selection process.

"We don't rush anything, and I don't think any solid companies would hurry the process. It takes a long time, but in the end, it's worth the extra time."

One of Molina's interview practices includes bringing potential members in to lecture or make a subject matter presentation to the board, to gauge chemistry and fit, but also as a group education project.

"A lot of boards hire speakers on topics, but we invite top executives we want to get to know, in order to see if they meet our criteria for a future board member. Can you talk about trends? Projections? Regulatory environment? Strategy? My rule of thumb is: If I could hire a person as a consultant, I don't need him or her on our board. But if a speaker or subject-matter expert brings value, we do consider them as possible director candidates."

Having come from a non-traditional background, Romney views herself as an out-of-the-box problem solver.

"I'm always thinking of different ways to skin the cat. I don't like to be boxed in or limited. While the traditional path to a board seat starts by being a young hotshot at a corporation, I think age, far from being a deterrent, is an asset. On our boards, we want the wisdom that comes from experience, not the brashness that comes with youth."

Romney's message to those who are retired or nearing retirement is to play into that invaluable experience and accumulation of knowledge.

"Time, talent, energy, enthusiasm, expertise: this makes a huge difference. The ability to keep calm during crisis—and believe me, there are many crises in corporate America—that's what we're looking for. It's a certain 'been there, survived that' attitude."

Romney's political background shaped her ability to become acclimated to the board environment.

"When I went into politics, there were very few women. It wasn't easy. I used to go to meetings in hotels, thrilled that I was even invited, only to see breakfast or lunch dishes outside the rooms. I realized I hadn't been invited to the first-tier meeting—it had already happened. I vowed never to run my campaigns like that. So when I was in my U.S. Senate race, I maintained an open-door policy with my entire staff. The political candidate sets the tone the same way the lead director or CEO does on a board."

If the name sounds familiar, Ronna Romney's daughter, with the same first and last name, was elected to chair the Republican National Committee in 2017, after making a name for herself managing campaigns in Michigan.

"Just one shining example' of how far a young woman can go following her mother's advice and counsel," Romney smiles.

Get Prior Board Experience

For most women board members, prior board experience, particularly on a well-established and credible nonprofit board, was the key to ultimately serving on a for-profit board. Serving on a government commission or an advisory board, and on university boards, provides valuable lessons in governance, committee work, financial oversight, and how to advise and guide a CEO and senior management.

Find an issue or a cause that has great meaning for you. If your family has been touched by cancer or Alzheimer's, if your childhood was enriched by Scouts or Boys and Girls Clubs, if you are passionate about the arts, if you are devoted to global needs, if you are engaged with your alma mater, there are thousands of worthy and well-run nonprofit organizations that welcome capable professional volunteer board members. You will benefit, as will those you are helping.

Wanda Austin, Adrian Brown, Phyllis Campbell, Monica Lozano, Maria Salinas, and Judy Olian are women who have made a real difference on their very diverse corporate boards. And their successes are due in large part to their prior work on nonprofit boards and in university environments.

WANDA AUSTIN, PhD

❝ Through my nonprofits, I learned what the role of a board member can and should be. ❞

Even as Wanda Austin, PhD was building a stellar career in the aerospace industry, she was also actively engaged on several high-visibility nonprofit boards of directors. The board members she came to know at those important nonprofits made personal introductions that led to her first corporate board seat at Chevron, after she retired as CEO of The Aerospace Corporation in 2016. Later, she was chosen as interim president of the University of Southern California (USC) because she knew the organization well by having served on its board.

WANDA AUSTIN, PhD
  Los Angeles, California

Corporate/Select Nonprofit Boards:
  Chevron Corporation
  Amgen, Inc.
  University of Southern California
  National Geographic Society
  National Academy of Engineering

Career History:
  University of Southern California: Interim President
  MakingSpace, Inc.: STEM consulting firm, Founder
  The Aerospace Corporation: President and CEO (retired)
  Viterbi School of Engineering, USC: Research Professor

Education:
  PhD, Industrial and Systems Engineering, University of Southern
    California
  MS, Systems Engineering and Mathematics, University of Pittsburgh
  BA, Franklin and Marshall College

"Some discount the importance of nonprofit board work, but I would disagree vehemently. Through my nonprofits, I learned what the role of a board member can and should be. I started on a credit union board, then joined the board of the National Geographic Society. Then I was approached to serve on the board of the University of Southern California. Unequivocally, my path to corporate boards was built on nonprofit board experience, in addition to my experience with my own board of trustees at Aerospace."

Austin made time to serve on nonprofits while she was climbing the professional ladder to the highest rungs of success in the male-dominated field of aerospace. She enjoyed a thirty-seven-year career in national security space programs at The Aerospace Corporation, based in Los Angeles, a leading architect for the U.S. security space programs. Austin is a Fellow of the American Institute of Aeronautics and Astronautics and the author of *Making Space: Strategies for Leadership in a Complex World.*

As a former CEO, she is a qualified financial expert, and she is internationally recognized for her work in satellite and payload system acquisition, systems engineering, and system simulation. She served on the President's Council of Advisors on Science and Technology and the President's Review of U.S. Human Spaceflight Plans Committee.

It has been an unlikely path for an inner-city African American girl from the Bronx. But a seventh-grade math teacher told her something she always remembered: "You're good at math! Don't let anyone say you're not." Mentorship continued to help shape her career trajectory, including the conversations that propelled Austin to her corporate board positions.

Early in her career, a previous CEO of The Aerospace Corporation recommended she go back to university studies and get her PhD. "Once you do that, the world is your oyster," was his sage advice.

"Further along, there were bosses who wanted to give me a chance to learn, so they advocated for promotions for me."

Her first public company board seat at Chevron came about through similarly strong advocacy and serendipity. "It was not a fast courtship. I talked to them for eighteen months before joining Chevron's board. I had first been approached by the head of human resources, then I also happened to bump into the Chevron president while I was serving on a special study group for the National Science Foundation. I mentioned to the president that I had been approached for his board. Meeting someone in person, like that, makes a difference. You can have all the right boxes checked on your professional profile, but making an in-person connection is critical."

The CEO of Amgen was also a colleague on the USC board and invited Austin to be considered for Amgen's board. Austin is adamant about the due diligence needed on the part of the prospective board member. "You can get excited about the opportunity to join a board, but you need to recognize that it is a two-way street. You also need to select them. Boards, like companies, have a personality. You need to be comfortable with how they conduct business. Do your own assessment before you accept—don't just take any board seat. You want to make sure it's a good fit for both parties.

"Once a CEO phoned me and said, 'We have to have some diversity, so I thought I'd give you a call.' He was fairly direct in saying that they didn't really expect me to do or say anything. I politely said no, because I want boards where I can be a valuable contributor to running the business, not just brought on for diversity." The CEO was undoubtedly taken aback.

"As exciting as a board may seem, it is important you understand why you're being asked. Find out about the business issues they are facing and how they feel you can help. Make sure their ethics and values are the same as yours."

Austin's leadership skills were honed in her early days at Aerospace. "I realized that the thing I'm good at is enabling teams of people to be successful. I was about mid-career at Aerospace when I learned I could accomplish much more through teams rather than working individually. That was my realization about leadership. I didn't decide to be a CEO—I was actually enjoying all of my positions. But helping teams to be successful was what I loved."

Her corporate boards all have several women members. "All are very smart, and I learn from them. Having multiple women members ensures that women's views are heard and that a woman's ideas are credited to her. I believe that women are more willing to question. Rather than just checking the automatic box, they will say, 'Why can't we try something different?' Women tend to view issues through a slightly different lens. They look at problems differently and are willing to try different approaches.

"Three or more women are very effective on a board. We women don't always agree. But we do tend to bring a viewpoint that says, 'Let's make sure everyone

is heard. And let's not dismiss an idea just because we haven't done it before.'"
At Chevron, she serves on the nominating and governance committee, and chairs public policy. At Amgen, she is on the audit committee and corporate compliance committee, and the audit committee at USC.

Her advice to women serving on corporate boards: don't overcompensate. "Women sometimes want to prove we're there for the right reason. If you're on the board, you've already proven you've got the credentials. So be thoughtful; don't feel like you have to own the room—don't comment on everything—or try to prove you're the smartest. The management team is responsible for running the company. But you have an obligation to speak up when you have an opinion that can make a difference. Governance is a very serious issue."

Austin says she believes she has made a difference in three areas:

"One, I help CEOs communicate about diversity. This is not something you're taught in school. It is very tough for a male CEO to talk about unconscious biases or grapple with how he must make sure that the culture of the company is inclusive. This can be hard for a CEO, and it helps having women on the board to whom he can turn for counsel."

Two, her positive impact as a role model can't be quantified—her presence is a tremendous boon for any board she serves. "Employees are encouraged when they see board members who are diverse. Also, shareholders pay attention—they want to see evidence that there is inclusion on the board."

Three, her mentoring with leadership teams. "I like to visit locations and meet the up-and-coming leaders of the companies where I serve on the board. I talk to them about their work and challenges. I ask about risk and strategies to assess their insights. All boards are tackling difficult issues, and they need people on the board who are asking the right questions and helping management to identify potential solutions. That means you have to be willing to do your homework. I'm the one who says, 'Give me that document—I'd like to read it.'"

Clearly, Dr. Austin brings value as a leader to all her boards, both corporate and nonprofit. After all, she worked all her life with astronauts and physicists—all brilliant people, she says. She may not bring the wisdom of the universe, but she helps her boards see the logical, mathematical, down-to-earth answers to business issues.

ADRIANE M. BROWN

We have survived the challenges that women face and bring to the boardroom a deep knowledge and understanding of challenging issues and opportunities.

Adriane Brown's first board experience—with Harman International—and the three that followed, came through relationships solidified over her more than thirty years of ever-increasing responsibility in global industries.

ADRIANE M. BROWN
Seattle, Washington

Corporate/Select Nonprofit Boards:
Raytheon Company
eBay, Inc.
Allergan plc
Harman International
Pacific Science Center
Jobs for America's Graduates
Washington Research Foundation

Career History:
Intellectual Ventures Management, LLC: President and COO
Honeywell Transportation Systems: President and CEO
Honeywell Aerospace: VP and GM, Engine Systems and Accessories
Honeywell Aerospace: VP and GM, Aircraft Landing Systems
Corning, Inc.: VP and GM, Environmental Products Division

Education:
Honorary doctorate: Humane Letters, Old Dominion University
MS, Management, Massachusetts Institute of Technology
BS, Environmental Health, Old Dominion University

Brown served as president and chief operating officer for Intellectual Ventures from January 2010 through July 2017, where her team delivered more than $3 billion in revenue, spun out fourteen companies and joint ventures, and established Global Good and Research, which innovates for global health and development. Previously, she spent ten years at Honeywell in leadership positions serving the aerospace and automotive markets.

Her career was forged through nineteen years at Corning, where she rose from a shift supervisor into sales, customer service, and product management roles, and became vice president and general manager of Corning's environmental products division. At Corning, during a leadership workshop, she met her "board guru," a consultant who would later advise her on potential board seats.

"I had received some interesting calls about serving on boards along the way, but my time was totally committed to my job and family. It seemed like just when they called, I was early in a new job and new location. I moved nine times over my thirty-eight professional years, so I have been on quite a journey."

To settle into new cities and environments, Brown joined local, large, nonprofit boards.

"As a new executive in a new location, I reached out to the community to grow some new roots. I always found community service rewarding, and it was also a way to build new networks of friends and local influencers in each city. I still spent much of my time at my day job and family life, with my husband and daughter. I found my nonprofit boards served me well in preparing me for the corporate boards that would come later.

"As I was deciding to take the leap out of the corporate, into the entrepreneurial world, I asked the CEO at Intellectual Ventures, during my interview, if he had any issues with me serving on an outside corporate board. If he had said yes, that would have been a dealbreaker for me. Thankfully, he hired me and encouraged me to serve on the board of a good company.

"My first board service was Harman International, where I found my voice in the boardroom. I was one of three women, where the lead director was a woman. It was no coincidence that my first board would be very well functioning, and a good company, indeed.

But three years later, Harman was purchased by Samsung and the board was disbanded.

"As we were going through the purchase, I knew if it closed, I was going to lose my beloved board." Coincidentally, it was precisely at that same time when the call came from a recruiter about the board of Allergan, the global biopharmaceutical company that specializes in medical aesthetics, including the well-known Botox, eye care, central nervous system, and gastrointestinal therapeutic areas.

"I did not immediately say 'yes.' I was not generally interested in the pharmaceutical industry, but as I did my research, I became intrigued with Allergan, whose motto was 'Bold for Life.'

"I met with the CEO and several board members, fully realized the impact and breadth of their products, and confirmed that they did not do things the traditional way. They really were bold, and I wanted to be on this board."

The very day that the Samsung purchase of Harman was announced, Allergan announced that Adriane Brown was joining its board.

"Talk about karma."

In fact, one of her Harman board colleagues had been asked for, and had given, a glowing recommendation to Allergan, which Brown emphasizes is critically important.

"Recruiters and boards will do in-depth outreach and vetting to learn as much as possible about you before they make a decision. Beyond the names you provide for recommendation, they will look deeper and even ask board members you've served with how you function in the boardroom."

Shortly after Brown joined the Allergan board, eBay's board recruiter approached her, based on a recommendation from a former executive colleague. After several rounds of interviews, she received a call stating, "We have good news and great news." The good news was that eBay invited her onto the board, and the great news was that they had identified a second highly qualified woman in the process who would join at the same time. The eBay board now has four women directors.

"I was interested in eBay because of its pioneering history, its recent split with PayPal, and the opportunity to participate in the strategic direction of one of Silicon Valley's finest companies. It would be a period of great change for eBay, not only from the perspective of new technology, but also in transforming its approach to its well-developed global marketplace." At eBay, Brown serves on the audit committee.

At Allergan, she has served on the audit committee, as well as the quality/innovation committee, which deals with the development of new products and operations. How does she deal with the multiple responsibilities and meetings?

"Boards tend to have a cadence. I looked at both board calendars first before beginning any board process, which is pretty standard. It is very important to compare your existing commitments against the new board opportunity."

Brown is adamant about meeting the responsibilities of her boards, which can include ten or more hours of preparation for each meeting. "The most important thing is to come in prepared, having given thought to the topics well before the live discussion. It's my job, and I aspire to not only meet expectations but to go above and beyond on behalf of shareowners."

After joining the eBay and Allergan boards, Brown says she thought she was done for a while. Unexpectedly, she was contacted to be considered for a coveted board seat at Raytheon. She was not looking, but this was an industry that she knew well from her years at Honeywell. So, once she confirmed that the calendars of the three boards were compatible, she went through the process and was asked to join the Raytheon board in late 2017. At Raytheon, she serves on the management development and compensation committee.

Brown says it is no surprise that all three of her boards have at least three women members, and in fact, two of them have four.

"At this time in my career, I find that having a voice and having a perspective comes naturally to me. Given my career experiences, I feel valued and powerful. Women with whom I serve have broken through many barriers throughout their careers. We have survived the challenges that women face and bring to the boardroom a deep knowledge and understanding of challenging issues and opportunities. We ask informed questions. We have an impact on every aspect of the businesses. I'm fortunate to serve on such great boards where the notion of men vs. women is not present. We respect each other and our responsibilities in the boardroom."

Brown's impressive list of awards and recognition added depth to her board profile. The University of Washington Women's Center honored her as a Woman of Courage; the National Diversity Council presented her with the 2016 Washington Leadership Excellence Award; and in 2015, she received MIT's Martin Luther King Jr. Leadership Award. In 2012, STEMconnector recognized Brown as one of 100 Women Leaders in STEM, and she was named one of *Black Enterprise* magazine's 100 Most Powerful Executives.

Brown is also the board chair of Seattle's prestigious Pacific Science Center, which she joined two years after moving there. Overall, with three corporate boards, a large nonprofit, and a foundation board, Brown is full speed ahead at breakneck pace, because "it's a pure pleasure. I can't get used to the 'R' word— Retirement. I'm having too much fun!"

PHYLLIS CAMPBELL

Serve on large nonprofit boards, if possible. The directors in those networks are ideal for forming relationships because they have seen you in action on their boards.

Well-known in Seattle for her service on four brand-name corporate boards—Alaska Airlines, Nordstrom, Puget Sound Energy, and Safeco Insurance—and boards of many large nonprofits, and as CEO of the Seattle Foundation, Phyllis Campbell says she was not born with the leadership gene. She had to learn how to lead, and practice it over and over.

PHYLLIS CAMPBELL
Seattle, Washington

Corporate/Select Nonprofit Boards:
Alaska Air Group, Inc.
Toyota Motor Corporation: North American
    Diversity Advisory Board
Pacific Science Center
Nordstrom, Inc.
Puget Energy, Inc.
Safeco Insurance Company of America, Inc.
Seattle Metropolitan Chamber of Commerce
Seattle Foundation
Washington Roundtable

Career History:
JPMorgan Chase & Co.: Vice Chair
Seattle Foundation: President and CEO
U.S. Bank of Washington: President and CEO
U.S. Bancorp: EVP
U.S. Bank of Oregon: EVP

Education:
MBA, University of Washington
BA, Business Administration, Washington State University

"As a Japanese American woman, I was always told growing up, 'Don't ruffle feathers,' 'Don't rock the boat.' I was very shy and insecure. Later in high school, my father pushed me to get out of my shell and run for student government. That was way out of my comfort zone, but I gradually gained confidence. Through trial and error, I found my opinion had value, and so I started pushing myself to achieve.

"Thankfully, there were many mentors in my life, starting with my father, who saw more in me than I did in myself. 'Get ready to walk through when the door opens,' he would say. Emotionally, mentally, be prepared. Take good advice, then jump into areas way out of your comfort zone."

Campbell has now served on boards in four different industries where she had no previous experience. It was uncomfortable at first, but after many years of experience, she is revered as a role model for women.

"Getting on corporate boards is all about working your network in a purposeful way. Before asking you to join their board, other directors want to know you, how you think, what your interests and background are, and most of all—how you will fit into their unique culture."

Her first board was Puget Sound Energy, which happened through a friend Campbell met when she was in upper-middle management, not yet VP, at a bank. Turns out, this friend became head of human resources for the investor-owned utility, PSE. Having observed Campbell in business over the years, this friend wanted to introduce her to the CEO as a board candidate. The CEO then introduced her to the other board members. "Really the first three to four months, we were getting to know one another—the board members talked more about me than about the strategy of the company. So it was clearly the culture fit that they wanted to assess."

Campbell's second board was Safeco Insurance, now acquired by Liberty Mutual. Both the utility, and now the insurance company, were in male-dominated industries. She reiterates having a sense of humor is critically important for women to thrive on a male-dominated board.

"Someone would say, 'Please stand when speaking,' and I would say, 'Well, I am standing!'" This always got a laugh because of her short stature. "Humor establishes that I'm not trying to prove I'm the smartest person in the room. A board member once told me he enjoyed having me on board because of my sense of humor."

So how can a woman become known for how she would fit into a board culture? "Serve on large nonprofit boards, if possible. The directors in those networks are ideal for forming relationships because they have seen you in action on their boards." Campbell was asked to join the Nordstrom board through her community contacts. She had been chair of the Seattle Chamber board, the Seattle Foundation, and many other civic organizations and nonprofits. "Boards are looking for leadership, so they have to have seen you in action.

"Learning how to work on committees is how you can make a difference. Become the chair of committees in nonprofits and on corporate boards, then work your way up to being the independent lead director."

One of the Nordstrom patriarchs approached her for the board, saying he knew she was a leader with a financial background. Nordstrom was looking for a financial expert to eventually chair the audit committee. So the first step was recognizing the valuable leadership Campbell had displayed in her finance career and nonprofit volunteer boards, then introducing her to the board members and to the Nordstrom family. From banking, she already understood the basic dynamics of family ownership, which impressed the board.

The CEO of Alaska Airlines also noticed Campbell in her nonprofit leadership role at the Washington Roundtable. He reached out and asked her to join his board. First she said no, because of time constraints. But two years later, Alaska Airlines came back again, and this time, Campbell accepted.

Campbell says it is important not to stay on boards too long. She stepped down from Nordstrom after eleven years, one year past the informal one-decade limit. While serving more than fourteen years on the Alaska Airlines board, she served as lead director for five of those years before turning the role over to another woman.

"It's no accident that we have gender diversity—three women on the Alaska board. Gender diversity is a true competitive advantage for the business."

Very active in corporate diversity efforts, Campbell was appointed to the Toyota North America Diversity Advisory Board, which counsels Toyota on reinforcing diversity as a true asset of the company, in marketing outreach as well as management and operations. "We have crafted governance as well as marketing guidelines, and made a significant difference. Sometimes I'm concerned that members might view me as the one who's constantly bringing up diversity. That doesn't change my focus, but it reminds me to cultivate allies. Especially if you are an ethnic woman on the board, find allies. Sometimes, even still, I am the lone voice. But don't apologize. Every business needs different points of view in order to be more competitive and really perform better."

Campbell's advice for getting a first board appointment is not just to market yourself, but to be very articulate about your specific areas of passion and expertise. Remind your contacts about more than just the obvious. "Boards have sought me out for my finance, audit, and enterprise-risk credentials, but I am most passionate about diversity in leadership succession planning, and employee and customer engagement. This goes all the way back to my early days working in my father's dry-cleaning business, focusing on customers.

"I've carried that through my whole life, focusing on employee development and mentoring. It's all about competitive advantage for the company. I recommend from my own experience not to succumb to obvious stereotyping. When you have the chance, remind women on other boards to bring up diversity, not because you are the woman on the board, but because diversity is a competitive advantage. That's most effective."

Once proactive outreach and career experience garner board consideration, then take Campbell's advice. She gives three pointers on how to be successful on the board:

- Do your due diligence before joining. Focus on finding out whether the independent directors actually influence decision-making.
- Get a "Board Buddy." Campbell cultivated a more senior woman director to be her informal board mentor. This woman provided counsel on the flow and cadence of board dynamics.
- Understand gender dynamics—they're always present, even outside the boardroom. The independent lead director should play a role in calling upon the women directors for their opinions.

So what is good leadership on a board? According to Campbell: having high emotional intelligence, also known as EQ, to understand the dynamics of board flow and management. Trusting that EQ is also really important when on a board.

"My biggest lesson learned was distinguishing the difference between governance and management. Board members are not there to manage, but to counsel the CEO, who leads and empowers the workforce. The board is also the keeper of culture—how does management measure and reward performance?

Look to more senior board members you can learn from. Give your best counsel while not being disruptive."

"There are countless women executives who are well qualified and have self-confidence in their own jobs but simply do not think of themselves as ready for board service." To them, Campbell says: "Do try to overcome the fear of being an imposter. Women never think they are ready enough, but men think they are ready anytime, even if they are not. Just remember, you have been getting ready for years. So step through that door!"

MONICA LOZANO

66 *Effective directors have to be over-prepared, learn as much as they can about the industry, and become immersed in the challenges, trends, growth opportunities, and strategic risks facing the company.* 99

Monica Lozano is the scion of the legendary Hispanic newspaper *La Opinión*. Her grandfather Ignacio Lozano started the newspaper more than ninety years ago in Los Angeles, and her father Ignacio Jr. led the newspaper for more than forty years. She has guided the publishing empire through the modern era, dealing with far-reaching industry disruption as print has been revolutionized by the advent of digital technology and the Internet. She joined the family business early in her career and over the years became editor, then publisher, then CEO of ImpreMedia, the newspaper's holding company with media properties nationwide.

Without realizing that community visibility would eventually lead to selection for corporate boards, Lozano began volunteering on nonprofit boards in her thirties. She was recommended to her first corporate board by a fellow board member at the YMCA of Greater Los Angeles. Before that, she had helped many community organizations grow, including March of Dimes SoCal.

"Becoming visible in civic organizations early in a career, in addition to working hard at your own job, contributes to building important networks, and your reputation grows gradually."

Her first corporate board was First Interstate Bank of California, which was later acquired by Wells Fargo. With bank board credentials, she was recruited to the board of Union Bank of California, but when her company ImpreMedia went national in 2004, her work duties greatly expanded nationwide, so she stepped down from the board.

In 2006, Ken Lewis, president and CEO of Bank of America at the time, called her to discuss a board position. Her prior experience on regional bank boards was invaluable.

"Because of the regulatory environment, my previous banking expertise was a great asset. After the financial crisis of 2008, the board was reconstituted and I—along with three other directors—was asked to stay on."

During her years on the board at Bank of America, Lozano has seen the addition of four more women directors to the BofA board, including Sharon Allen, Linda Hudson, Sue Bies, and Maria Zuber.

MONICA LOZANO
Los Angeles, California

Corporate/Select Nonprofit Boards:
Bank of America Corporation
Target Brands, Inc.
Weingart Foundation
University of California Board of Regents
The Rockefeller Foundation
The Walt Disney Company
The Aspen Institute
Tenet Healthcare Corporation
Union Bank of California
First Interstate BancSystem
California Health Care Foundation
UnidosUS (formerly National Council of La Raza)
University of Southern California

Career History:
College Futures Foundation: President and CEO
U.S. Hispanic Media, Inc.: Chair
ImpreMedia, LLC: Chair and CEO
La Opinión: Publisher and CEO
President's Council on Jobs and Competitiveness
President's Economic Recovery Advisory Board

"Bank of America is one of only a handful of companies with five female directors, and two of the four committees (audit and compensation) are chaired by women."

In 2000, Lozano joined the board of The Walt Disney Company. She had met Michael Eisner, then-CEO of Disney, through her father, who had served on the Disney board years earlier.

"Michael called me one day completely unexpectedly. Those were the days before [the] Sarbanes–Oxley [Act], and the CEO carried significant influence over the selection of board members."

In addition to her corporate boards, Lozano served on nonprofit boards: the University of California Board of Regents, the Weingart Foundation (as chair), and The Rockefeller Foundation. She reiterates that women who aspire to serve on corporate boards should intentionally serve as volunteers on large nonprofit boards in order to build relationships.

For The Aspen Institute, she founded a new policy program called Latinos in Society and serves as chair of the program's advisory board. She had been asked by the CEO of Aspen to design and launch a program that would highlight how Latinos are impacting America's future, and she jumped at the chance to collaborate with such a prestigious and influential institution. The program has become a valuable incubator of cultural knowledge and policy since June 2014.

"After two decades on corporate boards, I've learned how important it is to foster open debate and discussion and to surface distinct points of view. As an independent director, your number-one duty is to build shareholder value, and this requires a high-functioning, independent board of directors who are actively engaged at a strategic level with the CEO and senior management. All boards grapple with difficult strategic decisions, and you want board culture to promote open and candid dialogue.

"Committees are where much of the work of the board happens. I chair the Bank of America compensation committee, and we make every effort to not just review compensation but evaluate how our employment practices support the development of our workforce. How do we ensure that individuals can grow and thrive in the company, and what workforce practices do we have in place that attract, retain, and develop diverse talent? As a Latina, I know how important diversity and inclusion are to building a sustainable business—especially important for consumer-facing companies."

Sheryl Sandberg and Susan Arnold served with Lozano on the Disney board, and Maria Elena Lagomasino succeeded Lozano at the end of her term in 2016.

"Disney cares a lot about good corporate governance, and having three women on the board does make a difference."

When Lozano stepped down, she was immediately recruited to Target Corporation, where she was named to the governance and audit committees. As an expert in the Hispanic media market with inside knowledge on how to reach Latino consumers, Lozano was an ideal choice as a new director.

"Effective directors have to be over-prepared, learn as much as they can about the industry, and become immersed in the challenges, trends, growth opportunities, and strategic risks facing the company."

Lozano says it is especially important to voice your opinion.

"You are there to help the company. You were selected by your fellow board members, elected by shareholders, and you have the responsibility to exert your influence and independent judgment. Find your voice and use it. Of course, you don't want to be pegged as the female board member who only talks about women's issues. But don't suppress your background and experience; build from it to help make the company stronger and more inclusive."

Where did that spark of leadership first show up in Lozano's early life?

"I went to an all-girls Catholic high school that instilled in us a great sense of confidence. We were expected to actively participate and learn to solve complex problems. Girls become female leaders. Of course, I didn't want to go to an all-girls school at the time, but I've come to realize how that experience gave me a foundation that is extremely valuable.

"I know now that success cannot be built on passion alone—your passion must be married to a sense of purpose. If one's professional life can support both, that's the winning combination. For me, it's that sense of making a difference, of having impact whether in a boardroom or running a company. When you get recruited to join a board, make sure the company's philosophy and values reflect yours. That's what the right fit is all about."

MARIA S. SALINAS

> *A nonprofit board is a great place to achieve two essential elements: relationships and governance experience.*

Serving on nonprofit boards was the key to the relationships that led Maria S. Salinas to her first public board, ProAmérica Bank, where she was a founding board member and then board chair until the ten-year-old bank was sold. Salinas was the first woman and first Latina to be named CEO of the Los Angeles Area Chamber of Commerce.

MARIA S. SALINAS
  Los Angeles, California

Corporate/Select Nonprofit Boards:
  First Choice Bank
  Pacific Commerce Bank (acquired by First Choice Bank)
  ProAmérica Bank (acquired by Pacific Commerce Bank)
  Loyola Marymount University
  Kaiser Permanente School of Medicine
  UnidosUS (formerly National Council of La Raza)
  California Student Aid Commission
  Los Angeles Universal Preschool
  San Gabriel Pomona Valley Chapter, American Red Cross
  Angeles Girl Scout Council (Girl Scouts of Greater Los Angeles)
  Hispanas Organized for Political Equality (HOPE)

Career History:
  Los Angeles Area Chamber of Commerce: President and CEO
  Salinas Consulting, LLC: President and Founder
  Disney Consumer Products and Interactive Media: Director, Finance
  The Walt Disney Company: Manager, Corporate Controllership
  Ernst & Young, LLP: Audit Manager

Education:
  BS, Accounting, Loyola Marymount University

Salinas stayed on the board of the acquiring banks (ProAmérica Bank was acquired by Pacific Commerce Bank, which was in turn acquired by First Choice Bank), a tribute to her leadership and business acumen. More often than not, board members of the acquired entity do not stay on the board after the acquisition. But Salinas, a finance professional, brought added value with her exceptional career in finance, governance expertise, knowledge of the Hispanic market, and long history with ProAmérica Bank and Pacific Commerce Bank.

"It was my nonprofit networks and relationships that led to being invited to my first public company board at ProAmérica Bank." Early in her career, she recognized the importance of building strong relationships, so she engaged with nonprofit organizations where she felt personally connected, such as HOPE (Hispanas Organized for Political Equality). HOPE set the stage for her impressive and inspirational board career. She not only helped found the organization but went on to become its president, building lasting relationships in the community along the way. She served on other nonprofit boards, assuming expanded roles.

"Every nonprofit board experience I've had has been meaningful and given me the opportunity to learn a new area. On the Angeles Girl Scout Council, I served on the investment committee, a new area for me. It was intimidating at first, but I worked hard to become proficient in the area so that I could contribute to defining the strategy." Salinas advises women aspiring to serve on a public-company board not to fear taking on something new, as it all leads to developing well-rounded board experience.

"Through my involvement in community organizations, in addition to gaining governance experience, I developed great professional relationships. Relationships matter, and in my board career, my professional relationships have made a pivotal difference."

Salinas encourages women to consider serving on nonprofit boards. "A nonprofit board is a great place to achieve two essential elements in seeking a public-company board position: relationships and governance experience."

In 2018, she was named CEO of the Los Angeles Chamber of Commerce—the first woman and first Latina to be hired to lead one of the largest chambers in the country. Her business acumen and political savvy are a result of years of hard work in her profession and in the community.

At Disney, she climbed the ranks from corporate-level management to director of the controllership department in the consumer products division, always striving to excel in each role. Salinas thrived in a supportive corporate environment while balancing family life.

After Disney, she ventured into entrepreneurship, launching her own finance-and-accounting consulting company; soon thereafter, she was invited to join the board of a newly forming bank focused on the Latino market, ProAmérica Bank. Salinas' invitation to the board came from her community relationships, and her candidacy was supported by several board members who knew of her leadership in the nonprofit sector.

"I hesitated initially because I was not familiar with the banking industry. After speaking with the CEO, I understood that it was my financial expertise, governance experience, and relationships in the Hispanic community that made sense for them."

Having served on several significant nonprofit boards—Angeles Girl Scout Council and San Gabriel Pomona Valley American Red Cross—Salinas had a well-suited foundation in governance that appealed to the ProAmérica Bank board.

Salinas accepted the ProAmérica Bank board seat in 2005, a year before the bank officially opened in November of 2006. This unique opportunity allowed Salinas to be part of the launch of a financial institution, going through all the regulatory requirements, and later, the *de novo* phase. This phase is designated by federal regulators as between the date a new bank is chartered and the date regulators clear the bank from additional levels of regulatory review. Due to the economic recession, the *de novo* phase for new banks was extended to seven years instead of the customary three.

The new bank faced regulatory scrutiny during the economic recession. "We created a special compliance committee, which I chaired, to address regulatory inquiries. As chair of the ad hoc committee, I frequently met with regulators to respond about our progress."

Calling it one of the most difficult and grueling exercises of her professional career, Salinas is nevertheless thankful for the incredible learning experience that has made her a better executive today. "Once we got past all the regulatory matters, we were on a solid path. The silver lining was that I developed a good relationship with the regulators that would serve me well later on when I became chairwoman." Over the years, Salinas served on all of the bank's standing committees, including nominating and governance, and as chair of the audit committee.

Salinas was appointed chairwoman of the board for her deep knowledge of the bank, her strategic thinking, and her extensive relationships in the business community. "It was an incredible honor to be appointed chairwoman and to have the confidence of my fellow board members. As chairwoman, I drew on the support of key mentors both on the bank board and outside of the bank. The encouragement from so many came from many years of cultivating relationships. It clearly gave me the courage for the enormous task of being at the helm of the board of a financial institution."

In her first year as chair, Salinas expanded the board and recruited two women directors. She led the board through strategic-planning efforts, including leading the bank's mergers-and-acquisitions committee during the sale process.

"When we were presented with an opportunity to merge, the board looked to me to lead." She tackled the complexities of selling a financial institution, which included negotiations, due diligence, and all aspects of the regulatory review, culminating with shareholder approval. "It was an empowering experience to successfully close on a transaction that yielded value to our shareholders."

In 2017, Salinas was invited to the founding board of the Kaiser Permanente School of Medicine, and she served as chair of the audit committee. Salinas was sought out because of her extensive governance experience at ProAmérica Bank, and her business and community relationships.

Her work on a public-company board, on various nonprofit boards, and as an entrepreneur has been a convergence of experiences that have contributed to her robust board career.

"Serving on a public-company board gives you a great opportunity to influence decision making at the highest level. Having a seat at the table is important, but being prepared and having the courage to contribute to the dialogue in the boardroom is even more impactful."

JUDY OLIAN

❝ You want to be both helpful and challenging—an independent board member who is a truth teller. ❞

Dr. Judy Olian is a nationally recognized academic leader preparing students to succeed as business professionals. So it comes as no surprise that she is a successful corporate board member, bringing her expertise in management to the boardrooms of companies with very diverse missions.

JUDY OLIAN
Hamden, Connecticut

Corporate/Select Nonprofit Boards:
Mattel
Ares Management, LP
United Therapeutics Corporation
Catalyst, Inc.
United States Studies Centre, University of Sydney

Career History:
Quinnipiac University: President
UCLA Anderson School of Management: Dean; John E. Anderson
    Chair in Management
Smeal College of Business, The Pennsylvania State University: Dean;
    Professor
Robert H. Smith School of Business, University of Maryland:
    Professor; Senior Associate Dean

Education:
PhD, Industrial Relations, University of Wisconsin
MS, Industrial Relations, University of Wisconsin
BS, Hebrew University of Jerusalem

Olian serves on the boards of Mattel, the iconic toy manufacturer of Barbie and Hot Wheels; Ares Management, an independent investment firm specializing in leveraged loans, high-yield bonds, private debt, private equity, and other types of investments; and United Therapeutics Corporation, a biotechnology company focused on the development and commercialization of products for patients with chronic and life-threatening conditions.

For all her boards, recommendations for Olian as a board candidate came through her extensive network of business connections. As dean of UCLA Anderson School of Management for twelve years, her circle of contacts included many senior business executives who were familiar with both her management expertise and what she defines as her EQ, emotional quotient.

Olian's experience taught her that when nominating committees are searching for candidates, they are looking for more than just the specific criteria that come across on resumes. That's why the personal interviews become so important.

"People want to have a sense of confidence in you. The CEOs knew me in terms of both my work and my demeanor. You certainly have to bring your experience, background, and expertise to the boardroom. But you also must have compatibility with the board and with the company's senior leadership team.... Board members can check off all the correct boxes, but you don't want to be bringing in board members who create uncertainties that are unhelpful. You want to be both helpful and challenging—an independent board member who is a truth teller."

Olian emphasizes two basic qualities critical to getting a board seat.

"First, you should be known for your accomplishments. You need to be seen as credible for the work you have done. And second, you need to be known in the network of people who respect you for your demeanor. A board is a team, and interfacing well with that team, as well as with management and the chairman, is critical."

Olian's tenure at UCLA Anderson School of Management generated a long list of accomplishments that point to her business acumen. She brought dozens of outstanding new scholars and content to the research and teaching programs. She oversaw the launch of four new research centers, introduced and expanded degree programs, and promoted hybrid coursework combining online and in-classroom instruction. She recruited top business executives to the Anderson board and raised $450 million in philanthropic support. She is also credited with having greatly increased the faculty and student gender diversity during her tenure. In 2018, she left Anderson to become president of the renowned private Quinnipiac University in Connecticut, an institution internationally known for its political research and survey data related to political campaigns.

Over the course of her academic career, Olian made herself visible. She is widely published in journals on human resources management, top-management team composition, and the business alignment of management systems, all areas of expertise sought by high-functioning companies and boards.

She joined the Mattel board after changes in CEOs had led to less-than-robust results, so she wanted to be part of its turnaround team. The board of Ares is a non-controlling board, which means that several standard board committees are not required, such as a compensation committee. It does, however, require all members to serve on the audit committee. On the United Therapeutics board, Olian sits on the compensation committee.

"I believe that all committees can be influential—nominating and governance, audit, finance, compensation. It's valuable to be where you think you can make a contribution and also learn."

Olian worked with a very powerful board of trustees at UCLA Anderson.

"I've been on the management side of the relationship, so I'm sensitive to the board's oversight role. I think in every instance, management takes the primary role and the board is advisory. It should be questioning and, depending on the issues, bring in independent counsel. A board should be primarily influential around asking questions and soliciting further review around an issue."

Academic and nonprofit boards follow the same guidelines, rules, and structure that govern publicly traded company boards. And Olian made that point clear when she addressed nominating committees and when she is advising women who are interested in joining boards.

"Knowing the distinction between board and management, advising without intruding, asking the provocative questions, avoiding 'groupthink,' paying attention to profit and loss—these are all similar issues on profit and nonprofit boards, especially the larger nonprofits. The only real difference is around compliance. A well-functioning nonprofit board can provide board members quite relevant experience and preparation to serve on public boards."

The for-profit companies for which Olian serves on the boards are vastly dissimilar in their products, and she admits that neither financial investment nor medical treatments are within her experience set.

"So what I can bring are the bigger-picture issues—organizational structure, global expansion, mergers and acquisitions, human resources questions. You learn the basics of the business, and then you try to help the organization where it needs your expertise, where you can step back and give a bigger perspective. In the case of Ares, the board has a good number of financial experts; at United Therapeutics, there are several medical experts. I have impact in other consequential conversations."

On the Ares board, Olian is the only woman, while the United Therapeutics board has two women plus a woman founder and CEO.

Even though her personal experience has been positive, she's aware that many women face gender bias not just in the workplace, but also on boards.

"Data tell us that women are more apt than men to be judged against a likability factor in any role—not just on boards."

Olian says she believes her leadership skills were honed by taking on challenges.

"I simply said 'yes' to a lot of things. I'm one of those people who will take assignments that nobody else has time or the interest in doing. This way you expand your repertoire, your network of people, and your knowledge. Saying 'yes' means more opportunity, even though it's more work. Each time you get bigger and bigger responsibility. Before you know it, you're leading things. Leadership comes from having the opportunity and willingness to take on more."

Use LinkedIn to Your Advantage

> **LONG** before people ask you for a resume, they look at your **LinkedIn profile**

In the years since my first book, *The Board Game,* was published, LinkedIn has become far more important in successful self-promotion. Smart women (and men!) must use this tool to their best advantage in their quest for a corporate board seat.

"Really?" you ask. Yes. LinkedIn is considered the professional and business online site that every executive search firm and board-nominating committee looks at first to find out about individuals and their business connections. If you are not currently using LinkedIn, build a profile that is always updated, well-written, thorough, and takes full advantage of the options available in the LinkedIn profile template.

Your LinkedIn profile should contain the strongest, most relevant points from your board candidate profile (see Chapter 8) and should exemplify the value added that you would bring to a board. Be sure to state specifically that you are seeking a board position.

Describe previous board experience, both corporate and nonprofit, at the top of your profile. Use revenues, numbers of employees and people served, geographic reach, and any other statistics that have impact for a reader. Your career chronology should highlight your achievements that demonstrate strategic leadership, rather than your skills as you would list them on a resume. Each company name should be listed first, then your title.

List all your degrees and the institutions you attended, as well as your areas of specialty. Why? Because your LinkedIn profile may be the way board members and CEOs "meet" you; it may provide their first impression of you. Long before people ask you for a resume, they look at your LinkedIn profile. If your profile is not professional and specific about your pursuit of board membership, it could be their last impression. They won't interview you if your profile doesn't demonstrate how dynamic you are.

Diana Ingram made certain her LinkedIn profile stressed her track record with cybersecurity technology, since she was well aware that this area is of prime concern to boards. See Chapter 8 for more specific ideas on shaping your LinkedIn profile to appeal to the companies you are targeting. Diana Ingram and Dany St-Pierre are two successful women board members who can point directly to LinkedIn as a key to attaining their first board seats.

DIANA INGRAM

> **Your LinkedIn profile is more important than you ever thought.**

Diana Ingram is the only woman director we know who was contacted for her board position through LinkedIn. As a result, she advises all women seeking board positions be certain their LinkedIn profiles are updated and present their professional photo and background to exemplify the value added they can bring to boards. And this is really no joke in today's online environment.

DIANA INGRAM
  Los Angeles, California

Corporate/Select Nonprofit Boards:
  Rexford Industrial Realty, Inc.
  Goodwill Southern California
  ECMC Group, Inc.
  International Women's Forum, (Trusteeship)
    Southern California
  Big Brothers Big Sisters of Greater Los Angeles
  Los Angeles Urban League
  Coalition for Clean Air

Career History:
  Oracle: Technology Consulting Services
  IBT, S.A./Realtime: EVP, Head of Operations, U.S.
  IBM: Director, Security and Privacy Services U.S.; VP, Global Sales
    and Wireless E-business Solutions; VP, Telecommunications/
    Media Sector, Latin America; Director, Enterprise Content-
    management Software Sales, Americas
  Kinko's, Inc. (now FedEx Kinko's International, Inc.): SVP; GM,
    Operations, West Region

Education:
  MBA, Marketing and Finance, Kellogg Graduate School of
    Management, Northwestern University
  BA, Human Biology, Stanford University

"Out of the blue, I received a LinkedIn message from the CEO of Rexford; I didn't respond because I thought it was someone playing a joke, or worse, trying to perpetrate some sort of scam."

Several days later, her assistant at Oracle, where Ingram leads the company's technology consulting services in Los Angeles, passed on a message from the president's assistant at Rexford. Only then did Ingram realize she should explore this unusual approach. She returned the call, and today she sits on the board of this $3 billion company, proof positive that a well-constructed LinkedIn profile and professional headshot is a must for women seeking board positions.

Rexford Industrial is a leading Southern California-based industrial real-estate investment firm, publicly held, with eight board members. She is the only woman, the only African American, and the only director with cybersecurity knowledge.

Ingram has a long career as a senior leader in business development, sales, marketing, and information technology in the U.S., Latin America, and other global markets. She has led organizations with eight thousand employees and revenues exceeding $2 billion. At Oracle, she is focused on helping corporate clients accelerate their transition to cloud computing and enhance their IT security. Previously, she was executive vice president and head of operations for the U.S. start-up of networking software company, IBT/Realtime. She built her early career at IBM.

Here's how CEO Michael Frankel said he found Ingram on LinkedIn: "I was looking for successful women executives with certain levels of achievement, including senior operating roles, board roles, and involvement with community-oriented organizations. My keywords included director, president, and vice-president, then industries focused on technology, and finally community-based nonprofit organizations. After finding several profiles that fit, I then delved into their affiliations, associations, and relationships. Some of my best results and serious leads came from searching the endless trees of relationships and affiliations. For example, if one interesting woman was affiliated with a given organization, I'd then look at that organization's entire list of board members, committee members, honorees, and event speakers. LinkedIn is a pretty amazing resource. That's how I found Diana, so I called her to get to know her by phone, then invited her to meet."

Ingram adds, "If it were not for LinkedIn, I would not be here today. My profile highlighted my track record of business achievements and experience with cybersecurity technology. The Rexford board was keen to add a member outside the real-estate and financial-services industries that were well represented by the current directors. With the increasing importance of IT to the business and interest in enhancing its cybersecurity posture, I felt confident I could bring immediate value to the corporation."

Despite being the first woman on the board, Ingram felt welcomed and appreciated from her first meeting. As one of the two board members who did not come from the financial-services industry, it was essential that she gain a deeper understanding of the business and how the work actually gets done. She asked to meet with all of the department heads and their teams.

"I asked questions about how the work gets done; how technology serves their jobs.

"I was impressed that the Rexford workforce seemed pleased to have a board member demonstrate great interest in how their teams work. One of the executives told me, 'You've already distinguished yourself!' by seeking them out and engaging with them. Because of my background, I do tend to ask different kinds of questions, and the employees appreciate the opportunity to talk about their work."

Ingram spent many hours learning about Rexford in preparation for her nomination. "I made it very clear in my meetings with the nominating/governance committee that I didn't have real-estate experience. They made it clear that they wanted to bring different skills and expertise on the board. They were already doing a lot with technology that other real-estate companies hadn't done, and that gave us common connection points. The nominating process was quite rigorous, including meetings with a consultant,- and a battery of assessment tests to understand my leadership and decision-making processes."

Those leadership qualities first showed up in her early days.

"Way back in junior high school, I was elected captain of the softball team,- and had to determine which player should be assigned to which position to build a winning team. I found I enjoyed building effective teams. And I was able to put people who weren't always chosen for other teams into roles where they could shine. Of course, I enjoy winning, but I really like winning as a team."

Ingram says that another key to her career success was developing her Spanish-language skills.

"I always dreamed of studying and possibly working overseas in a Spanish-speaking country. I studied the language in junior high and high school and continued to take classes when I was at Stanford. I spent most of my junior year abroad at the Universidad de Salamanca, one of Europe's oldest universities. It was an amazing, life-changing experience for me. It built my confidence that I could thrive in environments far different from the U.S. Years later, during my MBA studies at Kellogg, I returned to Spain for a one-quarter program in Barcelona at IESE Business School." It was there where Ingram first experienced the sense of being seen as a curiosity.

"Out of 108 students, only five were women. One of my classmates with whom I had become friends asked me in all earnestness why I was in an MBA program rather than focusing on getting married."

Years later, as an executive at IBM, she was appointed to lead a business unit of IBM Latin America. "As I moved into the role, a few men told me that I'd face a couple of challenges—being a woman and a person of color.

"Since those are attributes I cannot change, I didn't focus on them. Instead, I concentrated on working with teams on the objectives we had in common— driving the business. My Spanish-language skills were definitely a great asset and made it easier for me to learn conversational Portuguese." Through that Latin American assignment, she developed a large social network, one that she still credits with helping to advance her career.

Ingram says serving on nonprofit boards, including Goodwill Southern California, Big Brothers Big Sisters, and the Los Angeles Urban League, has helped her move onto a corporate board. "That experience was so important and so valuable, particularly regarding fiduciary responsibility and connections."

Ingram wanted to serve on corporate boards, so she took the certification course offered by the National Association of Corporate Directors, a program she highly recommends. To validate her cybersecurity expertise, she studied for and passed the Certified Information Systems Security Professional exam. And she cited that certification prominently on her LinkedIn profile.

"There are no absolutes in this pursuit. Women don't need to have been a CEO to serve on a corporate board. Your board resume is very important, and it should be unique, reflecting who you are. Your LinkedIn profile is more important than you ever thought. Even if you don't care to create a network of contacts through LinkedIn, you must have a profile that's readable and experienced-based, and that shows achievements in your career—and your headshot has to be professional. It's part of your personal brand. Boards and search firms get their first impression of your board readiness through LinkedIn—even when you don't know they are looking at you. If your profile does not show your value to corporate boards, that first impression might be the last."

DANY ST-PIERRE

> **Every woman who wants to serve on boards should make her LinkedIn profile very compelling and complete.**

American women executives seeking their first board seats often look to Europe, where quotas have been in place for several years. But perhaps more women should look to the north for a board seat in Canada, which is much closer than Europe, and traveling there is easier from many U.S. cities. Canada was especially appealing to Dany St-Pierre, who has lived in the U.S. since 1990 but was born in Quebec. She has dual citizenship and speaks English and French.

DANY ST-PIERRE
Chicago, Illinois

Current Boards:
Logistec Corporation
Boralex, Inc.
Women of Renewable Industries and Sustainable
    Energy

Career History:
Cleantech Expansion, LLC: President
Nordex USA, Inc.: VP, Sales
Alstom: Director, Sales
Siemens Corporation: Strategic Marketing Manager; Sales Manager
Bombardier: Director, Global Marketing

Education:
MBA, Université Laval
BBA, Marketing, University of Quebec

St-Pierre says she highly recommends that women reach out to Canadian corporations that are in their industries. She also advises that director compensation is paid in Canadian dollars. "But that's a reasonable trade-off to secure your first publicly held corporate board seat."

St-Pierre actually used LinkedIn to find her first corporate board. She wrote an impressive profile on LinkedIn about her long career in the renewable-energy industry in the Americas, from Canada to Chile, and in Europe.

"I was very intentional about putting together my profile. I made sure to include all the industry buzzwords and fully described my achievements. A headhunter found my profile on LinkedIn when she was developing a list of candidates to present to Boralex, Inc. in Montreal. The company happened to be seeking a woman for its board of directors who had energy-industry knowledge and was familiar with the Canadian and U.S. markets.

"There were some people in my LinkedIn network who were mutual connections with the headhunter, so I received an introductory message asking if I wanted to talk to her. I know this is not the usual pathway to boards. But my story shows that every woman who wants to serve on boards should pay special attention to making her LinkedIn profile very compelling and complete. You never know!"

After the headhunter presented several candidates, St-Pierre was invited for a face-to-face interview with four board members plus the recruiter.

"The fit was great from the start—very comfortable, good chemistry, and it just felt natural. They were really focused on finding a woman in renewable energy."

Several days after the interview, the board sent her a proposal, then she went back to meet with the CEO, with whom she had an immediate rapport. And St-Pierre became the second woman on the board.

Her own company, Cleantech Expansion, advises C-level executives and investors on mergers and acquisitions, projects, and opportunities in the renewable-energy sector. Previously in her leadership roles at Bombardier, Siemens, Alstom, and Nordex, she launched multiple new products and brands, opened new markets in more than seventy-five countries, and built and managed international sales organizations. ("Of course, I felt I had to give up any clients that posed a perceived conflict of interest.")

Before ever starting her board search, St-Pierre had taken important training programs to prepare herself for future board candidacy. First, a simple Google search led her to find the WomenCorporateDirectors (WCD) organization, based in New York, which offered an OnBoard Bootcamp in Chicago. That helped her build up her profile and high-impact statement. Second, she enrolled in an executive-training program at the Université Laval in Quebec City. By the time she joined the Boralex board in May of 2016, she had learned a great deal about corporate governance in the U.S. and Canada.

"The best advice I can offer women is to have curiosity to learn. When you realize you need more training, find every resource possible to educate yourself. Before taking the training programs, I had presented at board meetings, but never was inside the board when decisions were made. So I needed to learn about corporate governance."

At Boralex, St-Pierre serves on the nominating/governance committee, as well as the environmental health and safety committee. This last committee is typically present in energy or construction companies, since technical field labor carries a high level of risk.

"My largest contributions to the board have been in risk assessment, compensation, and governance. I am productive in governance because I keep up with the latest information about board composition. For example, my board did not have rules about tenure when I joined. I helped create the current term-limit policy of fifteen years. I'm also really good at discerning, defining, mitigating, and preventing risk—something I learned in my former corporate career.

"And making a difference for women is a personal cause. Annually, the board reviews the highest-paid positions in the company—which include women officers. I monitor their status and ask questions as needed to make sure they are treated equally and paid what they should be. I know about compensation from my own corporate career. I was always personally ambitious for career advancement, and over time, I managed more and more employees."

According to St-Pierre, board members from the United States bring a different perspective to foreign companies, especially concerning organizational structure and people management—functions that corporations in other countries want to know more about.

"When it comes to insurance, taxation, human resources, marketing, sales, industry knowledge—almost anything really—we Americans have a unique way of looking at business. International companies love that."

When developing their unique selling proposition for board applications for foreign countries, St-Pierre says women need to spell out what differentiates them.

"My sales-and-marketing background in Canada, the U.S., and Europe is truly the added value I bring to Boralex. Canada, with its thirty-five million people, is a relatively small market, so companies that want to grow need to market to other countries, and they would benefit from having directors with successful sales track records in those markets."

As a leader in the renewable-energy industry, St-Pierre has been instrumental in creating opportunities for women to advance in their careers. She has been active since 2005 in the national trade association of the thirty-five-chapter nonprofit Women of Renewable Industries and Sustainable Energy (WRISE); she is now a member of its executive committee and serves as treasurer. St-Pierre has served as president of her local Chicago chapter and continues to actively build the organization.

"The energy business is probably more male-dominated than most. So retention and advancement of women is a huge issue. Our nonprofit WRISE was created to help women navigate their careers in energy. Our annual conference provides direction, tools, and training for women to succeed."

And it's no wonder—since her earliest recollections during childhood, St-Pierre shouldered the responsibility of being the leader. With two younger siblings, she recalls her mother always reminded her to be the example.

"I hear my mother's voice constantly. I do what I say I'm going to do. I always reach my objective—it's just that simple. Thanks, Mom."

GO IMMEDIATELY TO

Chapter 7

7 Traditional or Non-Traditional CAREER

Boards Need

EXPERIENCE —
Both

THERE IS NO SINGLE PATHWAY TO CORPORATE BOARDS. It's the rich fabric of experience a woman weaves together and the leadership she develops throughout her career that lead to a director's seat. Throughout this book, you've read about career pathways that were followed by future women directors in finance, banking/private equity, public service, and academia as well as corporate CEOs and business owners. As young women contemplate which academic fields of study and career choices to pursue, let's look at additional professional tracks that have produced successful women board members.

Operations

Susan Salka and Terry Bayer functioned as the key operational executives in their respective careers, both in healthcare industries. Salka leveraged her finance and accounting skills to become a CEO and built and operated a huge healthcare staffing firm. Bayer served as a chief operating officer (COO) in several established health-related companies. Most often, a corporate COO is a C-suite executive reporting to the CEO, marshaling the company's resources for maximum value and prioritizing customer, employee, and organizational requirements. In the case of both Bayer and Salka, deep experience juggling the myriad details and needs that constitute operating a large company was a key factor in their being selected for corporate board service.

SUSAN SALKA

" *When you sit on the board, you have to think "What are the biggest risks to this company?* "

Susan Salka, CEO, president, and director of AMN Healthcare Services, Inc. in San Diego, started her career in a not-so-glamorous job in Lincoln, Nebraska. How did a woman from a town of a hundred people in the middle of the Sandhills of Nebraska go on to become CEO of a large public company and serve on major boards?

SUSAN SALKA
San Diego, California

Corporate/Select Nonprofit Boards:
AMN Healthcare Services, Inc.
McKesson Corporation
Beckman Coulter, Inc.
Playtex Products, LLC

Career History:
AMN Healthcare Services, Inc.: CEO, President, and Director
Medical Express: President
BioVest Partners: Finance Manager
Hybritech, Inc.: Financial Analyst

Education:
MBA, Finance, San Diego State University
BA, Accounting and Economics, Chadron State College

"After college, I worked for a year as an auditor for the Nebraska Department of Revenue. It was a wonderful first job—I was just happy I could pay my rent! But I always knew there was something more out there."

Not knowing what or where that something would be, Salka packed up her belongings and drove to find warmer weather in California, where she looked for another job while spending nights at the homes of friends.

A San Diego biotechnology company, Hybritech, hired Salka as an entry-level accounting-and-finance analyst. However, the company was acquired by Eli Lilly within the year, and the former CEO and CFO left to start their own venture-capital firm focused on seed capital for biotech start-ups. They asked Salka to join their start-up, BioVest Partners, as finance manager, a sort of early-stage CFO position.

Salka says this was just a fortuitous offer that turned out to be the decision that shaped her future career as an executive and a board member.

"It was an incredible experience, one in which I started really understanding the world of mergers and acquisitions, what it's like to start a company, the role of the board of directors—everything."

While working at BioVest, Salka encountered a nearby staffing company, American Mobile Nurses, which needed help getting its finances together. She soon was offered a job as employee number nineteen, and as its first vice president of finance. She undertook the task of updating the organization from green sheets to a digital accounting system.

"I never dreamed healthcare would be my career, but it became my passion. By working with people to place clinicians and physicians in temporary and permanent positions, and working with their healthcare providers to enable excellent services and care, I realized we were impacting people's lives at the most critical times."

Hers was the kind of passion that she says, "gets in your veins."

By bringing a level of sophistication, business acumen, and scale to the day-to-day operations of the business, Salka and her team grew the company's revenues from $5 million to $2 billion annually.

"It wasn't necessarily that I had the skills or the background. But it was that I wore a lot of hats and was willing to do whatever was needed.

"Everything from doing the manual bookkeeping to showing up at networking events, because showing up and participating *always* inevitably leads to something—even if that something comes five or even ten years later."

From when she joined AMN in 1990, through its sale by the owners in

1997 and ownership by Dallas-based private-investment firm Haas-Wheat in 1999, through its IPO in 2001, Salka experienced firsthand the growing pains and triumphs of a fast-paced company.

Even before her appointment as CEO, Salka was the primary management member in touch with the board—a board that had changed drastically for the better as the company went from private to public.

Only 40% of board searches are handled by executive search firms

Salka interfaced frequently with the board and fostered relationships with the directors. It was Chairman Doug Wheat, sharing Salka's passion and enthusiasm for the mission of AMN, who recommended Salka for her first board position outside AMN. Wheat's private-equity firm, which owned AMN, also had investments in several other companies, including Connecticut-based Playtex, which manufactures feminine products and owns Banana Boat sunscreen.

"There was only one other woman on the Playtex board. Haas-Wheat had the power to nominate directors because of its ownership stake in the business. They wanted someone they could trust, and they wanted a woman. Until then, the board was mainly composed of men discussing how to manufacture and sell feminine products—a supreme irony."

Though Salka had worked with the members of the private board, this was her first appointment to a public corporation's board. She says the key to her success was "knowing when to ask the right questions."

One of the most important questions Salka asked while on the Playtex board was regarding transparency. As a result, the board, and the company, moved toward a more open and transparent communication model—something other board members later thanked her for.

"Though the other directors had been on the board for several years, no one really asked the question. But I was also in a unique position as chair of the audit committee to ask—and get answers."

Chairing the audit committee at Playtex was a particularly high-pressure but equally rewarding position for Salka, and soon the company was sold to Energizer and also went through CEO-succession planning shortly after she joined.

The next board position came via a recruiter for Beckman Coulter, a medical-device company in Orange County, California. The company was seeking a sitting executive of a public company, a woman with prior audit-committee experience.

"It helped that I was in close geographic proximity. I interviewed with the directors and with CEO Scott Beck, and they selected me."

While the Beckman Coulter board was transparent, the company itself was far more complex, with $4 billion in annual revenues and a host of regulatory requirements.

"When you sit on the board, you have to think: 'What are the biggest risks to this company?' For us, it was quality-related issues that could trigger FDA investigations or sanctions."

Another acquisition came a few years after Salka joined the board—Beckman Coulter was bought by Danaher.

On her next board, McKesson—a global healthcare and pharmaceutical-distribution company ranking as Fortune #5 company with nearly $200 billion in revenue—Salk learned that having another woman at the table is very helpful when you're new. At McKesson, her mentors were Marie Knowles and Christine Jacobs (see Christine Jacobs profile, page 191).

"Chris was very attentive to the needs a woman director would have on the board, especially during the first year. Sometimes it's the small things—like Chris called me before my first meeting as I was packing for the trip and said, 'Bring something warm, because the meeting rooms are always freezing.' She and Marie are tremendous executives and always available to give me the history on things."

Serving on the audit and governance committees at McKesson, Salka says a surefire way to make a positive impact with regard to bringing more women on boards is to have more women sit on the nominating committees.

"When women are on the nominating committee, the board becomes more open to considering women outside their immediate circles of friends as potential candidates."

Her best advice for how to acclimate to new board dynamics is to make time for one-on-one meetings with each of the directors. Finding ways to bond outside the boardroom, be it over site visits, cocktails, or shopping, helps inform the perspectives people bring to the boardroom.

"Sure, you can always make excuses not to make the effort—meetings, emails, no time. But to have the best chance to fit into the board dynamics, you just have to *make* time."

When it comes to board chemistry, Salka pinpoints information flow as one of the top priorities. Things like how much data is provided in the board book sent to directors before each meeting, or how frequently members communicate with the chairman and/or CEO, help shape the board dynamics.

Her positive mindset—to show up, be present, do your best—has paid off for Salka throughout her tenure as CEO and board member of public and private companies.

"When there is a tough job, I am the first to say I will do it."

Many years after she joined BioVest, Salka was invited to the CFO's house for dinner, where she finally had the courage to ask why he recruited her in the first place. "Because you've got moxie," he told her.

Salka says her moxie started to emerge in high school, when she was rejected for membership on the cheerleading squad. So she decided to start her own alternative cheerleading team. That type of moxie caused an accountant in Nebraska to drive to California, seeking a dream that led to being CEO and board member of multibillion-dollar public companies.

That type of moxie perhaps not all are born with, but all can learn from Susan Salka.

"When I think about the leaps we've taken as a company at AMN, I see that that's been a theme. We've never followed the industry, always done better, and taken a different, often more challenging, direction. You have to be willing to take those risks, to persevere and achieve what might not be so obvious or easy."

TERRY BAYER

❝ *I always ask: 'How can I add more value?'* ❞

Former chief operating officer of Molina Healthcare, Terry Bayer received her master's degree in public health from the University of California, Berkeley. Her career started at a healthcare clinic in San Jose, where a coworker told her she could "motivate a stone."

TERRY BAYER
Long Beach, California

Corporate Boards:
California Water Service Group (CalWater)
Apria Healthcare Group, Inc.

Career History:
Molina Healthcare, Inc.: COO
AccentCare West: President
Praxis (Sechrist) Clinical Services, Inc.: President and COO
Matria Healthcare, Inc.: EVP
Lincoln National Life Insurance Company: VP and GM
Partners National Health Plans of North Carolina, Inc.: Regional VP
Maxicare Health Plans, Inc.: Regional VP; National Director, Provider
　　Relations
FHP International Corporation: Associate Director of Operations

Education:
JD, Stanford University
MPH, University of California, Berkeley
BS, Communications, Northwestern University

"I call it my persuasive capability. I've always been very committed to making sure the people around me grow and flourish individually and as a team."

Inherently energetic, positive, and persuasive, Bayer has climbed the ladder to the executive rung and been named to several corporate board seats along the way.

Bayer's path to her first public board, Apria Healthcare, began long before she realized she wanted to be a director. Through business connections, she met a woman from the senior management team at Apria, a healthcare company that provides oxygen and home care for chronically ill, homebound patients.

"We seemed to click on a personal and professional level. It was a business situation in which we had to work closely together. That's why she remembered me when the Apria board began a search."

Bayer says she thinks it was this woman who brought her name up for the search team to consider.

"The chairman of the Apria board also happened to be an investor at a company where I had worked previously. I don't think he put my name forward, but when it was suggested, he endorsed my candidacy because he knew my work.

"My best advice is to be your strongest professional self and recognize that at all times, you are interacting with people who may one day simply suggest your name for a board search. When I joined Apria, I wasn't looking for a board seat. It was just a natural consequence."

Bayer joined the Apria board in 2006 alongside Mahvash Yazdi, then the chief information officer for Southern California Edison. With her extensive background in the highly regulated healthcare industry, Bayer was well suited to sit on the compliance and compensation committees.

"I was a subject matter expert, but I also brought the perspective of being a customer, because my employer was one of Apria's customers." Bayer also understood the importance of demonstrating value in a company reliant on revenue from a government healthcare program.

Bayer left the Apria board in 2008, when home oxygen and healthcare providers were under market pressures, and Apria reverted to a private company. All existing directors resigned, allowing the investors to create a new board. Bayer's time at Apria was valuable, however. In the boardroom, she met and worked with many very experienced board members and executives who taught her transferable skills in the realm of board leadership and good governance.

Additionally, Bayer completed the Director Training and Certification Program at the UCLA Anderson School of Management, and she later attended the Stanford Law School Directors' College.

"Having the director certification has really helped me in the course of my board career. It's not a mandatory requirement for joining a board, but I recommend that women take some course or certification. It's a useful credential that provides really great insight into the many obligations, fiduciary and more, that come with a board seat."

Bayer's most important takeaway from the UCLA course was the importance of confidence.

"You have to be confident enough to speak your mind in the boardroom. You can't hold back. If you don't agree with something that is being said, you have to speak your mind."

Bayer joined the board of California Water Service Group in 2015.

"They called me at just the right time—when I had an interest in joining another board but wasn't actively looking. My name surfaced for the firm conducting the search for CalWater. CalWater was specifically looking for a woman with operations experience who worked in a regulated industry."

The CEO of Molina encouraged Bayer to join the CalWater board.

"It is essential to have a very supportive boss. He told me I would gain experience from being on an outside board and bring back value to our company."

As a sitting COO, Bayer was careful to use paid time off when she traveled to attend board meetings.

"When you're new on the board, being vocal can be a little awkward until you become acclimated. It's best not to talk for the sake of hearing yourself talk. I already knew this group was collegial, however. So when a dynamic compensation issue arose, I felt comfortable telling the compensation committee that while I understood the rationale behind the decision, we had to be aware of how that decision might be viewed by management. I stated that I believed management would agree with me."

This, Bayer says, is called "optics"—looking at things from the perspective of public reputation as well as internal equity.

Part of the reason Bayer felt so comfortable speaking up at CalWater is her due diligence prior to joining the board. From socializing with existing board members at various lunches, dinners, and business meetings, Bayer was able to get a good understanding of the board dynamics before accepting the position.

"The best advice I can give is that you have to like your fellow board members and feel comfortable. If your gut tells you otherwise, trust it. When you're the right candidate, it's as much about the board deciding that you are a fit as it is about you feeling that way."

Utilities are highly regulated, like the healthcare industry. Though Bayer worked outside the water industry, she brought the perspective of a C-suite executive of a publicly traded company to the board.

"Frequently, boards are composed of retired individuals heavy on finance and audit. I bring a current perspective on everything from operating issues, employee issues, and compensation and benefits, to succession planning and organization structure.

"There's enough commonality but also enough difference. I also bring a certain amount of humility, willingness to learn, and eagerness to contribute. I always ask: 'How can I add more value? What more can I learn?'"

Part of Bayer's education about the water utility industry has included visiting plants, meeting with construction workers, and learning how wells are utilized.

At CalWater, Bayer serves on the organization and compensation, nominating/governance, and audit committees. She has supported change by working closely with the head of human resources on health benefits renewals.

"At Molina, we were beneficiaries of the Affordable Care Act, from the expanded Medicaid program. Since I have health insurance and employee benefits in my background, as a board member, I was able to team up with CalWater HR on health insurance changes.

"Most companies are spending so much on employee healthcare today, anyone who understands health benefits or the selection and administration of health benefits is of value to the executive team."

Bayer has benefitted from the mentorship and guidance of other women directors such as Bonnie Hill. At CalWater, Bayer was the third woman to join the board, alongside Hill and Linda Meier.

"When I joined the CalWater board and met Bonnie and Linda, both women directors became mentors who taught me how to bring value by speaking from my own experience.

"I've learned that if you can take a message and translate it for a variety of audiences, such an ability to communicate is a huge part of leadership. If you're able to see the world through someone else's eyes, you're able to mobilize them. The boardroom is not that different. With ten directors, there are ten different worldviews—you have to have the insight to meet people where they are without judgment."

Bayer says her path to corporate boards has been paved by a certain amount of luck and serendipity. However, she advises that if a director position is a woman's goal, start by saying it out loud:

"I intend to be on a public board in the next three to five years.

"Cultivate your relationships. As soon as you hear someone say they're on a corporate board, ask that person if he or she would be willing to recommend your name the next time they look for a board member. Be intentional, be focused, and you can get there."

Expertise in the Digital World

Too many board members who have served for decades on corporate boards do not have the digital expertise and knowledge to advise a company on navigating today's ways of doing business. In many cases, long-term board members lack even basic computer skills; some still have their assistants print their emails so they can read them on paper. They don't use social media, and although they may understand the power of a "tweet" because they read today's headlines, they would have no idea about the different characteristics of Facebook, Instagram, Twitter, and myriad platforms that can affect their companies.

Today corporate boards must have at least one director with the expertise to help guide their companies in maximizing digital technology and managing digital challenges. For example, long-seated board members may not be comfortable with the technology that has completely altered financial transactions in the companies they serve. While older board members are still carrying their checkbooks, Millennials are immersed in seamless mobile payment systems like Venmo, Zelle, Google Wallet, or Apple Pay in business and in their everyday lives. This is an opportunity for Millennial women candidates to be considered as potential "digital directors" because they not only have career experience in this critical marketing arena, they also have an inherent facility with digital tools.

If you have digital expertise, use it as your calling card. Your digital knowledge is the primary value-add you would bring to the board. In your networking conversations, lead with this important asset and discuss how you have helped a client or your own company rise above the competition by engaging digital technology for strategic solutions.

The transition to digital e-commerce has upended traditional customer interactions. We have already read about digital marketing experts like Shellye Archambeau, Susan Thronson, and Cynthia Cleveland, whose work has helped position companies for customer growth. Leslie Ireland, Barbara Faulkenberry, and Linda Hudson are experts on the threats that digital technology in the wrong hands can impose on companies (See Chapter 4).

With the volatility and dynamic changes of the modern digital world, technology and digital experts like Dr. Cheemin Bo-Linn and Liane Pelletier truly make a difference on boards. They became visible and respected for their careers in the digital sector. Bo-Linn studied information systems and orchestrated a career trajectory in that sector that led her to corporate boards. Pelletier studied economics and management before segueing to technology and communications. Both women cut their teeth in digital communications, and now help boards grapple with the challenging technological issues of today.

CHEEMIN BO-LINN

Credibility and performance will outshine any doubt about why you are on the board.

Dr. Cheemin Bo-Linn is the personification of what boards today call a "digital director"—the business leader who understands how technology, especially newer digital technology, changes everything about industry dynamics, from disrupting business models to creating new competitors and increasing market risks.

CHEEMIN BO-LINN
San Jose, California

Corporate Boards:
BMC Stock Holdings, Inc.
Sphere 3D
SNOMED International
EvenaMed
Violin Memory, Inc.
NetLine Corporation
TechAmerica / AeA (American Electronics Association)

Career History:
Peritus Partners, Inc.: President and CEO
IBM: VP, Electronics, Consumer, Technology, and Industrial Sectors
NetLine Corporation: CMO; Chief Revenue Officer

Education:
JEdD, Computer-based Management Information Systems and Organizational Change, University of Houston
Executive Program, Graduate School of Business, Stanford University

Digital directors have experience in leveraging technology to improve operational costs, gain insight, and provide the digital experience consumers demand. Bo-Linn's digital transformation leadership is key to how a board views its company's business strategy when impacted by digital forces such as mobile, e-commerce, data analytics, social networks, and cybersecurity. Her additional background in finance, operations, and marketing is a plus. This unique combination of skills and experience led to Bo-Linn's quick recruitment to her first two public company boards, her chairmanship of two public company audit committees, and her appointments to private boards.

From partner at a major mergers-and-acquisitions investment firm to vice president at IBM and chief marketing officer and chief revenue officer at a leading mobile applications and marketing company, Bo-Linn has leveraged her doctorate in computer-based information systems, analysis, and organizational change to navigate her way toward corporate boards. As president and CEO of Peritus Partners, Inc., Bo-Linn has directed a global business consultancy with back-end data analytics software that helps small- to mid-cap companies improve their valuation, leading up to next-level growth or an initial public offering (IPO) or acquisition.

For Bo-Linn's board leadership, she was named to the 2018 Directors to Watch list in *Directors & Boards Magazine.* Further recognized as a thought leader, Bo-Linn was inducted into the Women in Technology International Hall of Fame and celebrated as one of the organization's Top 100 CEO Leaders in STEM. She gained visibility by speaking at the United Nations on global growth, at the Dow Jones Global Compliance Symposium on future risks and resiliency, and as the keynote speaker at CIO and cybersecurity conferences. At top financial services (UBS, Barclays) and private-equity conferences, she shares her views on digital transformation and cutting-edge technologies. She is also visiting professor of digital transformation and analytics at the Executive MBA and MBA Asia Program, held jointly by the London Business School, Hong Kong University, and Columbia University. After speaking at a private-equity conference, she was asked to join the board of Evena Medical, a privately held, Northern California-based "smart" consumer-wearable, digital-imaging company in the medical field.

Bo-Linn's advice to all women executives is to perform at the highest level in an executive role.

"It's because of that visibility that board opportunities will surface. Executive search firms follow trade media, and board members ask their industry networks, so when you're recognized or honored, you may end up on their radar."

That's also how she secured her first two public company board seats at Violin Memory, a data storage- solution company, and Sphere 3D, a software company. Both companies deliver solutions facilitated by the growth of digital applications. The Violin Memory chairman of the board called her directly, even though she did not know anyone on the board. The board wanted a technology veteran with a strong financial services background, who was SEC-qualified, to chair the audit committee and bring more digital expertise. Through her previous operating vice president roles at top Fortune 500 companies, she had developed a reputation for building winning business and financial strategies and was responsible for multibillion-dollar profit-and-loss statements. She also brought hands-on marketing experience as a CMO, and in digital technology, operations, and finance—a rare combination of skill sets.

It wasn't merely past experience that cemented Bo-Linn as a strong candidate, but also good chemistry with the board.

"You get to the door because you have all the outstanding qualifications and experience. But you get through the door because there's good chemistry between you and the other board members."

Over her tenure on several boards, she has been asked to chair audit committees and has served on all major board committees, including compensation, nominations, governance, and risk.

Besides conducting self-assessments, yearly evaluations by the complete board are essential to measure the impact of individual contributions and the board's overall effectiveness. Bo-Linn considers four key elements for board evaluations:

- Ask questions that are thoughtful, but not disruptive. "Boards benefit from members who can listen, internalize, and come up with a broad range of questions to help filter through a plan of action, and having a diverse board brings different perspectives."

- Take a strategic approach. "Bringing up a pre-mortem perspective is helpful. Everyone can learn from a post-mortem, but thoughtful discussions can improve the strategy and risk oversight."
- Be collaborative. "When issues arise, we discuss amongst us directors, the bigger market-disruptor picture and its impact. Working as a team, our collective view is better than a siloed approach."
- Be innovative. "With management, we discuss how we can increase shareholder value and accelerate customer acquisition and loyalty while protecting the brand from cyber threats."

These elements are also key ingredients to strong leadership and an effective board.

"As board members, we also have to look at enterprise risk at all times. Cybersecurity is a huge issue right now."

With her digital technology and cybersecurity background, boards have asked her to also focus on cyber, since it's important to companies and all directors.

"Innovation and leadership bring imagination to reality—a winning combination. Being an Asian American woman with an unusual name, I have had to back up my innovation and operations knowledge with my own personal brand of courage. When I take on challenging situations, I remember that above all, credibility and performance will outshine any doubt about why you are on the board."

LIANE PELLETIER

" Strong boards are essential. We all understand that when we read certain headlines and ask, 'Where was the board?' "

After a long and successful career in telecommunications as a senior vice president at Sprint and later as chairman, president, and chief executive officer of Alaska Communications, Liane Pelletier has made her next career full-time corporate board work, currently serving as director on the boards of Expeditors International and ATN International, both companies with operations that span the globe. Her career moves took her to the furthest corners of the United States, and Pelletier wouldn't have it any other way.

LIANE PELLETIER
Bellevue, Washington

Corporate/Select Nonprofit Boards:
Frontdoor, Inc.
Expeditors International of Washington, Inc.
ATN International, Inc.
Alaska Communications
Icicle Seafoods, Inc.
Washington Federal
WJ Communications, Inc.

Career History:
Alaska Communications: President, CEO, and Chair of the Board
Sprint Corporation: SVP, Strategic Planning and Corporate
  Development
Touche Ross & Co. (now Deloitte)

Education:
MS, Management, MIT Sloan School of Management
BA, Economics, Wellesley College

"I did both my undergraduate and graduate degrees in Boston at Wellesley and MIT. Boston is where I really grew into my own, and if I hadn't kicked myself out, I would have stayed there my entire life. There's nothing wrong with that, but I truly have a hunger for challenge and an adventurous spirit. I wanted to experience, live, and work in different parts of the country."

Pelletier first moved halfway across the country, to Dallas after graduate school to take a consulting role. Then after two years, she followed her instincts to accept a role at what was then a huge "industry-disrupter" brand in the rapidly evolving telecommunications industry. "That meant relocating to Kansas City to work at Sprint HQ, where they recruited 'athletes' rather than industry veterans."

It was at Sprint where Pelletier's spark of leadership burst into a powerful blaze. She was working in product management, where all of her work and the work of her colleagues was "backed up" in IT, since the firm was struggling with its back-office infrastructure and facing a major overhaul of its billing system. Spotting an opportunity to help work on something nearly existential, she temporarily left product management to advise the IT development team so she could meet product managers' future needs with new information systems.

"I always took on extra assignments, from early on while in school, and also at work, on top of my day job. At Sprint, that habit was probably why I was named to the inaugural Leadership Challenge Program. The CEO and the other top senior executives in the corporation invested in young talent who seemed promising for the long term. The Challenge was on-the-job training in leadership, and I was attached to the president of the Sprint Long Distance Division, Ron LeMay, as his executive assistant. He is well-known as a work-dominated guy, so that meant a seven-day-a-week assignment for me. He was (and still is) an amazing mentor—not because he spoon-fed me a darn thing, but because he was unbelievably generous with his time and let me ask him a million questions. I wanted to learn how, why, and what he did as a division president and member of the executive committee. The two years I was his executive assistant translated to about ten years of development for me."

Pelletier's next promotion was to vice president, where she started and led a customer-retention unit. "We were losing far too many customers, and my job was to figure out how to stem the tide. I came to appreciate my stress-management strengths—how to stay composed while facing uncertainty and pressure, and to help lift non-productive pressures off others who need to stay focused on tasks."

After rotating through another two executive roles, she ultimately moved to Sprint corporate headquarters as the SVP of corporate strategy and business development. Suddenly she was a peer, sitting next to her mentor and former boss, both now reporting to the CEO and chairman. This role gave her tremendous insight into the mindset of a CEO and chairman, and notably, exposure to the board. She made frequent presentations to Sprint directors about the industry landscape, competition, possible mergers-and-acquisitions moves, and essential business strategies.

These rapidly earned leadership experiences, combined with an appetite for challenge, made her the ideal candidate for a first-time CEO role at a company that needed fresh eyes and focused work in both strategy and execution. "In early 2003, Alaska Communications Systems was searching for a CEO, and I fit the specifications perfectly." Pelletier took about six months to make her final decision, so board members of the Alaska company would fly through Kansas City to engage in long conversations with her until they convinced her to make the move.

"Moving that far away was difficult to wrap my head around, but I was compelled by the challenge. I thought I could make the company better. I was not married, I had no one else to worry about, and my adventurous spirit kicked in. At that point, I had been in the telecom industry seventeen years. I knew how the industry makes money, I knew the technology, and I knew the national regulations. What I didn't yet know— the employees, customers, and market in Alaska. I thought that would be fascinating to learn and hoped I could bring fresh ideas to the state."

> It is **essential** to have both an insatiable appetite to learn and the strength that comes from lifelong learning. **With both, you have the confidence to meet all challenges head-on**

"Finally, when we negotiated a five-year commitment, the contract showed only the CEO role, while the incumbent I would replace held both CEO and chairman titles. I was hauling myself to Alaska for at least five years, so I wanted to put every possible measure in place to make this board and company successful. I needed to hold both roles, and I was able to convince them."

As both CEO and chair, Pelletier worked with the board to identify or recruit an independent lead director who would liaise with her when she could not be in the room. "I knew about board dynamics and knew a lead director would be a healthy addition, especially because I anticipated major overhauls of strategy, operations, and even the board composition." The board chose new member Annette Jacobs, who lived in Seattle, to be lead director. Jacobs had two decades of operational experience in telecom and would be the second woman on the board.

Pelletier stayed two-and-a-half years beyond her five-year contract in order to manage her own succession, so that she could return to the "lower-forty-eight" states. She wanted her next career phase to be serving on corporate boards. Just stating that goal opened up her first opportunity, even while still CEO and chairman of Alaska Communications Systems. One of the early investors had witnessed her in action and thought she could bring value to a first-time CEO of a firm in their investment portfolio. He invited her to join the board of Icicle Seafoods in Seattle. "It is important to focus on where you add value when joining a private-equity-backed firm. Since the investor/owners are in the room, they don't need you to focus on them. The value I brought was my experience as a former CEO, knowing operations and board governance."

Pelletier wanted to stay in the Northwest, where her cravings for outdoor adventure were easily satisfied. Once in Seattle, she left no stone unturned when it came to networking to find another board. She called on her contacts from across the country, asking for email introductions to leaders in Seattle, and set out each day that first summer in 2011 with nothing but "coffee meetings" on her agenda. She worked her networks at director events held by the National Association of Corporate Directors (NACD), KPMG, Deloitte, and others, and followed up with every contact made.

At a KPMG function, she happened to meet a director on the board of Expeditors International, and that ultimately led to her becoming the first woman on that global logistics board.

Where to make a difference? "In my opinion, the nominating/governance committee is a wonderful place to sit and serve. You have to be clear on the corporate strategy, since that shapes your nominations work for succession planning. And while potential nominees must add valued experience, they must also be culturally coherent. The governance side keeps looking toward the horizon and contemplates actions that could help the corporation well before external pressures come bearing down. Strong boards are essential. I think we all understand that when we read certain headlines and ask, 'Where was the board?'"

When it comes to board chemistry, Pelletier advises walking into the first few meetings with your emotional quotient (EQ) levels turned up, always observing other board members' body language and reactions.

"It can be helpful to find a buddy to help interpret the scene early on. I think boards expect 'early returns' on your role, but it is important to know the culture in the room before you offer your contributions."

Pelletier has never been one to shy away from a challenge.

"The more I challenge myself, the more I justify the continuous learning I want to do. I may be a geek. But in today's boardroom, it is essential to have both an insatiable appetite to learn and the strength that comes from lifelong learning. With both, you have the confidence to meet all challenges head-on."

STEM Fields (Science, Technology, Engineering and Mathematics)

Women scientists, engineers, and mathematicians have an excellent chance to parlay their knowledge and achievements into board service. More and more women with STEM careers, previously considered the domain of men only, are sought after for boards. There's a certain comfort level for many men talking to women who understand engineering or math—they use the same lingo. Thankfully, from kindergarten through college, girls and young women are now consistently encouraged to pursue their interests in science, technology, engineering, and math. The opportunities available to women educated in STEM fields are seemingly endless.

608 total board seats were **gained by women** in Russell 3000 companies in 2018

Barbara Barrett and Linda Rosenstock, M.D. built careers in the sciences and have ultimately made a difference on their corporate boards. Barrett began with a math degree that evolved into an impressive career in aeronautics and aviation. Rosenstock began her career in internal medicine and found that her expertise was sought by government and academic institutions, and her knowledge plus her vast experience led her to seats on corporate boards.

BARBARA M. BARRETT

*"Success derives from being attentive to the talent around
the table."*

From losing her father when she was just thirteen years old and having to
support her mother and five siblings, to qualifying to go to the International
Space Station, Barbara Barrett has accomplished seemingly impossible feats
throughout her life and professional career. Today, she's chair of The Aerospace
Corporation and a board member at the California Institute of Technology, RAND
Corporation, and the Smithsonian Institution.

Barrett experienced the first sparks of leadership as a young child. "Ironically,
disadvantages may have their advantages. A benefit derives from figuring out
how to overcome hurdles and move forward despite adversity."

This must-do attitude led Barrett to a long and impressive career as a respected
board member on more than fifty corporate and nonprofit boards, as well as
such personal successes as climbing Mt. Kilimanjaro, cycling across Finland, and
operating one of the world's foremost luxury ranch lodges. Her love of horses
is a carryover from her childhood, when she managed the family farm upon her
father's death in support of her mother, brothers, and sisters. "It's amazing what
people can do if they simply have to get it done."

Barrett began her board career in the nonprofit sector by serving on local
boards including the Red Cross, Big Sisters, and hospitals. She was appointed
to her first corporate board through a professional friend who knew of her
legal and aviation background. It was the board of a portfolio company that
was emerging from bankruptcy with a contentious relationship between its
investment house and its creditors. Barrett added value from the outset as an
objective, respected third-party intermediary who amicably and profitably could
resolve disagreements. "I was the arbiter of peace in a gentleman's war. In
the end, the company became profitable, all debts were paid, investors were
rewarded, and their product enriched users' lives."

In addition to her law degree and government experience, Barrett also has
a background in aviation. She earned her pilot license instrument rating from

Lufthansa, the German airline that trains its new pilots in the bright, clear skies over her home state of Arizona. Later, she earned her certification to go to space at Russia's Gagarin Cosmonaut Training Center outside Moscow, which catapults her profile to extraordinary.

BARBARA M. BARRETT
Paradise Valley, Arizona

Corporate/Select Nonprofit Boards:
The Aerospace Corporation, Chairman
California Institute of Technology (Caltech)
RAND Corporation
Smithsonian Institution
Horatio Alger Association of Distinguished
    Americans, Inc.
Albert and Mary Lasker Foundation
Raytheon Company
Valley National Bank of Arizona, Founding Chairman
Piper Aircraft, Inc.
Mayo Clinic
Exponent, Inc.
The Space Foundation
Hershey Trust Company

Career History:
Thunderbird School of Global Management, Arizona State University:
    Interim President
U.S. Ambassador to Finland
Harvard University: Fellow
American Management Association: President and CEO
Federal Aviation Administration: Deputy Administrator
U.S. Civil Aeronautics Board: Vice Chair
U.S. Mission to the United Nations: Senior Advisor
Triple Creek Ranch: CEO

Education:
Honorary doctorates: Arizona State University, Thunderbird School
    of Global Management; Embry-Riddle Aeronautical University;
    University of South Carolina; Pepperdine University; Finlandia
    University
JD, Arizona State University
MPA, Arizona State University
BA, Mathematics, Political Science, Arizona State University

Barrett acknowledges that her board positions comprise a diverse set of companies—from Raytheon, Aerospace, and Piper, to Valley National Bank, Mayo Clinic, and the American Management Association. "Because I had experience that many leaders respect—flying and training for space travel—I was welcomed into the boardroom. My pilot credentials and flying experience were unusual and set me apart from the crowd. Any candidate would benefit from having a respected credential that is memorable."

While a memorable credential or relevant experience may help land a coveted board seat, Barrett says women must have the basics to do the job of corporate governance: an understanding of governance principles, the courage to ask questions and challenge presumptions, a collegial demeanor, the ability to run a meeting, and an inquiring, strategic mind. She has chaired every committee on her boards, including executive, compensation, nominating and governance, strategic planning, corporate responsibility, and quality assurance.

"You don't need any particular background or credential to serve on a demanding board and run meetings effectively. Instead, success derives from being attentive to the talent around the table, keeping discussion on topics germane to the agreed agenda, moving the agenda along, and engaging diverse opinions to fashion the best solutions. You can learn these skills anywhere: at your corporate job, on nonprofit boards, or even in family meetings."

She points out that running a meeting well requires thoughtful preparation, a tightly focused agenda, assignment of responsibilities, focus on outcomes, and respect for the time of each participant. When it comes to effective meetings, Barrett stresses the importance of participants approaching challenges with a bona fide intent to fashion a mutually agreeable solution.

In preparing for board or committee meetings, Barrett advises that every board member has the responsibilities to prepare by reading the distributed materials, know the business, and participate with thoughtful questions and comments. Barrett's handy checklist for an effective meeting has four key elements; the chairman should ensure that each participant in any meeting:

- Gives something
- Gets something
- Learns something
- Has fun

"I prefer board or committee members who bring diverse talents and perspectives to the table. If other factors are equal, diverse perspectives usually enrich a board's or committee's success and produce better results."

Part of Barrett's own diverse professional experience was a formative internship with the Arizona State Senate, where she observed future Supreme Court Justice Sandra Day O'Connor.

"I watched how effectively Justice O'Connor got things done, and I attempted to emulate her practices. Still today, on both big boards and small, I apply lessons I learned from Justice O'Connor's handling of divergent opinions and group dynamics."

In 1994, Barrett ran for governor of Arizona. Though she didn't win the election, she attributes some of her subsequent professional roles to the experience and visibility she gained during her campaign.

Barrett confirms that her successful working relationships led to her election as a director on business boards. Her global business, military, nonprofit, government, and personal experience set the stage for her appointment as U.S. Ambassador to Finland. She is also vice chairman of the Jet Propulsion Laboratory committee at Caltech.

When Barrett looks back on her philosophy of life, she reflects with a chuckle on the famous military advisor and author of The Principles of War, Carl von Clausewitz, who suggested that, "No plan survives the first contact with the enemy."

"No plan I could have envisioned would have included a tenth of the roles in my life. My corporate board service has been especially fulfilling. I take profound comfort knowing that I have contributed to the leadership and success of vital global enterprises through board work."

LINDA ROSENSTOCK, MD

❝ *I love being able to participate in the evolution of a company.* ❞

From doctor to director to dean, Dr. Linda Rosenstock has played an integral part in shaping American public health policy since she graduated with dual degrees in medicine and public health from Johns Hopkins University. As of the spring of 2018, she became chair of the board of TS03 (a publicly traded Canadian medical-technology company) and serves on the board of Community

Psychiatry (a privately held physician-practice company), but her board career began many years ago, when she joined her first corporate board, PacifiCare.

LINDA ROSENSTOCK, MD
Los Angeles, California

Corporate/Select Nonprofit Boards:
SCAN Health Plan
TS03, Inc.
Community Psychiatry
EngenderHealth, Inc.
The Wild Center
Guided Therapeutics, Inc.
Skilled Healthcare Group, Inc.
PacifiCare Health Systems, LLC (now UnitedHealth Group, Inc.)

Career History:
UCLA: Professor, Health Policy and Management, Medicine, and
    Environmental Health Sciences
UCLA: Dean, UCLA Fielding School of Public Health
National Institute for Occupational Safety and Health: Director

Education:
Fellow, Robert Wood Johnson Clinical Scholar, University of
    Washington
MD, Johns Hopkins University
MPH, Johns Hopkins University
BA, Psychology, Brandeis University

Rosenstock's knack for leadership emerged when she became one of only three full-time women professors of medicine in a department of several hundred faculty at the University of Washington (UW), Seattle.

"After I finished my internal medicine residency, I joined the faculty at UW and founded a clinic in occupational medicine, offering for the first time there academic expertise in diagnosing and treating work-related disorders. A start-up of this type in medicine is unusual—offering a new clinical program that is also engaged in research and training—and it gave me the opportunity to work with hospital and medical-school leaders with whom I had to rationalize the new investment by explaining not just the need to treat this underserved population (workers) but also to assure that it could be economically viable.

"The clinic and the related research and teaching programs that came out of it became a success and brought me further responsibilities at UW. In some sense, as one of the few senior academic women, I was called on more often than my male peers, but I was also presented with opportunities I may not have had otherwise."

Those opportunities led to Rosenstock's appointment during the Clinton administration as director of the National Institute for Occupational Safety and Health in Washington, D.C. She remains in awe of how much can get accomplished at the national level, having led the agency's significant growth in scope, responsibilities, and budget, including creating an award-winning public and private partnership, the National Occupational Research Agenda. She left D.C. for Los Angeles to become dean of the UCLA School of Public Health in 2000. During her tenure as dean, Rosenstock received a call from an executive search firm about a board search for PacifiCare, the healthcare insurance provider that was acquired by UnitedHealth Group in 2005.

"I'd spent a long time working in academia and government, and it never occurred to me that I might want to sit on a corporate board. I didn't really know what that meant. But I appreciate new opportunities and challenges, so I did my due diligence and went through the interview process."

Soon, Rosenstock found herself in a search for a new woman director to fill the "woman's seat" on the board. In this case, there were two woman finalists being considered to fill the slot of a previous female director who had retired—Rosenstock and the former administrator of the Small Business Administration, Aida Alvarez, the first Hispanic woman to serve in the U.S. Cabinet.

"Both of us impressed the board search committee as well as the CEO, so rather than choosing just one woman to fill the seat, they took both of us. It was a great way to replace a retiring woman director by adding two women to the board."

Rosenstock and Alvarez (see the Aida Alvarez story on page 188) brought with them diverse perspectives to the Orange County, California-based company. Part of what made this first foray into the world of corporate boards an invaluable learning experience for Rosenstock was the fortuitous timing.

"I was less than three years into my board tenure—having experienced one of the steepest learning curves of my professional life—when the acquisition of PacifiCare by UnitedHealth was finalized."

As a physician, Rosenstock brought a much-sought-after perspective to boards and their committees. Several years after her PacifiCare experience, she joined the board of a long-term care company, Skilled Healthcare.

"At Skilled Healthcare, I was the first and only woman on the board, and the only physician until our acquisition five years later by the much larger Genesis HealthCare."

During her time on the board, the company expanded its reach into home and hospice centers, providing more opportunities to build upon leadership and mergers-and-acquisitions skills. Her clinical background and past service on PacifiCare's governance committee helped position her to chair the company's compliance, governance, nominating, and quality committees. During her tenure, "quality" assumed a much more prominent role in committee and full-board discussions.

Serving on the nominating committee, Rosenstock helped lay the groundwork for adding more women to the board, until yet another successful acquisition cut those plans short.

"I seem to have a knack for being part of big exits."

Rosenstock continued to focus on her duties as dean of the UCLA School of Public Health, and at doing what she does best: advocating for public-health reform. With the advent of the Affordable Care Act, she was appointed as chair of the preventive-services-for-women committee, which identified gaps in women's preventive services. After she stepped down from her position as dean in 2012, she continued as a full-time faculty member, primarily in the health policy and management department. Soon after, she was approached by a colleague and friend from Seattle, now an investor in a publicly traded company, Guided Therapeutics, to consider serving on that company's board.

Guided Therapeutics is a biomedical device company that focuses on developing technology for early-stage screening and detection of cervical cancer.

"My investor friend knew I'd been working in preventive services for women. I was very impressed with the technology—and also with the potential for the company to sell in parts of the world that don't have the capacity or ability to properly diagnose one of the leading causes of death in women of reproductive age." She served on the GT board for five years and learned much about global regulatory and sales issues facing medical-device companies.

These cumulative board experiences positioned her well when she was considered for a board seat on a Canadian-based publicly traded company board, TS03 Inc. The company is engaged in global sales of its FDA-approved medical sterilization processes for heat-sensitive medical devices. Rosenstock says she was excited to join the board in early 2017, and then, a year later, she was honored to be named chair, a rarity for women directors in Canada—just as it is in the U.S.

"I love being able to participate in the evolution of a company from its research-and-development origins to commercialization, and to see increasing global sales addressing one of the most difficult challenges in infection control: making it safe to reuse complex instruments, such as those used in GI endoscopy."

At about the same time, Rosenstock joined the board of California-based SCAN Health, a Medicare advantage plan serving hundreds of thousands of seniors.

"In many ways, it is the perfect hybrid between corporate and not-for-profit boards. The company has significant revenues of nearly $3 billion annually, but 501C3 status, so we directors have the responsibility of assuring the financial health of this complex, highly regulated entity and can also enjoy the opportunity to invest 'profits' back into overall community benefit. In some sense, this is the perfect double bottom line."

Rosenstock serves on the board of the privately held company Community Psychiatry, a California-based psychiatric group practice, one of the largest—if not *the* largest—independent practices of its kind in the U.S. This opportunity came about from a networking activity at a national healthcare conference. A brief but memorable meeting with a private-equity investor produced the opportunity, over a year later, for Rosenstock to enter the board of Community Psychiatry.

From government to nonprofits to private and public companies, Dr. Rosenstock has impacted the American healthcare system by making a measured and informed stand against the status quo. Leveraging her positions on various committees and boards, she's come up with smart solutions for difficult problems.

"Coming from nonprofits, I always had to worry about money and take the financial health of the organization seriously. When I transitioned to corporate boards, I brought my well-honed sense of fiduciary responsibility. One of my proudest moments at Skilled was using data to show that investing more in our workforce, who were often low-wage female workers, could improve our quality of services, our bottom line, and thus, our shareholder value.

"I still value equally highly the contributions I can make to my work for nonprofits, whether as chair of the executive committee of EngenderHealth, an organization that provides reproductive-health services to women in some of the poorest countries in the world, or as a trustee of The Wild Center, a highly innovative regional natural-history museum centered in the Adirondacks in upstate New York, where our family has a summer home."

While being a physician was not always critical to her role on corporate boards, Rosenstock says she was pleased to contribute her perspective when called for.

"As someone with decades of medical experience, I brought firsthand knowledge about providers in various healthcare settings, from the clinic to the hospital."

Attorneys

To be "value-added" to corporate boards, attorneys must bring specialized business experience that the company needs to best serve its shareholders—in areas such as real estate, banking, technology, intellectual property, government service, or mergers and acquisitions. It is often challenging for attorneys to be selected for corporate boards because CEOs pay millions for the services of large legal firms and typically do not want advice and counsel from an attorney on the board. Until they retire from their firms, attorneys usually are restricted from serving on corporate boards, due to potential conflicts of interest with other clients of the firm.

However, a corporate general counsel (GC) has a good chance of being considered for a board seat because she has direct involvement with business transactions and growth strategies. Because GCs are required to attend and support the board meetings of their own companies, they have valuable "prior board experience" that law firm partners generally don't. Likewise, the corporate secretaries of companies are often attorneys who attend every corporate board meeting of their employer. As board candidates, they bring valuable experience about governance as well as legal expertise to an outside board.

Kathleen Brown, Connie Collingsworth, and Christine Garvey each optimized their legal backgrounds to achieve success in business. These three attorneys became attractive to corporate boards due to their specialty areas and legal expertise as well as their strategic connections.

Collingsworth notes that internal general counsels are qualified C-suite executives who often may not get noticed for boards, but they possess the skills and experience to help boards be successful.

Understanding the value that legal expertise can bring to a corporate board, the American Bar Association launched a program specifically for women attorneys who aspire to board seats. That program was spun off as an independent organization called DirectWomen, based in Chicago, and provides board training programs in New York, Chicago, Houston, and other cities specifically for women general counsels and managing partners of law firms. DirectWomen also stages the annual Sandra Day O'Connor Awards Gala in New York to honor outstanding women attorneys who have become corporate board directors.

KATHLEEN BROWN

❝ You may have disagreements or opposing views, but if you treat people with respect, you will gain a reputation for integrity and knowledge. ❞

Kathleen Brown is a well-known name in California. Elected as state treasurer in 1990, she was the Democratic candidate for governor of California in 1992, an election she lost to the incumbent Governor Pete Wilson, who was the former U.S. senator from California. As state treasurer of California, Brown was responsible for managing California's multibillion-dollar budget, debt issuance, and cash management. She also served as trustee for two state pension funds, CalSTRS and CalPERS.

KATHLEEN BROWN
Los Angeles, California

Corporate Boards:
Sempra Energy
Stifel Financial Corp.
Renew Financial Group, LLC
Five Point Holdings, LLC
Forestar Group, Inc.
Countrywide Financial Corp.

Career History:
Manatt, Phelps & Phillips, LLC: Partner
Goldman Sachs: Head, Public Sector and Infrastructure Group, West Coast
Bank of America Corporation: President, Private Bank
State of California: Treasurer
City of Los Angeles Board of Public Works: Commissioner
O'Melveny & Myers, LLP
Los Angeles Unified School District Board of Education: Board Member

Education:
JD, Fordham University School of Law
BA, History, Stanford University

Public service forged the first half of her career. That should come as no surprise, since she is the daughter of the legendary Governor Edmund G. "Pat" Brown Sr., who was the chief executive of the state from 1959 to 1967, and her brother, Jerry Brown, served two terms as California's governor, from 1975 to 1983 and from 2011 to 2019.

Brown has served on several corporate boards, including Sempra Energy (the holding company for both Southern California Gas Company and San Diego Gas and Electric), Five Point Holdings (which went public in 2017), Stifel Financial Corp., and Renew Financial, which is privately held. She previously served on the boards of Forestar Group, Inc. and Countrywide Financial Corp.

After thirteen years working at Goldman Sachs, and a stint in Chicago as chair of Midwest Investment Banking, Brown wanted to come home to family in Los Angeles and to serve on the board of Sempra. She says she "flunked retirement" after six months and joined the respected law firm of Manatt, Phelps & Phillips, LLP. To avoid conflicts of interest, Manatt does not do business with any boards on which Brown serves. To protect all partners and the firm from conflicts, Manatt has a robust review process to analyze, approve, or disallow work for related businesses.

"It's in the conflicts and intake system to automatically review business opportunities, which would trigger certain actions if there may be a conflict. The general counsel would be called in to review any client that doesn't pass such conflicts review. This is true anywhere—at Goldman, or investment banks, they always review potential conflicts to make sure partners are not working with competitors or vendors and remain in compliance with various independence rules."

Sempra is the largest board Brown has served—a Fortune 500 company with a market cap of $30 billion. She was recommended by someone who knew her, who also was aware that Sempra was looking for a new board member who was familiar with California government, political, and regulatory environments.

The Sempra CEO first made overtures to Brown in 2007 when she was at Goldman Sachs. She says she was flattered, and admired the company, but she could not accept due to time constraints and potential conflicts of interest. The chair of the nominating and governance committee and the retiring CEO, who became chairman, both stayed in touch with her. Knowing she would retire someday from Goldman, Brown asked her contacts to keep her in mind for future openings. And they did.

"Coming from a political career is generally considered a negative when attempting to serve on corporate boards, since most boards believe politicians lack the business operations experience needed and are not considered a good 'cultural fit.' Elected politicians, especially Democrats, have even greater difficulty getting on corporate boards. Republicans are considered more business-friendly, so they have an easier time. It's often harder for Democratic women to get on boards. It's helpful if you are appointed to a major federal regulatory commission, especially if it's the SEC, which would be very attractive experience, or the FTC or Department of Transportation.

"Jane Garvey, the first woman to head the Federal Aviation Administration (FAA), is a great example of a woman in the world of politics who transitioned successfully—she has served on the United Airlines board and is chair, North America, for Meridiam, a global infrastructure fund. And there's Alana Peters, who was on the SEC and later served on several major Fortune 50 boards."

Brown brings a unique sensitivity to the dynamics of operating in a regulated environment by being keenly aware of the ripple effects decisions may have upon an organization and all the potential stakeholders.

"For public companies, in addition to my eighteen years of private-sector experiences in the financial services industry, I bring a heightened awareness of the reactions of shareholders, community and political leaders, and government regulators. Honed from my life in public service, I bring insights about public and government reaction to corporate events that others might not be aware of."

At Sempra, she serves on the environment, health, and technology committees as well as nominating and governance. She serves on the rights/governance committee at Stifel. And at Five Points, Brown chairs the conflicts committee, as well as serving on the audit committee.

During the Sempra board interviews, the issue was raised about her being the sister of the governor of California and knowing friends on the Public Utilities Commission and in the state legislature. Another long-term Sempra board member, Lynn Schenk, had served in Jerry Brown's first cabinet as the first woman secretary of business, transportation, and housing.

Kathleen Brown's long and independent career was the most important factor. She made it clear that she would have no dealings with the Public Utilities Commission and would not lobby the state administration on any matters related to Sempra.

"It is critically important to spell out the ground rules for any person considering any board position. Potential conflicts of interest must be discussed and cleared in advance."

CONNIE COLLINGSWORTH

66 As longer-tenured board members hit term and age limits, there is increasing attention and pressure to nominate more women to fill the vacancies. 99

Connie Collingsworth is the chief business operations officer at the Bill & Melinda Gates Foundation, based in Seattle, and she serves on the boards of Premera Blue Cross and the Banner Corporation. That's a long way from Nebraska, where she grew up in a close-knit family with three brothers.

CONNIE COLLINGSWORTH
Seattle, Washington

Corporate/Select Nonprofit Boards:
Banner Corporation
Premera Blue Cross
Attenex Corporation
Women's World Banking
Social Venture Partners
French American School of Puget Sound

Career History:
Bill & Melinda Gates Foundation: CBOO and CLO
K&L Gates, LLP (formerly Preston Gates & Ellis): Partner

Education:
LLM, International Business Legal Studies, University of Exeter, England
JD, University of Nebraska College of Law
BA, English, Andrews University

"From an early age, I was driven to speak up and ask questions. I am decisive, enjoy management, and do not shy away from the responsibilities of leadership. With a reputation for creative problem solving, I am not easily intimidated—these are attributes that have contributed to professional success in arenas that have traditionally been male dominated, including corporate boardrooms."

In her legal career, Collingsworth was often the lead lawyer on merger and acquisition deals, as well as the lead negotiator representing venture-capital firms investing in burgeoning startups during the dotcom boom.

"I found the dotcom era discouraging as I observed money being thrown around by venture capitalists who were primarily motivated to get rich or richer. When the position of general counsel was created at the Bill & Melinda Gates Foundation, I did not hesitate to apply for the role. I realized it offered an opportunity to do challenging, innovative work, while at the same time making a meaningful contribution to its mission, which is having amazing, long-term positive impact on the world."

Collingsworth got the job, becoming the foundation's first and only lawyer (at the time, that is). After growing the award-winning legal department to thirty-two employees, she was promoted to the role of chief business operations officer for the world's largest foundation, one with more than $45 billion in assets. She manages 250 employees and is responsible for information technology, grants and contracts services, global security, business design, and change management, as well as legal.

Collingsworth is a member of the foundation's executive leadership team and is also responsible for organizing the trustees' meetings for Bill and Melinda Gates and Warren Buffett. She advises the Gates Foundation on a range of critical issues including governance, risk management, intellectual property, strategic alliances, and international compliance. She explains that these responsibilities provide valuable insights for her board work and believes general counsels are a pool of qualified C-suite executives (those who report to the CEO) who are often overlooked by boards striving to diversify, both from a gender as well as talent perspective.

"The definition of a 'qualified' board candidate used to be limited to sitting or former CEOs." Not any more. Given the limited number of CEOs who are women, Collingsworth points out that boards need to expand their traditional approach to identifying qualified female candidates. The American Bar Association spun off a program called DirectWomen to educate and encourage female attorneys about serving on corporate boards.

DirectWomen helped Collingsworth develop a board profile that emphasizes the executive and strategic roles she has played and also stressed the importance of letting others know of her interest in serving on a board. She attributes intentionality as a key ingredient to her success in securing positions on corporate boards.

"I was proactive in networking with people, including those serving on boards, former law partners and business clients, as well as corporate headhunters, making them aware I was interested and qualified to serve on a corporate board."

As a result of actively seeking out and renewing connections with such individuals, Collingsworth was offered and accepted board seats at two corporations in the same month—Banner Corporation, a publicly traded corporation that is the holding company of Banner Bank, with more than $10 billion in assets; and Premera Blue Cross, the leading healthcare insurance company in the Northwest, with over two million members.

Her expertise in mergers and acquisitions was a skill set Banner had identified as important experience to add to the board, as it was planning to expand through acquisitions. Since joining the Banner board, the company has closed four transactions, including a merger with American West that doubled the size of the company to $10 billion.

As a result of another merger, the board grew to seventeen board members, but for a time, Collingsworth was the only woman. The board soon acknowledged the need to diversify, both in the traditional sense, as well as relative to skill sets, and she was asked to take on the role as chair of the governance/nominating committee to lead this effort. A specific priority was to identify potential board candidates with technology and cybersecurity expertise.

"Corporate boards are traditionally filled through networking activities. The challenge is that retired businessmen who have long board tenure are often not in the best position to identify new and diverse talent."

Relying on networking with intention, Collingsworth identified a Haitian American woman in her forties with deep technology background as a strong board candidate; she was selected. Additionally, through her involvement in the International Women's Forum, an international organization for executive women, Collingsworth was introduced to a former executive of the Federal Reserve Bank, who was recruited to join the Banner board to add regulatory expertise and insights.

Similarly, the Premera board was eager to further diversify, as well as add a board member with financial expertise. By actively participating in forums such as DirectWomen and WomenCorporateDirectors, Collingsworth was introduced to, and able to recommend, a female CFO who was added as a director on the Premera board.

"These examples are why I am optimistic that progress is and will continue to be made in diversifying boards. As women get onto corporate boards, they are in a position to suggest other qualified women, making incremental progress."

At Premera, Collingsworth joined the audit and governance committees and was appointed chair of the compensation committee. Although she did not have previous expertise with either the healthcare or banking industries, Collingsworth believes her background as a corporate lawyer and as general counsel has been valuable in positioning her to evaluate regulatory, risk management, governance, and compensation issues.

The expansion of her role at the Gates Foundation to include management of the IT department, as well as assuming responsibility for crisis management, further increased the insights she offers as a board member.

"I find my corporate board experience helps me become a more well-rounded executive in my day job, contributing positively to my strategic thinking as an executive at the Gates Foundation. For example, Premera suffered a cybersecurity attack a few years ago. The experience offered a unique opportunity for me to learn many best practices firsthand that I directly applied to protecting the foundation from potential cyber threats."

Serving on boards allows women directors to make a difference in numerous respects, and Collingsworth has clearly made a difference on both her boards. In addition to recruiting diverse, talented executives, she has also implemented annual board evaluations and expanded the director training program at Banner. She has shown she is willing to ask probing questions in an appropriate way as part of fulfilling the fiduciary obligations of a board member.

Collingsworth is serious about championing the cause of helping women succeed not only on corporate boards, but also in management and in the workforce generally. From her vantage point as board member, she has been a mentor and coach to many women employees who aspire to move up the corporate ladder.

As she reflects on her upbringing, she attributes being told she could do anything she set out to accomplish, as well as growing up around her brothers and their friends, to be some of the reasons she has confidence in her ability to make meaningful contributions.

"Whether it is advising the largest foundation in the world or sitting alongside sixteen men in a corporate boardroom, I can hold my own. And that's what I advise women—don't worry about being outnumbered. You are there for your value-added experience, and they need you."

CHRISTINE GARVEY

> *I spent a lot of time individually with each board director, getting to understand their point of view—that's simply part of collegiality.*

Lawyer and real estate executive Christine Garvey has a full-time career as director of the boards of Center Trust, Maguire Properties, HCP, Toll Brothers, and MUFG Americas Holdings Corporation. Inspired by her late father, who was also a lawyer, Garvey became one of the first one hundred women practicing law in the state of Vermont.

But even though she was successful with cases ranging from real estate law to women's abuse, Garvey soon realized she did not enjoy her legal career. So she scheduled a lunch meeting with an old high-school friend who was working at First Interstate Bank.

"I made my intentions very clear: I didn't want to practice law anymore. When you have a clear request, others are very willing to help. That's how I got started at First Interstate, which was acquired by Wells Fargo."

After ascending the ranks at Wells Fargo, thanks to the guidance of then-Chair David Petrone, Garvey was recommended for her first board. When the Los Angeles-based real estate holdings company Catellus Development Corporation was seeking to fill an open board seat, Petrone recommended Garvey.

"The first board is the springboard—it's the hardest to achieve. Most often, it happens when someone who knows, likes, and respects you recommends you. It's because that person has seen you in action and trusts your opinions and judgment. I was fortunate to have worked under David at Wells Fargo and greatly appreciated his recommending me for the Catellus board. Throughout my career, I am grateful for meeting so many people who were instrumental in my future career."

Once on the Catellus board, Garvey was deliberate in building relationships with the other directors.

"I believe it is imperative to do the background work outside of the boardroom, so that when the board is in session, no one is surprised or caught off guard. I spent a lot of time individually with each board director, getting to understand their point of view—that's simply part of collegiality."

CHRISTINE GARVEY
Santa Barbara, California

Corporate/Select Nonprofit Boards:
Montecito Bank & Trust
Center Trust, Inc.
Maguire Properties, Inc.
HCP, Inc.
Toll Brothers, Inc.
MUFG Americas Holdings Corporation
ProLogis, Inc.
Hilton Worldwide Holdings, Inc.
Union Bank of California
Pacific Gulf Properties, Inc.
Catellus Development Corporation
Immaculate Heart High School and Middle School
Sansum Clinic
Public Square Partners

Career History:
Deutsche Bank AG: Global Head, Corporate Real Estate Services
Bank of America National Trust & Savings Association: Group EVP
Cisco Systems, Inc.: VP, Worldwide Real Estate and Workplace Resources
Security Pacific Bank: SVP, OREO Division
Wells Fargo Bank: SVP, Corporate Real Estate
First Interstate BancSystem: Real Estate Portfolio Manager

Education:
JD, Suffolk University Law School
BA, Immaculate Heart College

As one of few women working in banking and serving on a board at the time, Garvey found common ground with her peers outside of the boardroom. "I played golf with my dad when I was younger and played tennis throughout high school and college. Being a team player is very important and helpful because that is part of board culture. You spend a lot of time with the guys on the board, so I wanted everyone to feel comfortable. Athletics brought us together."

The relationships Garvey developed at Catellus were key to later board opportunities. Fellow Catellus director Richard Farman asked her to join the Union Bank of California board. And another Catellus director, Steve Bollenbach, later asked her to join the Hilton Corporation board. Nelson Rising, who was CEO of Catellus during Garvey's tenure, connected her with Maguire Partners, who would eventually bring her onto its board as well.

"My backgrounds in both real estate and banking were my value-added experience, and Nelson was also an advocate for bringing more women onto the board and into senior-level positions."

About her early sparks of leadership, Garvey recalls attending Immaculate Heart, an all-girls Catholic high school in Los Angeles. Years after her graduation, she volunteered on its board and currently chairs the finance committee of the private school.

"There's a lot to be said for attending an all-girls school. There are no distractions, so developing and practicing leadership is encouraged. Expressing your point of view is applauded. That's what gave me a head start to conquer the challenges I would face in my career."

So where has she made a difference on corporate real-estate boards? Garvey's strong background in finance and law makes her the ideal candidate for audit committees.

"I've been on so many audit committees I can barely keep track. I chaired audit at ProLogis and HCP and served on the committee at Toll Brothers. Audit is a critically important position because you are dealing with the numbers of the company. All numbers are public and highly scrutinized, so you really get a sense of the operations and company status by being on audit."

Garvey says she has most enjoyed being chair of the risk committee. "At Union Bank, we were actually one of the first bank boards that instituted a risk committee. All banks deal with many risks. Whether it is cybersecurity, credit risk, operational or reputational risk, all risk assessments go through our committee.

I considered being chair of the risk committee a very important opportunity."

At Maguire, Garvey chairs the compensation committee. "Compensation can be difficult, considering you have outside forces that evaluate how your compensation practices measure up against total shareholder return. Just before I joined, there had been a proxy fight, and all existing board members were asked to resign. I came on as part of the new board."

When it comes to difficult situations, Garvey says women often have the best opinions, but they may not be heard because they are in the minority.

"I have observed that women are more apt to take lonelier positions. However, when women challenge the male majority on the board, their opinions are not always welcome." She recommends that every board be composed of at least 40% diverse directors to ensure that all opinions are equally weighed and considered.

"Being on a board is still difficult for women, but I believe as opportunities grow, and more boards advocate for diverse candidates, the next generation of women will make an even greater difference in numbers and influence."

GO IMMEDIATELY
TO

Chapter 8

8 AND NOW It's All

Up to You!

Be intentional. Be purposeful. Make *the* difference. Now it's time to launch your own campaign. You have gained important knowledge from impressive women corporate directors who have made *the* significant difference to the corporations each of them serves. Because you are highly capable and determined, harness your resources and leverage your own value-added experience to win the board seat where you will do the most good.

Plan and prepare for this future role as early as possible in your career. Gain industry visibility along with nonprofit board experience. Be intentional and focused on *how* to strategically add to your experience and strengthen the skills and qualities that will bring specific value to boards. From here forward, this is your ultimate career goal. You will practice talking about corporate boards and reinforce your X-factor—your value-added strengths that make you unique.

Two new approaches to filling board seats make this the perfect time for your expertise to shine. First, consider that, historically, CEOs have wanted other CEOs on their boards to benefit from the counsel of those who have been—or still are—at the top of their own companies. Logically, a CEO believes that another CEO knows what it's like to be the sole person at the apex of the corporate structure. But logical as that may seem, it's old-school thinking. No outside CEO can or should know everything an inside CEO needs today. A modern CEO must build a team of board members who bring specialized expertise and leadership strengths to govern the company. Today's CEO relies on those specialists and their various functions and perspectives. The CEO cannot possibly know everything that they need to know. A modern CEO depends on the fact that people who are making a difference in their own companies will help make the difference for his or her company as board members.

Next, keep in mind another important factor: the number of CEOs available to serve on outside boards is limited now since their own company boards (and shareholders) restrict CEOs from serving on more than one or two outside boards. In decades past, as recently as five years ago, some CEOs were serving on four or five boards, which left little time to focus on their own companies. The good news: fewer CEOs filling board seats translates to more opportunities for women like you who bring functional expertise as well as diversity of thought to the boardroom.

Answer the Question: Why Does a Board Need You?

Ask yourself the essential question: "What's the difference I can make on the board(s) I'm targeting?" Be ready to purposefully communicate a definitive answer about your expertise and that board seat could be yours.

We've talked about the value-added C-suite experience that CEOs and boards are looking for. Identify the areas in which you excel and determine where your experience fits the needs of the boards you would like to pursue. Think beyond the basic skill sets that have defined your traditional job description. Think instead about vision, strategy, and your leadership track record.

Stay current about disruption happening in your industry. Your knowledge, background, and experience will be even more useful to a corporate board that is undergoing dynamic shifts in its consumer base or product line. Everyone remembers the business-changing shifts from in-person to digital banking, brick-and-mortar stores to online shopping, taxis to Uber and Lyft. The world of commerce and consumers continues to undergo constant—and often disastrous—disruption. Boards of directors feel the pressure to stay ahead of business issues and potential crises, so you should, too—long before you become a board member.

Boards are often doing "board self-evaluations" these days to analyze important gaps where their current directors don't have the experience necessary to keep up with changing times. Often, individual directors are afraid to speak up about it—afraid of losing their seats. You have the opportunity to be a hero by convincing a board that you bring specific knowledge and expertise that will enhance the wisdom that already exists. At networking events, let directors know what specific key components you bring to the table that are necessary for any board to stay up-to-date and anticipate future growth, innovations, and challenges.

Which of the following experience categories will you bring—or develop in the near future—to become an asset to any board you serve? In which functions have you excelled and demonstrated achievements that relate to your target boards? Start thinking about these areas and others where you have (or can develop) a specialty:

- **Technology**
  Cybersecurity
  Robotics and artificial intelligence (AI)
- **Global**
  Regulatory compliance
  Compensation, benefits, and other human resource issues
  Capital markets
  Solid contacts in foreign countries where you have been based
- **Investments**
  Risk management
  Mergers and acquisitions (M&A)
  Turnaround experience
  Real estate and REITS
  Securities
- **Financial**
  Audit committee service on other boards
  Accounting
  Banking
- **Business**
  Governance

Operations
Legal specialization
Competitive turnarounds
- **Marketing**
  Digital marketing
  Social media
- **Government Affairs**
  Advocacy
  Federal/state contracting
  Environment

California Corporate Boards **must add 1,060** seats for Women Directors **by year-end 2021**

Create High-Impact Sound Bites That Focus On Your Achievements

Once you have identified your areas of expertise, develop three or four specific, concise phrases that articulate your achievements. (Write a script for your own personal use—keep it in your purse, on an index card, or in your smartphone.) I call these "High-Impact Sound Bites," and you will use them in conversations at cocktail parties, business meetings, or social gatherings. These sound bites are the essence of what you say about yourself—a way to toot your own horn, without bragging. Your sound bites will be the foundation for some of the most important interactions you will have during your search for the perfect board.

These conversations can happen at a moment's notice, so be prepared. Commit your High-Impact Sound Bites to memory. You will call upon these points in business meetings, while networking at industry events, during keynote speaking opportunities, and when you are talking with your corporate director friends over coffee to ask for their feedback on your profile. Use your sound bites in short exchanges whenever you need to talk about yourself, so that people will remember you.

Your High-Impact Sound Bites must be ingrained in your brain, ready to use whenever you need to impress an influential person about your immediate qualifications for board consideration. I can't reiterate this enough.

To create your sound bites, first of all, consider your achievements throughout your career—your key success stories that produced specific results. Organize these achievements into a succinct and short list of two or three bullet points.

Sound bites have the highest impact when they are short, to the point, and very specific.

Include specific data and dollars. Numbers have more impact and will be recalled more often in conversation than flowery adjectives, which in the end add up to meaningless, throwaway lines that are a waste of time. As an example, if you say you are a senior executive at "A large, successful retail company," no one will remember. Instead, state clearly and substantively: "I have finance and technology experience with (name of company), a $600 million-dollar retail company that grew by 42%, where I led a team of two hundred people to achieve strategic growth." When you include dollars and hard data, your sound bites command the attention of the person you are talking to. You are going to be remembered for these accomplishments. Use data that is relevant and indicates stature or growth: the size of your industry, the size of your own company, revenues, number of employees, geographic reach (even small companies can be global), the size of the budgets you have managed, or your best achievement in terms of financial growth or success.

Your High-Impact Sound Bites should include no more than *five* points. Here's the conversation starter that states your goal clearly and immediately captures attention:

I intend to serve on my first public corporate board in eighteen months (or two or three years). I am seeking the ideal board in the _____ industry where I would add value because:

1) I am a seasoned veteran in the _____ industry at a _____ (annual revenue) company where I have worked for ____(number) years.

2) My prior board experience comes from serving in the _____ (public, private, advisory, commissions, university, or nonprofit) sector, where I made presentations to boards, so I am very knowledgeable about board procedures and dynamics.

3) I am immediately qualified to serve on the _____(Audit, Compensation or Nominating/Governance) committee because of my experience and specialization in _____(cybersecurity, digital, compensation, real estate, M&A, operations, etc. Additionally, for CFOs and qualified finance professionals, add that you are a "financial expert" as defined by the SEC) saying "I can bring that valuable experience directly to a board in your industry."

4) My career achievement that I'm most proud of is _____(leading growth, increasing value, managing a significant crisis—try to put these in dollar terms. Other career achievements could be leading the team on mergers or acquisitions, risk management, digital accomplishments, or achieving global employment increases related to revenue generation or strategic growth.)

5) Close the conversation anecdotally—such as "Today, public company boards are looking for women directors. This is because of new developments I'm sure you are aware of, but isn't it interesting that (use any of the following examples)…

   • California passed a new law requiring all California-based public companies to have at least one woman director on their boards by year-end 2019, and total of three by year-end 2021.
   • There is a growing demand for women directors over the next few years as Baby Boomer directors reach the retirement age of seventy-five.
   • Shareholders are clamoring for more women directors because research shows corporations with women on their boards are more profitable and productive than companies with all-male boards.

Your High-Impact Sound Bites should end with a memorable and personal request along these lines:

So, Bob, when your friends call you to ask if you know any well-qualified women candidates, please remember me. Remember that *(say it once more)* I could immediately serve on the (Compensation, Audit/Finance or Nominating/Governance) committee of the board. I welcome your advice and counsel when you have a moment. May I email you my board profile?

Your Linkedin Presence Makes Your First Impression

Many women are surprised to learn how critically important their LinkedIn profiles are. Search firms and nominating committees look at LinkedIn profiles as soon as they hear about a potential woman candidate, or are intrigued by her High-Impact Sounds Bites when they meet her. They will refer to LinkedIn to see how she presents herself, not how many connections she has. However, they may check to see if people they know are among your connections. We discussed this in Chapter 6, but I want to emphasize again how important

LinkedIn is to your board pursuit. Diana Ingram (read about Diana in Chapter 6) tells how her LinkedIn profile helped her land a corporate board seat.

The sound bites that you have created about yourself should be amplified in your LinkedIn profile. Focus on statistics, numbers, dollars, and hard data to underscore your specific accomplishments.

Nominating chairs searching LinkedIn are going to use several keywords that you should employ to lift your name to the top of the list: *Director*, *President*, *Chief Executive Officer*, *Vice President*. Users will also be probing for the areas that boards focus on, so emphasize your knowledge and experience in these key areas. List the associations and nonprofit board organizations that you belong to. Clicking down deeper into these organizations can provide pathways for a reader to see that you are connected to other colleagues or professionals that he or she knows who can attest to your qualifications and cultural fit for that board.

Do not overlook or underestimate important elements of your profile. An appropriate and professionally taken photograph (headshot) is an absolute must for both your LinkedIn profile and your board profile. This is not the time or place for cute casual shots with fluffy pets or wearing sundresses in picturesque vacation backgrounds. Hire a professional to take your business portrait specifically for your LinkedIn and your biographic profiles. There are many resources you can access by looking online for "Professional Corporate Headshots." Expect to spend at least $300 for a quality photographer, who will give you multiple poses and retouch the photo to your specifications. Even if you like doing your own makeup and hair, you should definitely consider hiring professionals to help you look your best for your photo shoot. Your headshot and how you present yourself are taken into consideration when search firms or other hiring professionals decide whether to reach out to you.

Just as LinkedIn is an invaluable tool, other social media platforms can have a negative effect on your pursuit of a corporate board seat. If you have been an active participant on social media, be aware that your posts, opinions, pictures, and responses are live and accessible for anyone who wants to learn more about you. If your posts on Facebook, Instagram, or other platforms reflect poorly on you, they diminish your image as a competent professional. You should remove them sooner, rather than later.

Your Board Profile: It's Different From Your Resume or Bio

Now that you are confident of your conversational sound bites and have built your LinkedIn profile to give you maximum advantage, it is important that your Board Profile is up to date and impactful. An effective Board Profile is separate and distinct from your professional resume. Your Board Profile highlights your areas of strength that boards are looking for. The profile should be no more than two pages if possible; keep it to the point. Highlight your most significant achievements with data and numbers and include your prior board experience, the list of companies where you were employed, and the range of years you worked at each company. The purpose is not to restate your resume, but to emphasize your key achievements in terms of leadership, vision, and growth strategies that can add value to a board. It should be easy for the recipient to read quickly and understand the most salient points.

Note your director experience and committee experience from past nonprofit boards or associations: Do you qualify as a "financial expert" per SEC rules, ready to serve on an audit committee? What other strengths would you bring to specific committees? This is where your governance experience with nonprofits, associations, or commissions should be clearly defined in a special section.

Use data and numbers to highlight your background; if the organization you served experienced growth, define it with statistics. Don't hesitate to highlight challenges or crises that your previous board may have encountered. Were you involved in handling or managing those crises? Define how your involvement positively impacted the outcomes.

Highlight your general reputation in the business community. You can point to favorable media coverage, industry awards, and speaking engagements, noting the size of the audience or the stature of the organization. If you have robust relationships with business and industry leaders, these are also important to highlight.

Be prepared to adjust your profile as needed for a specific board you have targeted. Make note of your connections and relationships with other directors and with members of the executive team. Make sure that there are no conflicts of interest. There are clear independence requirements that must be met if you have a specific board in mind. You must establish that you are not a former officer of that board's company, nor an employee of that company in the last five years. You must have no current material relationships with the company. You cannot have immediate family members related to officers or staff of the company, and the company may not use a contractor if you have earned income from that business, currently or in the past.

Guidelines for Writing YOUR Corporate Board Profile include:

1. Your value-added experience (key words) that captures your unique qualifications for target public corporations: Bullet your related experience (e.g., IT, M&A, HR, Cybersecurity, Finance, Digital Marketing) or career knowledge that boards need. Do you qualify as "financial expert" for an audit committee? Do you have compensation experience? Are you fluent or conversational in other languages?

2. Previous corporate board or large nonprofit board experience: What committees have you chaired in the past? Or, do you staff a board committee currently? Indicate growth. Did you gain crisis management experience? How much did you improve revenue? How many people served on the board?

3. Visibility in your industry or the general business community: List your media coverage, major speaking engagements, and industry awards.

4. It's not necessary to include references, but be mindful of the business and industry references that you can call upon to help. Networks count! Whom do you know on outside corporate boards? Do you know directors on your target boards? What other directors might endorse you with their connections? Be prepared to discuss these in person.

5. OPTIONAL CONSIDERATION: Perhaps include something personal that you have in common with board members: Golf? Hobbies? Other sports?

Corporate Board Profile Worksheet

NAME
(City of Residence)
Company name (and stock symbol) where you work

> Your professional headshot

Value-Added Experience for Corporate Boards

These are your conversational sound bites, now created as a written version for your Board Profile. Again, include revenues, size of gains in terms of dollars or percentage growth, and key statistics. The purpose is not to restate your resume, but to highlight your key experience in the areas of leadership, vision, and growth strategies.

The following are samples to select from. No profile will include all. Boards want specific expertise, for example:

- Works closely with the CEO and Board of Directors at ____ (name of company), a $___ (size) global corporation that _____ (explain what the business does). Reports directly to the CEO.
- Finance Experience, P&L Responsibility, M&A, and Divestitures: Leads a $____(million or billion) division, with ____employees (number), in ____countries (number).
- Digital Director: Strategic leadership of the company's online presence, including social media and content orchestration
- Executive Compensation: Supports the Board's Personnel and Compensation Committee on executive compensation and benefits, including compensation disclosure and analysis and "say on pay" voting; administrative responsibility for stock options, restricted stock, and other executive incentive plans; as plan administrative committee member, oversees defined benefit pension, and more.
- Regulatory, Environmental, Health and Safety Risk and Sustainability: Experience leading environmental and health and safety programs and managing compliance with federal EPA and other environmental agency

regulations, federal acquisition regulations, contracting, and compliance. Possesses U.S. Government security clearance.

- International Trade Compliance Expert and Frequent Speaker: Leads trade compliance programs for businesses in the United States, Canada, United Kingdom, Western and Northern Europe, and China; interactions with State Department and Commerce Department.
- Cybersecurity Experience: Familiar with intrusion detection and prevention and personnel awareness training, including interaction with government agencies regarding advanced persistent threats and investigations.
- Intellectual Property: Oversees intellectual property portfolio; responsible for patent and trademark prosecutions; unique cost-discipline approach to sale, licensing, or abandonment for cost containment or strategic growth opportunities.
- Global Human Resources: Leads human resources function; works closely with the board's compensation committee; workplace culture; legal responsibility for ensuring compliance with employment laws worldwide; negotiates with ___unions (number).
- Audit Experience: Supports the audit committee of the board of ____ (name of company) and served on ___previous boards (number).
- Global Business Knowledge: Leads business and product development and manufacturing in other countries, including China, Hong Kong, Brazil, Canada, Denmark, France, Germany, Mexico, and the United Kingdom.

Board Training:
- Board Training Programs at _____ (names of universities or professional associations)
- 2020 Women on Boards "Get on Board!" Workshops on _____ (dates)
- WomenCorporateDirectors (WCD) member; attended Global Conference in _____ (year)
- National Association of Corporate Directors (NACD) member, attended annual summit in Washington, D.C.

Career Chronology

Current Company (list company where you work or company you own with stock symbol. Include location, size of revenues, number of employees, and how many countries the company is located in	XXXX-Present

Previous Company (same info as above)	Year to Year
Previous Company (same info as above)	Year to Year
Previous Company (same info as above)	Year to Year

Education:

University.....MBA (list field of study)	Year of Degree
University.....BA (list major and minor)	Year of Degree

Build Your Board-Smart Networking Chart

Now you are going to put your High-Impact Sound Bites to work. Your LinkedIn Profile is accessible and you have your Board Profile ready. You are about to ramp up your networking skills into high gear. "Networking" may sound casual and non-essential—but believe me, networking has been the key to success in my career and to the careers of many successful women I know. I talked about the importance of networking in Chapter 6, and here I want to dive into the how-tos of successful networking. In pursuit of a seat on a corporate board, your networking must become very strategic and involve planning, precision, and both short- and long-term goals.

Take a look at our Board-Smart Networking Chart below. It is designed to help you focus with discipline on the people you already know—the contacts you currently have—to maximize those relationships and to ask these people to introduce you to people they know who might lead you to a board opportunity. Women who found their first board on their own have told me that they developed spreadsheets to track their networking progress, updated notes as they met and talked with contacts, and then added notes when they followed up.

Using our Board-Smart Networking Chart, write the names of the top twenty-five contacts you have made over your long and successful career. Identify influential people and relationships that you have cultivated. These should be the people who can best support your efforts to find a seat on your first board. There are four categories: your friends, your professional contacts, corporate leaders, and corporate board members you may know. Those are your Tier One contacts. Let these colleagues know that you are actively pursuing a seat on a board, and when you are in conversation, vocalize your High Impact Sound Bites. Ask for their feedback.

What feedback are you looking for? You want your colleagues to give you advice on your top three bullet points about the experience that you would bring to a board. Ask for their opinions: will your conversation points represent your value-added experience to a board's nominating chair? If they say no, how do your colleagues think you could talk about your experience to be more compelling and unforgettable? Ask their opinions about how your Board Profile presents your experience in writing. Are there any words you should change—or add—that would be more meaningful to the nominating committee? Then talk about the types of boards you have researched that are of interest to you. Be ready to talk about your realistic target list of companies—not the Fortune 500, but companies in the lower half of the Russell 3000 that have only one or zero women directors currently. Ask your colleagues for their opinions again: "Which of those firms do you think I am best suited for? Can you suggest other companies that might be of interest to me?" (To learn which corporations have none or only one woman director, go to the 2020 Women on Boards website 2020WOB.com, click on the Gender Diversity Directory, and filter for state, industry sector, and Ranking of "T" (for Transforming, meaning there's one woman) and "Z" (for Zero women).

During these first conversations with your Tier One contacts, ask them to introduce you to their contacts—the people *they* know—who will become your Tier Two contacts. These are the people who will broaden your network further by introducing you to their contacts, which become your Tier Three contacts. You get the picture.

I encourage you to develop your own Board-Smart Chart with the discipline and focus you would employ for a homework assignment. Fill in the blanks and add names, ideas, and contacts as you go. Keep detailed notes and update your follow-up spreadsheet as you develop your outreach. Writing names in this chart is an exercise that can reap huge dividends as you see your network of influential contacts grow. These are the people who will most likely lead you to your first board seat.

Keep this chart alongside your personal calendar and use it to systematically book coffee or lunch dates with the contacts you add. Be diligent, intentional, and bold in reaching out. This is not the time to be hesitant or modest. Schedule activities or events where you interact with contacts that you might have previously forgotten about. For example, if you met a person who was a speaker at an industry event or know that a person you worked with five years ago might today serve on a corporate board, definitely reach out to that person to meet up over coffee, or ask the person to review your board profile by email. Even if he or she says they don't have time right how, you have re-established a contact and can ask them again for their advice in the near future. Your goal is to help them remember you.

Be Strategic About Identifying Your Target Boards

This next exercise will help you identify ten or fifteen target companies that might be most appropriate for you as a potential board member. First, go to the website 2020WOB.com to see the Gender Diversity Directory. As you've read, 2020 Women on Boards analyzes extensive research every year to list every company in the Russell 3000 and cites how many women are on each board of directors. For your purposes, search for the "Z" companies to find those in your state or industry with no women directors. When you find one or several that you know of in your industry, check out the company website to see whom you might know on the board.

Based on this information, think about the type of company where you feel you would bring the most value and could make the biggest difference. In what sectors are you most interested? What size company are you interested in? Where do you already have personal contacts? As you expand your network into Tier Two and Tier Three, add the names of influential people who may have access to companies on your target list.

As with the Board-Smart Chart, be disciplined about keeping your spreadsheet up-to-date with new and old contacts and what their reaction was when you contacted them. List them together with type of business, company size, name of CEO, and the composition of the board, including the gender and longevity of the members. This information should be available on the company's website.

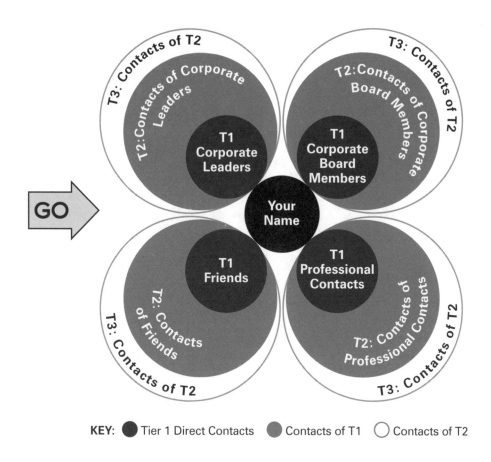

KEY: ⬤ Tier 1 Direct Contacts ⬤ Contacts of T1 ◯ Contacts of T2

Target 25 Contacts Who Know Directors—Start Reaching Out

Your strategic networking, your review of "Z" companies on the 2020 Women on Boards website, and the work you put into your Board-Smart Networking Chart will all help you identify some corporate directors with whom you probably already have a direct connection, even though you may not have realized it. Do your research about the board on which these directors serve, the mission of the company, the committees on which they serve, and the length of their term. Find names of their fellow board members on the company website (see the Investor Relations page) or research the person on LinkedIn.

Then be proactive about inviting each of those twenty-five people to lunch or coffee. Be frank and intentional; let them know you want to find a board seat. Ask about their own stories of how they got their first board seat and be prepared with your High-Impact Sound Bites so you can bring them up when it's appropriate in the conversation. Just as with your Tier One colleagues, ask for feedback. This is where you will learn from the people who actually serve on boards about how to polish your presentation and clarify the value-added experience you would bring to a board.

Your contacts will give you good guidance as to what types of boards you might be well suited for and what types of board culture would be a comfortable fit. Different boards, like different companies, have cultures that distinguish and define them. Conversations with a number of corporate directors from a variety of boards can help you identify the types of boards on which you would like to serve. Many of the women profiled in this book emphasize the importance of doing one's homework before pursuing a board seat. This is the phase when you are exploring boards that would be right for you. If you have any qualms about a company, its reputation, or its corporate culture, trust your gut and don't pursue it.

As the incredible women profiled in this book have shared openly through their stories, there are still some boards—amazingly enough!—with antiquated views about board diversity and inclusion. But every woman becomes a valuable addition to a board, whether she is the only woman serving or one of several women directors. She is helping to change that old-fashioned and unproductive notion. It can be exciting and energizing to be the "first" on a corporate board. It can also be challenging, if you are not treated with the respect that your credentials deserve. When you meet with your target corporate director contacts, ask them in an informational way to help you understand how to "fit" on a board. How did they determine the right fit for themselves as they pursued boards and how did they fit in once they sat on the boards they serve?

The old adage "Noses In, Fingers Out" relates to the hard line between how a board advises from a hands-off perspective, while the CEO and management actually manage the operations of the company. Given that demarcation, there are still some questions that you will want to ask to help you get a good picture of how you would "fit" with a particular board:

- How do the board meetings go? Is it mostly management presenting PowerPoints to the board, without much interaction? Or is there a good deal of time devoted to strategy discussion at the meetings? Is most of the meeting spent on compliance issues? Or does management brainstorm with board members to take advantage of the directors' expertise? Asking such questions will help you sort out how the board values the input of its directors, as well as whether or not you are going to be bored on this board. If management simply presents to the board and expects a rubber stamp approval, is that board worth your effort? Your name and reputation will ride on the success of this company.

- What crises have occurred in the business over the last three or five years and how has the board handled them? You want to know that crises have been resolved, as well as whether the board took a proper role in handling and advising the CEO as a collaborative team. Or did the board simply blame management? Of course, if you have done your homework—your due diligence—you already know what crises the company has faced. So you may be more specific about asking how the board handled a specific crisis. If, in your judgment, the directors interviewing you try to avoid answering questions about crises, that should raise a red flag. Maybe board members here have a head-in-the-sand mentality and don't want to face crises as advisors to the CEO. On the other hand, you may be impressed by how they handled a recent crisis, and you may tell them so.

- Describe the workplace culture at the company—are board members kept apprised of culture issues? Are there whistle-blower complaints? How are sexual harassment issues handled—is the board made aware of the problems and the solutions? In this era of the #MeToo generation and open discussion about how women are treated, it's important you know how the board handles these situations. If you have any reservations about the directors' commitment to monitor bad behavior at the company, or if they have paid exorbitant "hush money" to cover up issues, this is not the right board for you.

- Is this company very litigious? How many lawsuits are underway now? What is the nature of most of the lawsuits the company faces? When there is a lawsuit, the board's computers are always confiscated and directors are sometimes deposed by the courts. Has this happened in recent years? How has the board resolved its role?

  Understand that lawsuits are part of doing business today. Lawsuits are quite frequently filed over patent infringements, privacy violations, or vendor/contractor disputes. These could be considered the normal course of doing business at that company. But if the lawsuits are in process for especially egregious actions by the corporation or its executives, this should be another red flag for you. The majority of lawsuits include the names of the board members. If the company has what you consider to be quite a few lawsuits, this does not mean you will have to appear in court. But it could mean that your computer and emails will be subpoenaed often, which will cause general disruption of your already very busy schedule.

There's no way to predict everything that could turn into a lawsuit, but you can get a feel for the general attitude and involvement of a company. I once knew a CEO who quite regularly only paid his contractors half of what had been agreed to. He was clearly unethical and just figured that the few lawsuits the contractors might bring would cost him less in legal fees than paying the full bill. This person is no longer alive, so any resemblance to someone you know alive or dead is totally coincidental!

Increase Your Industry Visibility

Your impressive Board Profile and LinkedIn profile, and the attention-getting High-Impact Sound Bites that tell the story of your capabilities and achievements, are based on so much more than your "day job." As you have read in the profiles of our fifty-four talented women directors, the following actions and activities must be ongoing if your goal is a corporate board seat. Each of the women profiled in the book emphasizes how your visibility as an industry or functional expert is a key asset in your quest for a board seat. It is never too early to ramp-up your profile by offering your expertise more broadly. Here is a summary of the recommendations you read about in earlier chapters that were meaningful to the women who've shared their stories and advice:

- Join the associations within your industry and get to know the members. Over time, some of these people could become Tier One contacts on your Board-Smart Networking Chart.
- Build and moderate panels at industry events; this gives you access to experts and high-profile industry leaders. Volunteer to escort and assist

these guests so they have an opportunity to witness your skills and abilities.

- Run for elected board positions in your industry's associations and volunteer to head working committees. You will gain business contacts at the top levels of many companies in your field—people whom you might not have met otherwise—and you will gain leadership skills as well as board experience.
- Identify your area of expertise and build a powerful presentation on that topic. Solicit your own speaking engagements; offer yourself as an industry thought leader on your topic; then work to be featured at conferences, local chapter meetings of related organizations, or the Chamber of Commerce in your area. Be certain to have handouts that feature your bio and contact information.
- Post your speaking events on your LinkedIn page and include two paragraphs from your talk.
- Write bylined articles for trade publications or social media sites or blogs and make sure that these articles represent your area of expertise, then post them on LinkedIn; be sure to include your bio and contact information prominently.
- Accept queries from media representatives and reporters who might want comments or opinions related to your areas of expertise. Positive media exposure will be extremely impressive when a nominating committee member searches your name and finds articles and speeches quoting you. (Make sure your current employer is aware of your media work.)
- Volunteer for fundraising events for nonprofit organizations where people can observe your skills in hosting, organizing, and managing events. Be certain that you are included in photos with the speakers and organizers, so your presence will be seen and posted.

Boards Want To See "Prior Board Experience"— What Qualifies?

Prior board experience. Does that sound like a Catch-22 when you're looking for your first seat? It can be, but you can avoid it. Boards don't want new directors who need on-the-job training about how boards get things done. How can you get relevant board experience if you have not yet been on your first corporate board? Here is "prior board experience" you may not have thought of. And yes, this counts:

1. The company where you work: The most immediate avenue to "prior board experience" is inside your own company. You can facilitate developing this experience by volunteering to make presentations to your board on activities or projects within your division or participate in a board Q&A session about the areas you manage. Board retreats or orientations for new members are excellent opportunities for you to present insider knowledge of your department or function in the company, as well as make a memorable impression. Mention such board presentations in the "Board Experience" section at the top of your Board Profile. When you make presentations to your company's board or are included in the board meeting discussions, this qualifies as "Prior Board Experience."

    Additionally, having exposure to your company's board will provide invaluable lessons in board structures, procedures, responsibilities, and governance. Observing a well-functioning board or board committee can provide lessons that will enable you to hit the ground running in your own board work. Your board provides the opportunity to learn directly about board governance, finances, and budget management.

2. Nonprofit boards, including universities and hospitals: The majority of the women profiled in this book have had successful terms on nonprofit boards and I strongly urge you to pursue this path to your ultimate goal of corporate board work. As one successful corporate director put it, "A well-functioning nonprofit board can provide very relevant experience."

    University boards and large hospital boards have responsibilities closely aligned with those of for-profit companies. Governance issues, compensation and benefits, financial and audit oversight, mission, and strategic direction are all responsibilities of the boards of nonprofits. Committee work can be equally instructional and informative, whether it is on the audit committee, in marketing, in compensation, or in nominating and governance.

    If you volunteer with a nonprofit or university board that aligns with your own interests or passions, you're very likely to be successful as a fundraiser and remembered for your success. If you are a fan of the fine arts, music, or theater, there are countless 501c3 organizations where your professional skills would be welcomed. If personal or family experience has drawn you to a cause in a health-related or medical field, your commitment is bound to be of value to that nonprofit. Similarly, if you have been affiliated with your university or its alumni association, you will gain meaningful governing experience and visibility by serving on the board.

3. Government-appointed commissions: Whether at the city, county, or state levels, commissions provide excellent experience in governance and large budget oversight. For example, every government agency and every city fire or police department has a team of appointed commissioners that functions like a corporate board of directors, setting policies for the department and overseeing its operations. These commissions work in conjunction with the supervising body and the chief executive, who reports to the commission. You don't have to be a major contributor to a political candidate to be appointed to a commission. You simply need to apply online for the open appointments that any local- or state-elected official or agency may have open, then follow-up with the administrator in that office. Hundreds of positions (non-paid) open up when new elected officials enter office. It takes some homework to find them. Often, the websites of the governor, members of the legislature, county supervisors, or mayor list openings for a wide array of departments, and each has an "appointments secretary" responsible for naming people (like you) to those positions. Appointments secretaries are responsible for choosing people for commissions, not for scheduling.

4. Trade association boards: Industry trade groups are valuable entities for gaining governance experience. A trade association is an organization founded and funded by businesses that operate in a specific industry for the advancement of its corporate members and represent the industry's interests to federal, state, or local governments. These associations are nonprofit organizations governed by bylaws and directed by a board of directors. It's easy to get on boards in your industry; simply volunteer to help current board members get things done: manage an event, escort a speaker for the big fundraising event, be a spokesperson for an issue. Make yourself known to the industry leaders (graciously, of course!) at industry events.

5. Corporate advisory boards: Many corporations have volunteer advisory

groups that have the expertise to counsel the board. Often they represent specific communities important to the company like consumers, vendors, or diverse stakeholders. Advisory boards provide you with excellent experience as well as help you make important contacts as you ultimately seek to obtain a corporate board seat. Advisory boards, while not performing governance or fiduciary duties, frequently engage with executive leadership on issues dealing with community outreach or customer service. It is common for advisory boards to make presentations to the company's corporate board or interact with directors. Such access to the company's directors provides opportunities to demonstrate your skills and value to the company. Many successful women directors have gained their requisite "prior board experience" by first serving on an advisory board.

In Closing, Remember Your Girlfriends!

Everything you have read in my two books (*The Board Game* and *Winning the Board Game*) provides the launching pad for board membership. During your journey, you will find other resources that are critical to your success. Please, once you have made it to your coveted board position, remember your girlfriends coming up the pipeline!

It is your responsibility to help bring along the women behind you. As Bonnie Hill was retiring from her boards, she made sure that competent and talented women were considered to become her successors—and she propelled them to the front of the line. This is critical for you to remember as you finish this book and start the hard work of sitting on boards, to make your ideas and opinions heard. It is now on *your* shoulders to use your connections and communication skills to help more women secure seats on corporate boards of directors. You deserve the accolades you will receive when you work to establish gender diversity in the boardroom. And that's not just for the board seat you are leaving, but for other boards where you have or will have influence.

You may not realize it, but you are already a significant role model to the women in the workforce of the company where you sit at the directors' table.

Make sure you understand how women are treated in this company, because you want to serve on boards where women employees are considered vital to the culture and overall productivity of this business. If the workplace environment is not fair to women, this unfairness can manifest itself as a legal risk for your board and more importantly, it can impact your service on the board. Know that a company's character is revealed by the way it treats women and minorities. You are the agent of change for the better.

Thank you for listening and learning. Reading books is a challenge when you have a busy day balancing kids, husband, career, and your board pursuit. You are preparing for your later career, and what you do now will be critically important to that phase of your life. I know you are the woman who shoots for the stars, not the one who stays comfortably planted on the ground.

Good luck and Bon Voyage!!

—Betsy

GUIDE TO RESOURCES

Organizations

2020 Women on Boards is a global public awareness campaign (not a membership organization) to increase the number of women on corporate boards. When founded in 2010 in Boston, its goal was to raise the percentage of women on corporate boards in the U.S. to 20% or greater by the year 2020. Continuing after the year 2020, its goal is parity for women and men on boards. 2020WOB moved to Los Angeles in 2018, and named Betsy Berkhemer-Credaire as CEO. Focus has expanded globally, while tracking annual progress of the three thousand largest public companies in the U.S.

Every November, 2020 Women on Boards presents the National Conversation on Board Diversity simultaneously in dozens of cities across the country and internationally. The national and global events feature speakers and "Director/Coaches" who advise attendees how to use their networks to find a corporate-board seat. On this single day when most events are held, the latest statistics are unveiled, called 2020 Women on Boards Gender Diversity Index. 2020WOB sponsors educational "Get on Board!" workshops in major cities. These one-day intense workshops are customized for a limited enrollment to focus on individuals. (Online resource: 2020wob.com)

Athena Alliance is a national nonprofit membership organization started in 2016 to connect industries and executives with a qualified network of C-suite women candidates for boards, primarily in technology-related industries. Founder Coco Brown helps train and place professional women on boards. Athena Alliance has developed a network of more than 800 C-level women, venture capitalists and CEOs from more than 100 companies. (Online resource: athenaalliance.org)

The American College of Corporate Directors (ACCD) is a networking, educational, and credentialing organization for current directors of publicly held companies. Its mission is to provide members with a high standard of instruction, theory, and practice surrounding the issues facing public companies today. Membership is available to current public company directors. (Online resource: accdirectors.com)

DirectWomen is designed specifically for women attorneys and women general counsels to train them for corporate boards. Through educational programs, DirectWomen coaches women attorneys to serve on boards, and develops networks to help place them across the country. The DirectWomen Board Institute is held annually in New York, to provide networking among women attorneys who serve on boards with potential candidates, and honors women lawyers who have served with distinction as independent directors of public companies at its signature Sandra Day O'Connor Board Excellence Award Luncheon. (Online resource: directwomen.org)

Equilar Diversity Network: Diverse Director DataSource is a free resource where aspiring women and minority candidates may create their own online profiles free of charge, listing qualifications they deem relevant to corporate boards. Two-thirds of self-nominated candidates are women. Informally called the 3-D Database, this service was originated by CalPERS and CalSTRS, the two huge institutional investors managing retirement funds for California's retired employees and teachers. It is public information that can be accessed by companies, shareholders, and nonprofit boards seeking diversity candidates. (Online resource: marketing.equilar.com/24-equilar-diversity-network)

National Association of Corporate Directors (NACD) is a membership organization founded in 1977 and based in Washington, D.C., that helps corporate boards build collaboration among directors, investors, and governance stakeholders. NACD stages an annual educational conference. Board members of corporations (public and private) and large nonprofits qualify for membership. The NACD Fellows training programs are excellent for aspiring board members—men and women. (Online resource: nacdonline.org)

WomenCorporateDirectors (WCD) is a global, nonprofit, educational foundation whose members are current corporate directors on publicly traded companies, large privately held companies, or family-owned businesses, with minimum annual revenue of $200 million. WCD has chapters throughout the U.S. and internationally.

To help advance women not yet serving on a public or private board, WCD created BoardNext, with chapters in Los Angeles and New York, providing educational training, introductions to board members, search firms, and a peer-group network. (Online resource: womencorporatedirectors.org)

Private Directors Association (PDA) is a growing national network for directors of private company boards, where executives and professionals interested in private-board service can meet with current directors of non-public companies. "Private company boards are often a great first board for women because they focus more on strategy and less on compliance and regulatory issues," according to CEO Ken Hoganson, "We want to be the connecting link between private boards and people seeking to join them." PDA provides educational and performance insights, and publishes a magazine geared to private company directors. (Online resource: privatedirectorsassociation.org)

Inforum is Michigan's statewide nonprofit organization for women, providing networking, professional development programs, events, and forums, and board training. Headquartered in Detroit, Inforum offers twenty-five affinity groups in Southeast and West Michigan, as well as specialized industry groups in automotive, healthcare, manufacturing, and technology. In addition to board training, Inforum coaches emerging leaders, entrepreneurs, veterans, and offers leadership programs in collaboration with the University of Michigan's Ross School of Business. (Online resource: inforummichigan.org)

How Women Lead is a membership organization based in San Francisco, which offers training and support services to increase opportunities for professional advancement in corporate, public, philanthropic, and nonprofit sectors. Founded by Julie Castro Abrams, How Women Lead orchestrates board training for women, multiple programs in philanthropic activity, and provides grants and volunteers to Bay Area organizations helping women and girls in under-served communities. (Online resource: howwomenlead.com)

Paradigm for Parity is a nonprofit coalition of CEOs, senior executives, founders, board members, and education leaders committed to gender equality in U.S. corporations. Its goal is to achieve full gender-parity in corporations by 2030, with a near-term goal that women would hold at least 30% of senior leadership roles. The coalition invites corporate CEOs and influential leaders to pledge they will follow the Paradigm for Parity 5-Point Action Plan, steps designed to help companies increase the number of women of all ethnic backgrounds in leadership positions. (Online resource: paradigm4parity.com)

Women's Leadership Foundation of Colorado: BoardBound, headquartered in Denver, is a board leadership training program created by CEO Jo Lynne Whiting. It offers a year-long board-readiness program for C-suite women, or those with equivalent experience, who are positioned to join a corporate board of directors. BoardBound includes workshops with subject-matter experts and one-on-one matching with mentors who have corporate-board experience, as well as peer networking and support. (Online resource: womensleadershipfoundation.org)

The Thirty Percent Coalition focuses on private equity companies to generate board positions on their portfolio companies, most pre-IPO. Led by CEO Charlotte Laurent-Ottomane, The Thirty Percent Coalition has as its goal that women hold 30% or more of board seats across public companies. The Coalition includes public and private companies, private equity firms, institutional investors, professional service firms, advocacy and nonprofit organizations, state treasurers and other government officials. The Coalition meets twice annually in a unique forum to promote diversity on U.S. corporate boards. According to Laurent-Ottomane, private-equity firms and institutional investors understand the direct correlation of gender diversity to shareholder value. (Online resource: 30percentcoalition.org)

30% Club (global)

In 2010, the 30% Club was founded by Dame Helena Morrissey. It has evolved into a global mission with chapters in fourteen countries and regions. In 2016, Brenda Trenowden CBE was appointed the new leader for the UK chapter and Global Chair of the 30% Club, reflecting the increased reach and scale of the campaign since its launch. As of June 2019, Ann Cairns was named Global Co-Chair of the 30% Club, serving alongside Trenowden. (Online resource: 30percentclub.org)

30% Club of the United States

The U.S. chapter of 30% Club was formed in 2014. As an extension of the 30% Club Future Female Directors program, the 30% Club partners with the Catalyst Women on Board program which establishes connections to help women extend their networks. Qualified women board candidates are paired with seasoned corporate directors for two years of mentoring and networking. 30% Club members who are chairmen and CEOs volunteer as mentors in the Women on Board program. (Online resource: us.30percentclub.org)

Catalyst

Catalyst was founded in 1962, and may be the oldest and most well-known of organizations that encourage fair and equal treatment of women in the workplace. For many years, Catalyst has published its research to promote greater recognition of gender inequities at companies. Catalyst has launched several programs to advance women to corporate boards. Its board search service is based on corporate CEO endorsements of women executives they know personally, for potential board consideration by other CEOs. Catalyst also partners with the 30% Club of the U.S. to build the pipeline of qualified women candidates. (Online resource: catalystwomenonboard.org)

International Women's Forum of New York (IWF) offers board-training programs, with its centerpiece biennial event, Breakfast of Corporate Champions, honoring corporate CEOs in New York whose companies have 40% women directors on their boards. Janice Ellig, CEO of the Ellig Group executive search firm, is the founder and energy behind the event, which is very successful in raising visibility for primarily large corporations that are role models in the campaign to increase the number of women on boards. (Online resource: womensforumny.org/corporate-board-initiative)

African American Board Leadership Institute (AABLI) recruits, prepares and assists in placing African American business professionals on boards of public, private, and nonprofit organizations nationwide. (Online resource: www.aabli.org)

OnBoard Georgia tracks progress of women directors on Georgia public corporations, also develops and inspires Georgia women executives to become board members. (Online resource: www.OnBoardNow.org)

WEL Florida: Women Executive Leadership in Florida, the statewide nonprofit organization that educates and connects business women in Miami, Ft. Lauderdale and Tampa Bay toward corporate boards and career advancement. (Online resource: www.WELFlorida.org)

GLOSSARY

Activist Shareholder: a shareholder who uses an equity stake in a corporation to put pressure on management. The goals of activist shareholders range from financial to non-financial, often attempting to gain control of the company and replace management or force a major corporate change.

Board Committees:
- **Audit** — in charge of overseeing financial reporting and disclosure. All U.S. publicly traded companies must maintain a qualified audit committee in order to be listed on a stock exchange.
- **Compensation** — recommends, oversees, and approves compensation in the form of corporate equity, stocks, perquisites, and other benefits. It also oversees employment contracts in conjunction with board oversight and, under some circumstances, with shareholder approval.
- **Executive** — a leadership subset of the board, often comprised of committee chairs, who get together, often with little notice, to address pressing issues that affect the organization substantially, such as an emerging crisis. The executive committee has the power to act on behalf of the full board.
- **Governance** — responsible for ongoing review and recommendations to strengthen the board. Often works with nominating committee (or the two are merged as a single committee) to recruit new prospects and to educate all board members on their responsibilities. Five major areas of focus include board role, composition, knowledge, effectiveness and leadership.
- **Nominating** — evaluates the board of directors and examines the skills and characteristics needed in new board candidates. Determines and recommends qualified candidates for board membership.
- **Risk** — oversees the risk management infrastructure, addresses risk and strategy simultaneously, and supports Chief Risk Officer.

D & O Insurance: liability insurance covering a company's board of directors and officers in the event the insured suffers a loss as a result of a legal action brought for alleged wrongful acts in their capacity as directors and officers.

Dodd-Frank Act: signed into law in 2010 by President Barack Obama in response to the 2008 financial crisis. The law places strict regulations on lenders and banks to protect consumers and decrease risks in the U.S. financial system. Dodd-Frank also created several new agencies to oversee the regulatory process and by extension some aspects of the banking industry.

ESG (Environmental, Social and Governance): a phrase used to refer to three non-financial performance factors that help measure the sustainability and ethical impact of an investment in a business or company.

Financial Expert: As defined by the Securities and Exchange Commission (SEC), in accordance with the Sarbanes-Oxley Act of 2002, a financial expert is defined as a person who has all of the following attributes:
- an understanding of GAAP and financial statements
- an ability to assess the general application of such principles in connection with the accounting for estimates, accruals, and reserves
- experience preparing, auditing, analyzing, or evaluating financial statements that present a breadth and level of complexity of accounting issues that are generally comparable to the breadth and complexity of issues that can reasonably be expected to be raised by the registrant's financial statements, or experience actively supervising one or more persons engaged in such activities
- an understanding of internal controls and procedures for financial reporting
- an understanding of audit committee functions

Fin Tech: shorthand for "Financial Technology," defining the financial services industry disruption by technology. This digital disruption has the potential to shrink the role and relevance of today's banks, and simultaneously help them create better, faster, cheaper services that make them an even more essential part of everyday life for institutions and individuals.

FTSE: the Financial Times Stock Exchange 100 Index, also called the FTSE 100 Index, is a share index of the one hundred companies listed on the London Stock Exchange with the highest market capitalization. It is seen as a gauge of prosperity for businesses regulated by UK company law.

Governance: describes how institutions conduct their affairs and manage resources through a process of decision-making, and the process by which those decisions are or are not implemented. Good governance assumes a positive impact on development and growth, and is viewed as adhering to the following characteristics: participation, rule of law, transparency, responsiveness, consensus orientation, equity, effectiveness and efficiency, and accountability.

Independent Director or Member: sometimes known as an outside director, a member of a board of directors who does not have a consulting or familial relationship with the company or related persons, and is not paid fees for services, other than receiving compensation as a director.

Institutional Investor: an organization that invests on behalf of its member groups. Six categories of institutional investors are generally identified: pension funds, endowment funds, insurance companies, commercial banks, mutual funds, and hedge funds. CalSTRS (California State Teachers Retirement System), CalPERS (California Public Employees Retirement System) and the New York State Pension fund are examples of institutional investors.

Lead Director: an independent board member, usually elected by the other independent members of the board, who performs certain duties on behalf of the board. The lead director often serves as chair of the governance committee. This would be true for either a public or a private company board. Lead independent directors are liaisons between the CEO/chair and the board.

Market Capitalization: the value of all outstanding shares of a publicly traded company. Size of companies are generally referred to by their "market cap" such as:
- Nano Cap – Under $50 million
- Micro Cap – $50 million to $300 million
- Small Cap – $300 million to $1 billion
- Mid Cap – $1 billion to $5 billion
- Large Cap – Over $5 billion

Private Company: a firm held under private ownership. Private companies may issue stock and have shareholders, but their shares are not traded on public exchanges and are not issued through an initial public offering (IPO).

Private Equity (PE): capital that is not listed on a public exchange. Private equity is composed of funds and investors that directly invest in private companies, or that engage in buyouts of public companies that want to go private. Institutional and retail investors provide the capital for private equity funds. Private equity firms often place board members on their portfolio company boards to protect their investments, which can open opportunities for women who are known to PE firms.

Proxy Advisory Firms: consulting firms including Institutional Shareholder Services and Glass Lewis provide vote services and shareholder voting research primarily to institutional investors for voting their shares at annual meetings of public companies.

Public Company: a company that has issued securities through an initial public offering (IPO) and its stock is traded on at least one public exchange or in over-the-counter markets. A public company must have at least two independent directors.

Russell 3000: also called the Russell 3000 Index, a market-capitalization-weighted equity index that tracks the financial performance of the 3,000 largest U.S.-traded stocks, which represent about 98% of all U.S incorporated equity securities.

Sarbanes-Oxley Act: Congressional act passed in 2002 to protect investors from the possibility of fraudulent accounting activities by corporations. Also known as the Corporate Responsibility Act of 2002, it mandated strict reforms to improve financial disclosures from corporations and prevent accounting fraud.

Securities and Exchange Commission (SEC): the independent federal agency responsible for protecting investors, maintaining fair and orderly functioning of securities markets, and facilitating capital formation. It was created by Congress in 1934 as the first federal regulator of securities markets, promoting full public disclosure, protecting investors against fraudulent and manipulative practices in the market, and monitoring corporate takeover actions in the United States. The SEC has five appointed commissioners, two from each of the major parties, and the president appoints the chairperson, so that means the president's party usually is in the majority.

ACKNOWLEDGMENTS

I am grateful to all women corporate directors profiled in *Winning the Board Game* who granted me permission to interview and quote them about "How Women Make THE Difference."

Thank you to everyone listed here, without whom I could not have finished this second book in our *The Board Game* series:

Barbara Goen, my longtime friend and invaluable collaborator throughout the process on the interviews, writing, organizing, and editing this book.

Angel City Press for publishing both *The Board Game* and this book, and to its owners Paddy Calistro and Scott McAuley for their unlimited patience and care. Located in Santa Monica, Angel City Press is one of the largest woman-owned publishing companies in California, known for its beautiful and historic books. Now its editors are experts on the subject of women corporate directors.

Creative Director Hilary Lentini, owner of Lentini Design & Marketing in Los Angeles, and her hard-working staff, especially Lead Designer Leanna Hanson, for graphic design throughout.

Co-founders of 2020 Women on Boards, Stephanie Sonnabend, and Malli Gero, who selected me as CEO of their remarkable public awareness campaign in January 2018; to Breanna Bakke, director of finance and research; Tyra Butler, our program manager; and our national board of directors: Tracey Doi, Bonnie Hill, Julie Hill, Sharon Garrett, Robin Ferracone, John Iino, Joanna Lau, Steven Bock, Renee Fraser, Bridget Baker, Stephanie, and Malli. Thanks to our thirty-two campaign city chairs throughout the United States, plus London, Madrid, Mexico City, and Hong Kong.

My business partner for twenty-five years, Fred Clayton of Berkhemer Clayton Retained Executive Search in downtown Los Angeles, and to our hardworking senior management team, Ben Lambert, Shai Phillips, and Elaina Schmitz; and our client corporations, universities, and nonprofit organizations.

My close friend Renee Fraser, owner of Fraser Communications in Los Angeles, my year-round co-chair of the 2020WOB National Conversation on Board Diversity in Los Angeles, for her encouragement and marketing wisdom. And special thanks to our Los Angeles and Orange County Host Committee members for their volunteer support of 2020 Women on Boards.

State Senator Hannah-Beth Jackson (Santa Barbara) for carrying SB 826, the statewide board and eleven chapter leaders of the National Association of Women Business Owners-California (NAWBO-CA) for their sponsorship of SB826, the first law in the country requiring public companies to add more women directors to their boards. And of course, many thanks to Former California Governor Jerry Brown for signing SB 826 into law on September 30, 2018.

Cristina Rose, Billie Greer, Lori Kammerer, and Nora Lynn, my political friends, and Annalisa Barrett, for her governance research expertise and friendship—all helped develop and implement the strategies needed to secure passage of SB 826.

Charlotte Laurent-Ottomane in Florida, CEO of the Thirty Percent Coalition, and countless business owners, directors and NAWBO members who sent support letters to California Legislators and Governor Brown.

Susan Stautberg, founder and retired CEO of WomenCorporateDirectors, for engaging me as the Los Angeles/Orange County chapter chairperson for seventeen years until I was named CEO of 2020 Women on Boards. And to Susan Keating, the new global CEO of WomenCorporateDirectors, who is forging the next legacy for WCD.

Cate Goethals, adjunct professor at the University of Washington Foster School of Business, who invites me to speak at her Women Board Director programs, where I've met remarkable women directors from the Northwest, several profiled in this book.

Xavier Gutierrez, managing director of Clearlake Capital Group, and Jeri J. Harman, CEO and founder of Avante Capital Partners, who guided me through the world of private equity as pathways for women to seek pre-IPO board positions.

Linda Rabbitt—former CEO and founder of Rand Construction in Alexandria, Virginia, longtime board member of Willis Towers Watson, NACD Director of the Year, and founder of the Women Directors board-training program at Harvard Business School—for being my role model and for mentoring many women seeking corporate board seats.

Ken Hoganson, CEO and founder of Private Directors Association (PDA), for guidance that private companies are often ideal first boards for women.

Chris Mitchell, national board member of the National Association of Corporate Directors (NACD), for his insights about strategic networking with one's own business contacts in a systematic and disciplined way to seek out corporate board opportunities.

Virgil Roberts, entertainment and civil rights attorney, chairman of Broadway Financial Corporation, serving on university boards, and founder of the African American Board Leadership Institute (AABLI), mentor to women and men seeking board positions, whom I've known since we were in school together at Ventura/Buena High Schools, Ventura Community College, and UCLA.

My close friends Sally Jameson, Linda Deacon, Jackie Doud, and Sue Whitfield, for their encouragement.

Last, but certainly not least, I am so grateful for my sisters, Rosemary Joyce, Dorothy Perry, Bonnie Vincent, and Erica Brooks, as well as my nieces Anne Perry and Karen Brooks, who have all helped me as I recover from the untimely loss of my husband Cris.

INDEX

ABOUT THE AUTHOR

BETSY BERKHEMER-CREDAIRE is CEO of the 2020 Women on Boards global campaign and CEO/owner of Berkhemer Clayton Inc., the diversity-focused retained executive search firm in Los Angeles. Betsy shares behind-the-scenes facts about board searches to guide women to the top positions in global business. Her first book, *The Board Game: How Smart Women Become Corporate Directors,* was published in 2013. Now comes her second book, *Winning the Board Game: How Women Corporate Directors Make THE Difference,* expanding and exploring what women have accomplished on boards.

Remarkably, in mid-2019, 2020WOB achieved its ten-year goal a year early: women at last held 20% of the public company board seats in the U.S. After 2020, the campaign goal evolved to achieving parity for women on boards. The 2020WOB.com website is the only comprehensive resource open to the public online that tracks the Russell 3000 Index companies, citing how many women directors, if any, are on each corporation's board.

Before joining 2020WOB, Betsy was founding chair of the Los Angeles/Orange County chapter of WomenCorporateDirectors (WCD), a global nonprofit network of women serving on public and private boards. Since 2000, she has served on the statewide board of the National Association of Women Business Owners–California (NAWBO-CA), and was instrumental in passing SB 826 in 2018, the first law in the country to require adding women to public company boards in the state. Previously, she served on the California Utilities Diversity Council; nonprofit boards of Southern California Leadership Network (SCLN) for twenty-five years; and the advisory boards of SoCal Edison (SCE) and UCLA Medical Center.

A longtime member of the International Women's Forum, National Association of Corporate Directors, NAWBO-CA, and Los Angeles Chamber of Commerce, Betsy is also a lifetime member of both UCLA Alumni Association and Girl Scouts USA. Her career began in newspapers and television news, and then she joined the Walt Disney Company as a publicist. At age twenty-seven, she opened her first company, a public relations agency in Los Angeles, which was acquired by the global firm Golin Communications. She grew up in Ventura and Claremont, California, and graduated from UCLA with majors in history and journalism.

"My lifetime goal is to help as many women as possible advance their careers in business, and guide talented women executives and business owners toward becoming directors on corporate boards."